ROUTLEDGE LIBRARY EDITIONS:
INDUSTRIAL ECONOMICS

Volume 17

MONOPOLIES, CARTELS AND TRUSTS IN BRITISH INDUSTRY

MONOPOLIES, CARTELS AND TRUSTS IN BRITISH INDUSTRY

HERMANN LEVY

Routledge
Taylor & Francis Group
LONDON AND NEW YORK

First published in Germany in 1909 as "Monopole, Kartelle und Trusts" by Gustav Fischer, Jena
First published in English in 1927 by Macmillan and Co. Limited
Reissued in 1968 by Frank Cass

This edition first published in 2018
by Routledge
2 Park Square, Milton Park, Abingdon, Oxon OX14 4RN

and by Routledge
711 Third Avenue, New York, NY 10017

Routledge is an imprint of the Taylor & Francis Group, an informa business

British Library Cataloguing in Publication Data
A catalogue record for this book is available from the British Library

ISBN: 978-1-138-30830-5 (Set)
ISBN: 978-1-351-21102-4 (Set) (ebk)
ISBN: 978-0-8153-8009-2 (Volume 17) (hbk)
ISBN: 978-0-8153-8023-8 (Volume 17) (pbk)
ISBN: 978-1-351-21382-0 (Volume 17) (ebk)

Publisher's Note
The publisher has gone to great lengths to ensure the quality of this reprint but points out that some imperfections in the original copies may be apparent.

Disclaimer
The publisher has made every effort to trace copyright holders and would welcome correspondence from those they have been unable to trace.

MONOPOLIES, CARTELS AND TRUSTS IN BRITISH INDUSTRY

BY

HERMANN LEVY, Ph.D.

MACMILLAN AND CO., LIMITED
ST. MARTIN'S STREET, LONDON
1927

This book was first published under the title "Monopole, Kartelle und Trusts," by Gustav Fischer, Jena, in 1909. (Second German edition, 1927.) I owe my thanks to Messrs. Fischer for giving their consent to its translation.

TO MY FRIEND

SIR HUGH BELL, Bart.

IN GRATITUDE AND

RESPECT

PREFACE TO THE FIRST ENGLISH EDITION

This book was written and more especially translated in the hope of offering to Englishmen interested in the economic problems of their country, some account of its present industrial organisation. That organisation is characterised by monopolist tendencies which run counter to the hitherto prevailing régime of free competition. In England, the pioneer in economic history of competition, this development should excite the greatest interest; yet it is in England of all countries that the least recognition has been given to the economic importance of this new form of industry.

The present work attempts to explain the existing organisation of English industry by a study of the history of monopoly and competition, and at the same time to give an analysis of English cartels and trusts as they now are. I have tried to approach my subject without *parti pris*, and solely to describe and analyse. As I regard the historical alternation of monopoly and competition as an economic necessity which dogmas and evaluations unavoidably coloured by contemporary prejudice cannot affect, I have no personal bias to discount. It is, however, the duty of science to show what facts give or have given rise to these two systems of industrial economy respectively, and though itself without ulterior motive to assist those who wish to be guided by knowledge in the attainment of their objects.

I should be grateful for any corrections on points which

I have misunderstood or treated insufficiently; and I must in conclusion express my warmest thanks to my translator. To his energetic and intelligent assistance the appearance of this book in English is primarily due.

HERMANN LEVY.

HEIDELBERG, *April* 1911.

PREFACE

I HAVE no intention of writing a preface summarising the main ideas of the following enquiry. I should like, however, to explain shortly how the material was collected, on which my account of former and existing monopolies and my theoretical conclusions are based. I owe very much to the excellent work of various English economic historians, and most of the facts used in treating of existing monopolist associations to Mr. Macrosty's very instructive book. For Parts I. and III. of my essay there were many previous books, both general works and monographs, from which I could gather useful facts and hints and which suggested promising lines of enquiry; but for Part II. I found practically no precursor. The laborious pioneer work of extracting details of former English monopolist associations out of long-forgotten Parliamentary Reports was, however, lightened by the delight of being one of the first in the field.

It was, of course, necessary to spend a considerable time in England. For some years the British Museum and the Patent Office were my headquarters during my holidays. The library of the former provided me with the historical information I needed, and the trade papers preserved in the latter explained to me the present day. For investigation into English industrial conditions the examination of these papers is especially necessary.

We in Germany, if only by reason of the number of theses produced, possess a large collection of more or less useful studies of particular industries, but in England such things only exist, if at all, in the case of the main industries. It is extraordinary that there are no monographs on the economic position of such things as iron and salt mining, the cement trade, industrial spirit and whisky distilling, the tobacco trade or engine making. The enquirer must turn to trade papers for information on their economic or technical position, their geographical connections or their finances. To these I added prospectuses of large undertakings —often very instructive material for my purposes—and reports of important events in the Commercial and Financial Supplement to the 'Times,' the 'Financial Times,' the 'Manchester Guardian,' and that admirable paper, the 'Economist.' But such a collection, taken mostly from newspapers and interested parties, could not, of course, be used without considerable scientific caution, and required to be interpreted in the light of personal statements, of criticism from the opposing interests and of explanations from the leaders of the industries in question.

I cannot sufficiently acknowledge the assistance I have received from all kinds of persons, many of them friends gained at the time of my studies in rural economy who were all connected with urban industries. For valuable information as to the steel and iron trade, I have particularly to thank Sir Hugh Bell and the editor of the 'Iron and Coal Trades' Review,' Mr. Jeans; for the paper trade, Mr. Dykes Spicer, Sir Albert Spicer, and Lord Northcliffe; for tobacco, Mr. A. C. Churchman; for the salt and soda industries, Sir A. Mond, M.P.; for the tinplate trade, Lord Glantawe; for coal mining, Mr. D. A. Thomas, M.P. My attempts to gain information even of the most elementary kind from the directors of large textile undertakings generally failed, and I cannot help feeling that the leaders of these monopolist associations desire to avoid discussion. I am the more grateful to Mr. W. B. Morison, of the London Stock Exchange, for placing his great experience of the textile industry and its combinations at my disposal. My investigations led almost continually to comparisons between English conditions and tendencies with those of German and American monopolies, and I derived much help from the results of my former visits to America.

In conclusion I would draw attention to the Appendices, in which I have included certain documents which I could not quote in sufficient detail in the text and to which I would particularly direct the reader. More especially would I recommend even those who are otherwise unwilling to spend time in studying appendices to read Lord Furness's speech. It is a most excellent illustration of that movement towards the concentration and combination of large industrial undertakings which has led many English industries towards new organisation on a monopolist basis, and which will continue to do so in the future.

HERMANN LEVY.

HEIDELBERG, *October* 1909.

PREFACE TO THE SECOND EDITION

Seventeen years have passed since the first edition of this book appeared. Such a lapse of time is in itself very important in the quick movement of modern economic development. But the war and its aftermath have brought into English economic life such transformations as cannot be matched in previous decades. English national economy was to a great extent cut off during the war from its regular sources of imports. After the war it experienced an extraordinary boom, which quickly changed into a condition of chronic depression not yet dispelled. English industry in particular, like that of other countries, was subject during the war to State regulation, with motives and problems of organisation and production altogether different from those of entirely free enterprise. New industries have sprung up in England since 1914, or have waxed important where they were formerly insignificant. England has more or less gone over to Protection since 1925. New social conditions have appeared, attended by severe shocks—marked by the most important English strike ever known, the coal strike of 1926—and have altered the preliminary conditions of organising Production. All these changes called for a new examination of the development of English trusts and cartels at the present time. Nevertheless, I consider that even these great changes in the background of English industry and in the whole frame of the English economic structure, have little altered the underlying facts of the development of monopolistic organisation in England. Many new organisations, sufficiently described in this second edition, have arisen; many old conflicts between Competition and Monopoly are now settled and replaced by new problems; the statistics of the first edition have had to be supplemented. But the reader and economist will find that the movement towards concentration, described in 1909, has suffered no change in principle in its main tendency, but shows rather a continuous forward movement. There has been no change in the regularity of this development as it was before the war, but this new edition adduces a number of events which occurred between 1909 and 1926 and show the increased force and expansion of the process. Meanwhile official literature on English cartels and trusts has been increasing in an important degree, especially by the 'Report on Trusts,' 1919, which was reprinted in 1924. Shortly before the completion of my second edition appeared the book of Mr. Patrick Fitzgerald, who had contributed important articles on "combinations" to the 'Statist' from 1922 to 1924, and has now collected them into a volume, which I have utilised, full of information. But I have not found it necessary to change my theoretical judgments of English trusts and cartels in spite of the important changes and new facts brought to light. In contrast to Fitzgerald, whose work is primarily descriptive, I have endeavoured in my first, and still more in my second edition, to exhibit the whole problem of concentration in English industry as it appears to-day, in connection with the general problem of the organisation of English industry. The more imperatively the disorganisation of world economy after the war demands a reconciliation of the economic interests of Europe, the more important will be these problems to the national economy of Germany.

HERMANN LEVY.

BERLIN, *January* 1927.

CONTENTS

PART I. MONOPOLY IN THE DAYS OF EARLY INDUSTRIAL CAPITALISM

CHAPTER I

THE HISTORY OF EARLY CAPITALISM

CHAPTER II

THE ORGANISATION OF MONOPOLIES

CHAPTER III

EFFECTS OF MONOPOLIES—THEIR FALL

CHAPTER IX

EXISTING MONOPOLIST ORGANISATIONS IN ENGLISH INDUSTRY

APPENDICES

PART I

MONOPOLY IN THE DAYS OF EARLY INDUSTRIAL CAPITALISM

L.T.

CHAPTER I

THE HISTORY OF EARLY CAPITALISM

When the Industrial Revolution began in the second half of the eighteenth century, the organisation of English industry was better prepared for an advance than that of any other European state. It is true that, as elsewhere, industrial undertakings found their freedom of movement restricted by the survival, partly in law and partly in custom, of the gild system; but much as these restrictions were opposed to the interests of large capitalist industries, they could not repress the many enterprising spirits who were eager to use to the full the new developments of trade. Long before the actual repeal of the Statute of Apprentices and other gild regulations completed the freedom of English industry, the way had become open even within the bounds of industrial capitalism for individual activity and mutual competition. In other countries the productive activities of single economic units were limited not merely by the demands of the gild system, but in the majority of cases, even after that difficulty had been overcome, by privileges, concessions, monopolies and the official regulation of capitalist manufacture, which united to make individual operations difficult and often impossible.

In England also, at the time when industrial capitalism commenced, the system of granting privileges to particular persons prevented the growth of competition among many who were both willing and fitted to be leaders of industry. Only when that system, which gave advantages to the few at the cost of all the rest, fell after prolonged struggles at the end of the seventeenth century, did that most important factor in modern freedom of industry, the abolition of all legal recognition of private monopolies, come into play. Nearly a century later a new technical and economic movement began, but the significance in this connection of the earlier won industrial freedom was not observed by the English economists. They regarded the free play of competition as a natural phenomenon in capitalist industry, and the unsophisticated reader might well imagine from their writings that no other system had ever existed since the rise of capitalism. The more this earlier triumph of free industry was taken as a matter of course, the more content economists were to apply the expression "freedom of industry" solely to the delivery of industry from the fetters of the gild regulations. As a result classical economy and its pupils never examined the liberation of English industry from the rule of monopoly in all its bearings, nor gave it its true importance in economic history.

It is only now that in all countries, including England, a new form of monopoly is beginning to arise in industry, that attention is directed to the monopolies which saw the birth of early capitalism, and whose fall was the necessary preliminary of that epoch of free competition, which in its turn appears to be inevitably coming to an end through the action of cartels and trusts.

The period which can be marked out in the early history of English industrial capitalism as predominantly that of monopoly lasts from the end of the sixteenth century to about 1685. Not that trade monopolies were unknown before that time; on the contrary they were very common. What made the monopolies of the time of Elizabeth, James I. and Charles I. appear in many ways something new, was that they bore a purely capitalistic impress, and perhaps for this very reason represented national industrial organisations in contradistinction to the former trade monopolies [1] of the gilds which were of purely local importance.

The period starts with the rapid economic expansion at the end of the sixteenth century. During the reign of Queen Elizabeth, and even more in the first ten years of the seventeenth century, a great number of new industries were introduced into England partly by foreigners and partly by Englishmen.[2] The majority were from the beginning of a capitalistic character, and far removed from the domestic handicraft. The adventurers consisted in most cases of well-to-do foreigners acquainted with the new industries, native merchants or rich courtiers, and the amounts invested were often not inconsiderable even in comparison with modern times. The four capitalists who undertook the working of the Yorkshire alum deposits in 1607 put £20,000 to £30,000 into this undertaking within a short period. In 1612 it was estimated that any one of the six existing companies employed 60 hired labourers, not counting foremen and their assistants or the necessary mechanics. The total expenses of such a company were put at about £2100 yearly.[3]

Salt mining and the glass industry were also organised from the beginning on a capitalist basis.[4] The last—if we neglect primitive beginnings—first became important in 1619, when Sir Robert Mansell started to erect glass works in Newcastle, which still survived till about 1855. He undertook to make a yearly payment of £1000 to the Crown.[5] That he employed 4000 men is, no doubt, an exaggeration,[6] but it is clear that the whole enterprise was of a purely capitalist character. Soap was another industry

[1] H. Hyde Price, 'The English Patents of Monopoly,' Boston 1906, pp. 6 and 7; also G. Unwin, 'Industrial Organisation,' Oxford 1904, p. 175.

[2] W. Cunningham, 'The Growth of English Industry,' Cambridge 1907, p. 78 and following and p. 518.

[3] Price, pp. 82 and following, 88 and 89.

[4] Cunningham, p. 78.

[5] R. L. Galloway, 'History of Coal Mining,' London 1882, p. 38.

[6] Price, pp. 74 and 67-81, *passim*.

introduced in the time of Elizabeth, although the novelty in this case consisted chiefly in the adoption of an improved process of manufacture, which, it was hoped, would make England largely independent of imports.[1] As early as the first half of the seventeenth century soap boiling was no longer reckoned as one of the crafts which came under Elizabeth's Statute of Apprentices, but was "an art of mystery,"[2] which any free burgess, knowing the process and possessed of the necessary resources, might practise. In the middle of the eighteenth century a considerable sum, relatively speaking, was considered necessary, according to trustworthy evidence, for the initial capital of each concern, the work being done by "Labourers" and "Foremen," no longer by Journeymen.[3] There is no doubt that as early as the seventeenth century the manufacture of soap, where not carried out in private houses, was organised in a capitalist fashion. The Company of Soapmakers of Westminster incorporated in 1631 was prepared to deliver wholesale, and promised the Crown to supply 5000 tons of soap yearly. When the business was transferred in 1639 to another company the latter paid for plant and material a purchase price of £20,050.[4]

As a last example of the new capitalist organisation we may take the wire industry. While in Germany wire-drawing mills driven mechanically were introduced as early as the first half of the fourteenth century,[5] the use of water power for drawing wire was first brought into England by a German in the second half of the sixteenth century. Till then, though the wire industry was practised as a craft in various parts of England, and especially in the Forest of

[1] Cunningham, pp. 78 and 306.

[2] 'A Looking Glass for Sope Patenters,' London 1646, p. 5.

[3] 'The General Shop Book,' London 1750, under 'Soap.'

[4] 'A short and true Relation concerning the Soap Business,' London 1641, p. 3 and ff.; also G. Unwin, 'Gilds of London,' London 1908, p. 323.

[5] K. Knapmann, 'Das Eisen- und Stahldrahtgewerbe in Altena,' Leipzig 1907, pp. 8-9.

Dean, the main supply, both of wire and carding wire, had to be imported. On the introduction of the new process a large capitalist factory arose at Tintern, of which we are told that it often produced more in the year than it could dispose of in England. When leased in 1592 the factory commanded a rental of £1000 a year, and employed workmen who received as much as £80 a year in wages, and were attracted from a distance, besides "many thousand poor" who found employment in the works of the company incorporated in 1568. On the other hand the finishing processes remained in the hands of craftsmen, who drew their raw material from the capitalist factories.[1]

Contemporary mining shows another group of capitalist undertakings. At the end of the sixteenth century Cornish tin mining was in an unfavourable position; many works had come to a standstill owing to the increasing cost of working in deeper levels; [2] and the introduction of pumping machinery had become an essential preliminary to any increase of production. Presumably to bring the capital necessary for this purpose into the mining industry, Queen Elizabeth conceded her royal mining rights to a number of capitalists, a policy continued by the English kings until 1643.[3] As a consequence the producers, hitherto independent miners and smelters, became economically dependent on capitalists. In 1630 Judge Doderidge complains that "the mine-workers in respect of their poor Estate are eaten out by the hard and usurious contracts for tin" [4] (a state of affairs exactly parallel to the conditions ruling as early as the sixteenth century in German tin mining),[5] "as those poor labourers being not able to maintain themselves and their families . . . are by necessity compelled for a small sum of money to enter bonds with the said regraters of tin, in

[1] Price, pp. 55-58.

[2] 'The Tinners' Grievances,' London 1697, p. 2.

[3] G. R. Lewis, 'The Stannaries,' London 1908, p. 217.

[4] 'Tinners' Grievances,' London 1697, p. 217.

[5] Sombart, 'Der moderne Capitalismus,' Leipzig 1902, i. p. 401.

value much more than the money they had received from them."

The persons here called "mine-workers" must, it is true, be still regarded as formally independent, in spite of their name, as they produced their tin at their own cost and risk. But in reality they were nothing but the instruments of their capitalist purveyors, who sold to the "labouring tinners" at extortionate prices the necessary mining materials, receiving payment in tin at far beneath its market value.[1] Further, the smelters were compelled to have recourse to advances from capitalists[2] by the provisions of the law as to sales, which only allowed tin to be delivered twice a year, at Midsummer and Michaelmas.[3] On the other hand the producers, thus dependent on capitalist assistance, were in their turn employers, for the great mass of those employed in tin mining were ordinary labourers. As early as 1601 Sir Walter Raleigh, who knew tin mining well, spoke of the "poor workmen" who formerly received 2 shillings a week, but now 4 shillings.[4] A document of about the same time states[5] that "the most part of the workers of the black tin are very poor men, and, no doubt, that occupation can never make them rich . . . for they have no profit of their tin if they be hired men, for their masters have the tin."

The need of capital, therefore, brought with it a triple classification of the persons concerned in the industry—first, the capitalist trader; secondly, the producer or working master without resources of his own and drawing all his supplies from the capitalist; and lastly, the labourer he employed.[6] During the seventeenth century the state

[1] 'Aggravii Venetiani,' London 1697, p. 3 (Proposal to raise the prices, etc.).

[2] Unwin, p. 154.

[3] Lewis, pp. 149-150.

[4] 'Parliamentary History,' vol. i. Debate of November 20, 1601.

[5] 'Journal Royal Statistical Society,' 1838, p. 71.

[6] Lewis, p. 216. He distinguishes (1) 'merchant buyers'; (2) 'non-labouring shareholders,' 'small independent miners,' 'in some cases ore dealers'; (3) 'wage workers.'

of affairs so far changed that the capitalists became themselves "adventuring tinners" working their own mines, and further, had an interest "in most of the smelting-houses, which they either managed themselves or leased to poor smelters."[1] In this way there arose in tin mining after 1600 a class of capitalists who appeared on the one hand as traders under the name of "merchants," supplying independent working masters, and on the other hand gradually became themselves "masters," and laid aside the disguise of mere traders. The final stage of this development was reached when the London merchants' agents, who had formerly disposed of the tin to the finishers, were gradually extinguished, and the capitalist smelters took over the tin trade and sent their orders direct from London.[2] According to the statements of Mr. Lewis this system is still in vogue.

The most important factor in the early English industrial capitalism was, however, the development of North of England coal. The first authentic records go back to 1213.[3] About 1246 coal from the Newcastle district received the name 'sea coal,' which proves that already in those days it was carried by sea. From the end of the sixteenth century its hold on the more distant markets, more especially on London and the neighbourhood, continually increased. While, according to Harrison, export coals "had first taken up their innes in the greatest merchants' parlours" in 1577,[4] about 1640-50 an increase in the price of coal was already considered a great injury to the poor.[5] Originally only irregular shipments, the export of coal to France had so developed by 1552 that "France can lyve no more withoute" English coal "than the fische withoute

[1] 'Tinners' Grievances,' p. 4 and ff.; Lewis, p. 223.

[2] Unwin, p. 153; 'Grievances,' p. 4, and Lewis, p. 223.

[3] Th. Wood Bunning, 'The Duties on Coal,' Newcastle 1883, p. 1.

[4] M. Dunn, 'View of the Coal Trade,' Newcastle 1843, pp. 12-13.

[5] R. Gardiner, 'England's Grievance Discovered,' 2nd ed., Newcastle 1796 (an exact copy of the original edition of 1655), p. 193.

water"; [1] and in the days of Elizabeth the trade thus rapidly rising to importance was used for revenue purposes by the introduction of an export duty on coal.[2] But the chief increase in shipments took place in the seventeenth century.[3] The numerous statistics and figures of production given in various documents of the time appear on inspection so contradictory that they are not worth much, especially in view of the often uncertain details of weight. But it is a certain fact that the annual coasting trade was estimated in 1663 for revenue purposes at 160,000 chaldrons, or about 450,000 tons; [4] and according to an official return in 1871 the entire coal production of England in 1660 was about 2 million tons.[5] The statistics concerning the means of sea transport for coal are also striking. A single ship had a carrying capacity in 1421 of about 20 chaldrons (1 chaldron = about 2·6 tons), in 1653 six or seven times that amount was given as the average cargo.[6] In 1676 Sir William Petty put the tonnage of the vessels employed in the Newcastle coal carrying trade at 80,000 tons, and stated that it had increased fourfold in the last forty years.[7]

As the outlet for North of England coal in more distant markets increased, coal mining acquired the impress of a large capitalist undertaking. The Elswick mine, one of the most important, originally let by the Abbey of Tynemouth [8] in 1330 for a rent of £5 a year, brought in 200 years later only £20, but in 1538 £50. In 1582 Queen Elizabeth leased the manors of Gateshead and Wickham, which were rich in coal deposits, for £90 a year, and shortly afterwards transferred her lease to the town of Newcastle for a payment of £12,000.[9] The yearly output of a number of collieries on

[1] Galloway, 'History of Coal Mining,' p. 20.

[2] Bunning, p. 4.

[3] Brand, 'History of Newcastle.'

[4] Dunn, p. 18.

[5] Cunningham, i. p. 530.

[6] Dunn, p. 12, and Gardiner, p. 105.

[7] A. Anderson, 'Geschichte des Handels,' Riga 1778, part vi. pp. 17 and 18.

[8] Dunn, pp. 14 and 19.

[9] Gardiner, pp. 13 and 14.

the river Wear was valued in 1644, a year, it is true, of dear coal, at £3000.[1]

The great attraction which coal mines had for capitalists —often to their undoing—is shown by the following description by Gray in the year 1649.[2] "South Gentlemen have, upon great hope of profit, come into this Country to hazard their monies in Coale Pits. Master Beaumont, a Gentleman of great ingenuity and rare parts, adventured into our mines with his thirty thousand pounds; who brought with him many rare Engines, not known then in these parts, as the best to boore with, Iron Roddes to try the deepnesse and thicknesse of the Coale, rare Engines to draw water out of the Pits, to the Staithes, to the River, etc. Within few years he consumed all his money and rode home upon his Light Horse." The conditions of work at this time also show an entirely capitalist organisation. Gray relates that many thousand people were engaged in the coal trade, and that a single employer had 500 to 1000 persons "in his works." And in 1662, 2000 miners sent a petition to Parliament complaining of the injustice of their employers. At the beginning of the eighteenth century several hundred people were employed in single collieries.[3] When it is remembered that in 1754 the entire production of the Grafschaft Mark was only 35,000 tons, the number of miners 699, and each mine employed under seven men,[4] the very advanced state of coal mining in the North of England as early as the seventeenth century, both in the quantity of its production and in its capitalist system of management, becomes even clearer.

Finally, a large number of handicrafts were in the sixteenth century, and still more throughout the seventeenth

[1] Dunn, p. 16.

[2] W. Gray, 'Chorographia or a Survey of Newcastle-upon-Tyne,' 1649, p. 25.

[3] Dunn, pp. 17 and 23.

[4] Heymann, 'Die gemischten Werke im deutschen Grosseisengewerbe,' Stuttgart 1904, p. 108.

century, financed by capitalists,[1] and so gradually converted into capitalist industries. The extremely complicated process by which independent craftsmen came gradually into "indirect dependence on capital"[2] has been recently reconstructed with excellent illustrations from authorities by Mr. George Unwin. Traders in foreign goods, oversea merchants, and middlemen formed a new class of capitalists, which by its command of money gained the mastery over the craftsmen. Even at the beginning of the sixteenth century the Haberdashers, then still chiefly dealers in fine goods from abroad, employed a large number of London craftsmen, who are said to have been in the most pitiable condition; while well-to-do masters also assumed the part of capitalists and pressed on the small masters, who were crushed out—for instance, in felt-making and cloth-weaving—between the capitalist masters on the one side and the simple journeymen and labourers on the other. For a long while the small masters sought to maintain their independence against the capitalists, partly by trying through an organisation of their own—the yeomanry organisation—to win a place in the old corporations now gradually falling more and more under the sway of the capitalist masters, and partly by striving to create a corporation of their own.

[1] Translator's note. There is no adequate English translation for the German "Verlagsystem," "Verleger," etc. It means a special kind of *capitalist* organisation, and cannot therefore, as Mr Unwin has pointed out ('Industrial Organisation,' pp. 3-4), be well identified with the "domestic system" proper. The "Verlagsystem" differs from the "domestic system" in so far as it has a definite capitalist basis, and from the ordinary "factory system" in so far as the workman does his work at home. The capitalist (merchant, employer, factor, etc.) controls the domestic worker or craftsman by advancing him money or machinery or supplies of raw material, in return for which the worker delivers to him the bulk of his output. The system shows a good many variations, but the essential feature is always in domestic work in direct economic dependence on a capitalist entrepreneur. The "commission system" has been suggested as an equivalent, but in the absence of any recognised term I have thought it better as a rule to avoid the appearance of a technical expression.

[2] Sombart, 'Moderne Capitalismus,' i. pp. 203 and 401.

The craftsmen also made attempts by combined action to emancipate themselves from the capitalists. The felt-makers collected £5000 in 1611 to make themselves independent of middlemen in the purchase of raw material, and to prevent themselves being compelled by financial needs to cut prices. But this organisation—a kind of limited company—only lasted three years. In the middle of the seventeenth century there was a deep gulf fixed between the small masters and their richer brethren, with whom they had united in the " Project " against the capitalist middlemen. On the one side stood the rich felt-makers, many of whom employed " ten, twenty, or thirty persons and upwards in picking and carding wool, and preparing it for use, besides journeymen and apprentices." They had freed themselves from middlemen and become themselves capitalists. On the other side were the small masters, still dependent as before on the capital of others and faced with the certain fate of having to make way for the class of journeymen on daily wages. Other corporations had similarly tried to maintain their independence with the aid of co-operative undertakings and by attracting outside capital, and in every case the plea of finding work for poor members had been to the fore. It was so in the case of the horn-makers, the tin founders, and the cloth weavers, usually with the same eventual result as with the felt-makers.

A valuable document of 1618 ('State Papers, Domestic, James I.,' vol. lxxi. 13, year 1615) gives us some information as regards the capitalist organisation of the cloth trade at the beginning of the seventeenth century. It contained the following kinds of traders :

1. The rich clothier, who bought his wool direct from the wool countries and made his whole year's provision beforehand, had it spun in the winter by his own spinners, woven by his own weavers, and fulled by his own tuckers, all of whom he paid " at the lowest rate of wages."

2. The meaner clothier, who borrowed most of his wool "att the market," employed many "poor men," sold his cloth, and then paid his old debt. "Of this sort there are a great store that live well and growe riche and sett thousands on worke."
3. Clothiers who did not possess enough capital to buy wool in advance, but "doe weekely buy their yarn in the market," and make it into cloth and sell it themselves. The yarn is made by "spinners" "who buy their woolle in very small parcells," and put yarns on the market every week, for which they require the aid of chapmen.
4. Lastly, thousands of "poore people" who made coarse cloth "by theire great Industry and Skill," and were apparently in the same position as those named under 3.

The entire classification shows the opposition between the large capitalist makers, who provided themselves with raw materials and had them manufactured wholesale, partly on a domestic system and partly in factories, and the small independent master, who usually carried out only part of the process and relied on credit and middlemen. This opposition, whose existence in the fifteenth and sixteenth centuries is described by Prof. Ashley,[1] was permanently accentuated in the seventeenth,[2] though the complete extinction of the small master did not occur till the Industrial Revolution, with the rise of machinery and the final replacement of the domestic system of industry by the factory.[3]

[1] Ashley, 'History of English Industry,' Leipzig 1896, p. 230 ff. and p. 238 ff.

[2] We hear of small masters complaining in 1689 of "some merchants that keep journeymen, cloth workers, packers, dyers and others to work in their houses and not only employ them in doing their own work but also other merchants' clothes, which in the end will prove the ruine of many families in the working trade."

[3] Though Prof. Cunningham ('Growth of English Industry,' i. p. 499) is of opinion that handicraft "maintained its ground" in cloth weaving until the rise of factories, we can only understand him to mean in most cases a dubious struggle for existence against capitalism working partly with the domestic system and partly with the factory.

The attempts of the small master by some kind of organisation to maintain himself in the capitalist development of industry against those whom that development had aggrandised must be considered to have been hopeless by the time of the Civil War. By that time, wherever capitalism had introduced larger forms of industrial organisation, the poorer master craftsmen were a moribund class of independent producers who had no choice but to become day labourers.[1]

Thus the general expansion of the trade, commerce, and shipping of England in the seventeenth century brought a new organisation in the most diverse branches of industrial production. With the end of the sixteenth century, and then with every decade of the seventeenth century, industrial capitalism extended, most markedly in the industries newly introduced and in mining, slowly but steadily in trades till then entirely carried on by craftsmen.[2] In many cases the decisive influence was the extension of markets and the consequential increase in production. This in its turn required a larger accumulation of fixed capital, as for instance in mining or where increased machinery was required, and further necessitated the possession of capital by the manufacturer to enable him to obtain supplies of the necessary raw material where wholesale purchases were profitable. In this way capitalism, either by supporting

[1] Cf. for this statement Unwin, 'Industrial Organisation,' p. 73 ff., pp. 197 and 198, p. 199 ff., p. 209 and *passim*. For the classification of cloth weavers, *ibid.* pp. 234-36.

[2] This result contradicts the frequently repeated contention that industrial capitalism started in England in about 1760. For instance Toynbee (' Industrial Revolution,' London 1884, pp. 53-4) basing himself on observations concerning the domestic system in the wool and linen weaving of the eighteenth century says : " This was the nearest approach to the capitalist system before the beginning of the great technical discoveries." Like many other writers, Toynbee fixes his attention on the textile industry alone (besides the nail industry, which he admits to be worked on the factory system), and overlooks a great number of industries which, as we have shown above, had long been bound up with capitalism, and had in some cases even advanced beyond the system of depending on capitalists for supplies.

small industrial units, as in the case of domestic capitalist industries,[1] or by building up large undertakings gained command over the most important English industries of the time.

The special form of organisation which was characteristic of this early industrial capitalism up till the end of the seventeenth century was the monopoly.

[1] See Translator's note, *supra* p. 12.

CHAPTER II

THE ORGANISATION OF MONOPOLIES

THE legal foundation of monopoly rested on the grant by the Crown to individuals or corporations of the sole right to carry on a given trade. Under Queen Elizabeth the system of trade privileges, as is well known, grew rapidly. There was scarcely a commodity which was not the object of a monopoly. On one occasion, when a long series of concessions was recited in Parliament, a member exclaimed "Is not bread in the number?" And to the astonished cries of "Bread!" he replied, "Yes, I assure you, if affairs go on at this rate, we shall have bread reduced to a monopoly before the next Parliament." [1]

Elizabeth had repeatedly to promise the abolition of monopolies,[2] and finally, in 1601, after a Parliamentary debate in which most of the speakers expressed in the most unequivocal terms their exasperation with the existing privileges, a great number of exclusive rights were in fact suppressed.[3] But the era of monopoly was by no means ended thereby. The creation of grants, patents, etc., continued under James I. and reached a new high-water mark between 1614 and 1621.[4] The reply to this development was the well-known Anti-Monopoly Act of 1624.[5] The

[1] F. W. Hirst, 'Monopolies, Trusts and Cartels,' London, p. 17; and for particular cases of monopoly, C. Fisk Beach, 'Monopolies and Industrial Trusts,' St. Louis 1898, p. 10 and *seq.*; also Palgrave's 'Dictionary,' vol. ii. p. 802.

[2] 'Parliamentary History,' vol. i., London 1806, pp. 925 and 929.

[3] *Ibid.* p. 935. [4] 'Social England,' p. 192 and *seq.* [5] 21 Jac. i. cap. 3.

effect of this Act, which is still of importance to English lawyers, has often been wrongly estimated, so far as it concerned the actual creation of monopoly. M'Culloch, for instance, was of opinion [1] that it had given freedom of trade to English industry. The terms of the Act may no doubt have been inspired by doctrines akin to free trade, but it would be a mistake to imagine that it abruptly terminated the existence of monopolies, which, on the contrary, appear to have continued for decades afterwards in spite of this express prohibition. The explanation is this. In the first place the Act itself left a whole series of monopolies untouched, and secondly, it was divided into two parts, one of which consisted of an emphatic condemnation of all monopolist undertakings, while the other at the end of the statute (sections xii.-xiv.) sanctioned afresh certain important monopolies. As has been said, the entire statute is characteristic of its creator, James I., the prince "with a head of gold and feet of clay."

At the same time, the Act of 1624 would have greatly limited the power of monopoly, had it not been frequently transgressed subsequently. Charles I.'s claims to rule without Parliament and to be financially independent of Parliament, drove him to follow in the steps of his predecessors and to have recourse to the grant of patents. For this purpose especial use was made of the clause of the statute (section ix.) which excepted civic corporations and companies from its provisions. It is true that originally it was only permissible to set up a corporation of a monopolist character within the area of a given town, and that in that town membership of such a corporation might not be restricted without further formalities. But the enterprising spirits who wished to conceal under such a corporation a national monopoly soon found a way out. They obtained a grant by royal ordinance of the right of "superintendence" over the whole national production, and finally a right to suppress all outsiders. The traditional right of

[1] M'Culloch, 'Dictionary of Commerce,' London 1882, p. 895.

the free burgess, especially the free burgess of London, to enter any company for the practice of his trade was similarly suppressed. In this way the London Starch-makers' Company, an undertaking managed by a few capitalists, had already become a closed national monopoly even before the Anti-Monopoly Act.[1] The Act made this method of founding a monopoly very popular, and after 1624 numerous corporations arose with the express object of forming national monopolies.[2]

The provision of the Act (section vi.) which allowed a fourteen years' patent for new discoveries opened up a further possibility or point of departure for the grant of monopoly. Starting from this vantage ground the possessor of a patent could acquire all kinds of privileges. He could be given a patent for his particular process and at the same time the right "for the protection of his patent," to keep watch on all other producers, a measure which in practice led to the exercise of monopoly rights.[3] A later writer even complains bitterly that this clause had been stretched to cover imported goods, unknown to English manufacturers, so that anyone who promised to produce such commodities in England could obtain protection against both foreign and internal competition.[4] The use of the clause as to patents for purposes of monopoly was so general that the word "patentee" meant in the period from 1630 to 1650 "monopolist."

> "The Monopolist and the Patentee
> Did joyne hand in hand as here you see"

is the legend under the frontispiece to an anti-monopolist pamphlet of 1642.[5] With justice did a member of Parlia-

[1] Price, 'Patents of Monopoly,' pp. 37-8.

[2] Unwin, 'The Gilds and Companies of London,' London 1908, pp. 294-5 and pp. 317-8.

[3] Price, p. 119 and *passim*.

[4] 'Britannia Languens or a Discourse of Trade,' London 1680, p. 85.

[5] 'The Projectors' Downfall,' London 1842, title-page.

ment declare, in a debate in 1640:[1] "Better laws could not have been made than the Statute of Monopolies against Projectors; and yet, as if the law had been the author of them, there have been during these few years more monopolies and infringements of liberties than there have any year since the Conquest."[2]

In view of the Elizabethan monopolies, the last statement seems somewhat exaggerated, but the substance of the complaint is certainly true. The remarks of speakers from all parties during the debate prove the existence of a profusion of monopolists. The sarcastic speech of Sir John Colepepper in 1640 was famous. In one passage he declares that "these, like the frogs of Egypt, have gotten possession of our dwellings, and we have scarcely a room free from them. They sip in our cup; they dip in our dish; they sit by our fire. We find them in the dye vat, the washing bowl, and the powdering tub. They share with the butler in his bar. They have marked and sealed us from head to foot. They will not bate us a pin."[3]

It must especially be remembered, in considering the effect of the Monopoly Act, that the legal conditions in mining up till the end of the seventeenth century offered in many ways great advantages for the creation of monopolies. The right of the Crown to claim ownership of all mines in which silver and gold were found became a means of monopolising copper, lead, and zinc mines. Since the time of Elizabeth the Crown had exercised this contingent right, not without provoking many lawsuits,[4] and it led to

[1] 'Parliamentary History,' vol. ii. p. 650.

[2] Mr. F. C. Montague in his 'History of England' (London 1907, vol. vii. p. 181) thinks that the Act of 1624 was evaded on the pretext that it only relates to monopolies given to individuals. For this opinion he gave no evidence. It is clear that the Act forbade all monopolies, whether for individuals or bodies corporate or politic whatsoever. Also monopolies were granted to individuals after 1624, just as before, *e.g.* one for glass in 1634.

[3] 'Parliamentary History,' vol. ii. p. 654-5.

[4] Cf. detailed list of cases in Abbott, 'Essay on the Mines of England' (London 1833), pp. 218-9 ff., *seq.*; Lewis, 'Stannaries,' p. 76.

the formation of the great monopolies of that time.[1] No radical alteration in the law was made till the time of William III., in 1689, when the expression "mines royal" was unambiguously defined by a new law. "No mines of Copper, Tin, Iron or Lead shall hereafter be adjudged, reputed or taken to be a mine royal, although Gold and Silver may be extracted out of the same." [2]

Thus the mining rights in these metals were finally taken away from the Crown and assured to the landowner, and in consequence the *raison d'être* of the notorious mining monopolies, the Mines Royal, Mineral and Battery Works, and the later combination of these two, the Society of the Mines Royal,[3] was removed.[4] The right of pre-emption of the Crown in the case of the tin mines in Cornwall and Devonshire remained. But the abolition in principle of the mining monopoly was doubtless the reason why the Crown made no further use of this method of creating a monopoly. It was used once more in the reign of Queen Anne; but after 1717 vanished wholly from the history of English mining.[5]

The legal position reached at the end of the seventeenth century, therefore, no longer put any obstacle in the way of free competition in the extraction of minerals. In coal the ownership of the landowner had been the rule in most cases from time immemorial. The law of 1689 put copper, tin, iron and lead in a similar position.

An exception remained in the so-called "free mining districts," which were subject to the royal rights of the Crown. Free mining existed, for the Crown merely received dues and supervised the mine courts; but the mining villages had built up a complicated system of principles and regulations which influenced in various direc-

[1] Price, 'Patents of Monopoly,' p. 50.

[2] 1 William and Mary, cap. 30; also Palgrave, ii. p. 765.

[3] For details see Price, 'Patents,' p. 49 and *seq*. and p. 55 and *seq*.; also Cunningham, 'English Industries,' p. 59.

[4] Lewis, 'Stannaries,' p. 42. [5] *Ibid*. pp. 48-9, 220-221.

tions the organisation of each district. Generally speaking, no village in these districts set up a monopolist system of mining. Of the five free mining districts known to us, the Mendip Hills, Alston Moor, the tin districts in Devonshire and Cornwall, some parts of Derbyshire and the Forest of Dean, only the last was organised on the monopolist lines of a gild, while in all the others no special limitations seem to have been set by the local mining authorities on the grant of mining rights.[1] In the Forest of Dean, however, the Mine Law Court started after about 1660 to attempt monopolist control over production and markets in all kinds of ways—by attaching various conditions to the permission to mine as a "free miner," by fixing the prices, even by assigning definite prices to particular markets, and trying to limit the production of individual miners.[2] In 1675, however, this organisation seems to have been broken up by outsiders, who, in defiance of the Court, but also without interference from it, began to mine "with the express purpose of working against a coal monopoly." These "foreigners," as they were called, in contradistinction to the "free miners," became more and more numerous, especially when the Mine Court came to an end in 1777, and the "free miners" relinquished their property more and more to strangers.[3] Still the possibility of monopoly lasted longer here than elsewhere in English mining. The exception is, however, an inconsiderable one. In the other free mining districts, especially in the tin mines of Cornwall and Devon, there was no difficulty in acquiring mine concessions.[4] Mining rights went with the ownership of the

[1] Lewis, for coal, p. 78; for free mining, p. 76; for single districts, pp. 78-81; for the organisation in the Forest of Dean, pp. 79 and 173 *seq.*

[2] Thomas Sopwith, 'The Award of the Dean Forest Commissioners,' London 1841, pp. 12-20; Nicholls, 'Forest of Dean,' London 1858, p. 45 and *seq.*

[3] 'Fourth and Fifth Reports of Dean Forest Commissioners,' London 1835, pp. 44 and 7-10; also Nicholls, p. 116.

[4] Lewis, *op. cit.* p. 161 for details.

land, after the law of 1689 had finally settled and brought into general use this legal principle.

In the same year took place the final repeal of another legal enactment of the highest importance for the creation of monopolies. The claims of the Royal Prerogative to dispense with the law, by which Prerogative the Crown had granted monopolies over the head of Parliament by hair-splitting interpretations or even open evasion of the existing law, was abolished in the Bill of Rights. Even though the number of existing monopolies had in all probability greatly decreased since about 1650 or 1660—unfortunately we have no detailed record—the extinction of that right showed that Parliament had henceforth the power to prevent all private trade monopolies by means which could not legally be evaded. Only local monopolies based on gild and corporation rights and having nothing in common with the great national monopolies of the Tudor and early Stuarts could now exist, except where Parliament by its own act otherwise ordained. Great capitalist monopolies such as we have in view, controlling by legal privilege the entire national production of a given branch of industry, were once and for all impossible. The Long Parliament in 1640 had declared most of the monopolies void, and thereby taken upon itself functions in relation to the Crown for which it had no constitutional justification. After the Restoration the Crown found itself similarly hindered [1] by the increasing power of Parliament [2] in the exercise of its former custom of settling industrial questions on its own initiative. This state of affairs received recognition in theory by the abolition in 1689 of the Royal Prerogative, and the always latent [3] conflict between a Crown inclined to befriend monopolists and a Parliament that was bitterly hostile to them was thus finally decided in favour of the latter.

The legal conditions which were thus altered at the end

[1] Macaulay, p. 209. [2] Cunningham, vol. i. pp. 201 and 205.

[3] Unwin, 'Industrial Organisation,' p. 169. Interesting account of such a conflict in 1664.

of the seventeenth century had for about a century largely determined the creation of monopolies in its general aspect. But a number of other circumstances, such as the economic characteristics of the industries concerned, the various trade regulations, and the manner in which the laws relating to the trade were administered had no less influence on the actual development of the monopoly in individual cases. The forms of such monopolies were very various. They differed from one another, owing to the differences and permutations of the above and other circumstances, in structure, in the size of their sphere of action, and in economic potency. No correct estimate of the actual importance of the early monopolies in the economic life of the day can therefore be gained without an examination of individual monopolies and their special peculiarities.

Some of the most important, curiously overlooked by recent investigators,[1] are to be found in mining, and especially in coal mining. Even without the aid of the law the large consuming centres were limited for their supplies of mining products to particular producing areas, which either because of the primitive means of transport or from lack of any competing source of supply soon acquired a monopoly. London, for instance, could only get coal or tin from Newcastle and Cornwall even when the prices of those commodities rose very high. Clearly, if the exploitation of these natural monopolies was further delivered over by legal concession to a few individuals, or often to a single individual, a monopoly of unusual strength was possible.

We first hear of monopolies in the coal mines of the north in 1590. Their history is connected with the group of mines which, as has already been mentioned, belonged originally to Queen Elizabeth, and was then transferred to the town of Newcastle. The town made over its property to a company of free citizens called hostmen, and this company gave its rights to eighteen or twenty of its members,

[1] Neither Unwin nor Price mentions the coal monopoly.

who became coal miners and coal merchants in combination.[1] This concentration of the coal trade in a few hands much disturbed the London buyers, the more so as the price of coal rose greatly between 1582 and 1590.[2] Rumours of a monopolist ring among northern coal miners were in the air, and in 1590 the Lord Mayor of London made complaint to the Treasurer Burleigh that the hostmen had "engrossed" the mines, and petitioned that "all mines should be worked and a maximum price of seven shillings a chaldron fixed."[3]

No special privilege from the Crown had so far been necessary for the growth of a monopolist organisation of production. But it by no means followed that there was no desire for additional State protection. On the contrary, the stronger the agitation of the consuming interests became, the more anxious the monopolists were to see their organisation sanctioned by the Crown. After further complaints in 1597 against the excessive coal prices,[4] hostmen seized a chance opportunity[5] to attempt to obtain incorporation as a gild. The town of Newcastle had for a long while neglected an obligation existing since the days of Henry V. to pay a tax of 2d. a chaldron to the Crown. Queen Elizabeth claimed the debt, and the town made her the following proposal: the arrears to be struck off their debit account, and the queen further to grant a gild patent to a "brotherhood, called the free hostmen, for the sale of every kind of coal to the ships," in return for which she should receive 12d. for every chaldron of coal carried by sea. The queen accepted this proposal, and on March 22, 1600, the aforesaid brotherhood became an incorporated gild. It was protected by the gild statutes and its exclusive rights

[1] Brand, 'History of Newcastle,' p. 269.

[2] According to Dunn, 'View of the Coal Trade,' p. 21, coal on ship at Newcastle cost 6s. in 1582; 8s. in 1585, and 9s. in 1590.

[3] Brand, also Dunn, p. 13.

[4] J. D. Rogers in Palgrave, London 1899, vol. iii. p. 615 A.

[5] For authorities see my article on "English Cartels of the Past" in Schmoller's 'Jahrbucher,' 1907, p. 158.

from any external competition. On the one hand it had the monopoly of the most important mines; on the other it possessed the sole right to sell coal to the ships which entered the River Tyne, and held in its hands the entire export trade,[1] so that it could prevent the independent sale by possible outsiders of any coal they might produce. It held, in fact, a right of pre-emption sufficient to frighten off any competitor at the outset. The actual exercise of its rights was assured by the fact that most of the members of the gild held public offices, were free burgesses, and so on, and their influence served to maintain the gild's rights and privileges, and often to assert them by force. Accordingly we find the chief opponents of the gild identifying the hostmen with the corporation of Newcastle, and attacking the privileges of the town magistrates when their real objective is the gild patent and its exclusive rights.[2]

But external protection by no means secured the internal harmony of the gild. That had to be assured by ordinances limiting competition among the hostmen themselves. That this step was taken immediately after the incorporation of the gild is proved by the Gild Book of the coalowners in 1602. This book contains " An Ordinance and Common Agreement for the Sale of Coal " among twenty-nine, or, counting partners, twenty-four hostmen. These twenty-four, who were all coalowners,[3] were only a small committee of the gild which had in 1600 forty-four members, but their decisions were regarded as binding. Within this committee of the four and twenty there were again four groups, each member of which might only sell a given amount of coal, no member being allowed more than nine times the amount assigned to any other member.

[1] The Act of 1624 says they had privileges " concerning the *selling*, carrying, loading, disposing, shipping, *venting*, or trading *of* or *for* any sea coals, stone coals, or pit coals forth or out of the haven and river of Tyne."

[2] Levy. *op. cit.* p. 186; also Gardiner, ' England's Grievances,' 3rd ed. p. 85, note 1.

[3] Palgrave, ' Dictionary,' iii. p. 615.

In other words, within each group the sale of coal was so regulated that the smallest sale must be to the largest as 1 to 9.[1] This organisation was clearly an early attempt to create a division of production, based on figures of participation.

This system continued unchanged under James I., though the complaints against its control of the market had by no means ceased. We find in Gardiner [2] that about 1620 the Attorney-General filed a complaint in London against the town authorities of Newcastle concerning the free hostmen, that, having all the selling of coal in their hands, they compelled ships to take bad coal, and even delivered coal unfit for sale, to the great harm of the people.

In spite of this, the Coal Gild received further express recognition of its privileges by the Anti-Monopoly Act of 1624.[3] In 1638 Charles I. again renewed its patent, and decreed that it should be entitled to attach all coal exported by ship except through it. Gardiner's pamphlet, the origin of which we shall see later, proves that it continued to exist in 1650. The limitation of competition by the organisation of producers is again and again the subject of comment. For instance,[4] " Gentlemen and others in the counties of Northumberland and Durham are prohibited to sell their coals to ships to be transported to London, and all owners of collieries are compelled to sell their coal to them [the magistrates who were identical with the hostmen]. If any shall presume to sell their coals immediately to the ships, they seize upon such coals upon pretence that the owners of the coals are not free of their corporation. . . . Whereas if the owners of every colliery had free liberty to sell his coals to ships immediately Tinmouth haven would afford two hundred thousand chaldrons of coal in a year more than now are vented, which would reduce the late exorbitant rates of coal in the city of London."

[1] Palgrave, 'Dictionary,' iii. p. 615A; Brand, 'History of Newcastle,' p. 273 and *seq.*

[2] Gardiner, p. 49.

[3] 21 Jacob. I. cap. 3, xii.

[4] Gardiner, pp. 204, 205.

This apparently refers to the outsiders put down by the Coal Gild, and in whose interests Gardiner spoke. In the great petition laid before a Parliamentary Committee in 1653 he again advocates the liberty of persons hindered by the gild.[1] The Bill presented to Parliament by the committee in November 1653 states :[2] " To the end so useful a commodity as that of sea coal, wherein the poor of this commonwealth are so principally concerned, may come cheaper to the market and the coalowners may not be in a worse condition than the rest of the free people of this realm, be it enacted and ordained that the said coalowners in the respective counties may and have hereby liberty to let or lease of their coal pits and to sell their coals to whom they please, as well to ships as elsewhere, for the benefit of the public." This Bill, drawn up after hearing evidence, and at the vigorous instigation of the chief witness, Gardiner, never became law. Together with many other projects, it disappeared from the scene on the dissolution of Parliament by Cromwell in 1653.[3] The scanty documents which survive prove that in 1665 a coal gild no longer existed officially,[4] therefore between that date and the time of the above Bill the abolition of the Coal Gild's monopoly must have taken place.

The monopolies in the tin mines in the south-west of England were very different from those of the coal trade. In this case, as has been already remarked, monopoly arose from the Crown's right of pre-emption. At the end of Queen Elizabeth's reign this right was granted to private persons, and it remained the basis of the monopoly almost without intermission down to the outbreak of the Civil War. The monopoly was owned by capitalists. The capitalist form of the tin industry, as it appears at the end of the sixteenth century, has already been described. The lack of necessary capital had led to the dependence on the

[1] Levy in Schmoller's ' Jahrbuch,' p. 188 ; Gardiner, p. 9.

[2] Gardiner, p. 124. [3] ' Newcastle Weekly Chronicle,' July 21, 1894.

[4] Palgrave's ' Dictionary,' vol. iii. p. 615 B.

capitalist traders of the working mine owners and smelters, who in their turn employed a number of dependent miners. This process might have come about naturally, without the existence of a monopoly, but the special effect of the latter was to concentrate in the hands of one or more associated capitalists [1] the entire control of the trade capital, instead of leaving it as at the end of the sixteenth century [2] in those of several capitalists.[3]

For some years the tin monopoly was owned by the London Pewterers. They had "general supervision over the manufacture [of pewter] elsewhere in England," [4] and it seems quite intelligible therefore that they desired to be independent of the monopolists for their supplies of the raw metal. The simplest way was to take over the monopoly themselves. For that purpose it was necessary to have money, first to acquire the privilege from the Crown, and secondly, because the existing monopolists had made advances to the producers of tin and supplied all their needs, a practice which the Pewterers would have to imitate if they intended to gain control over the raw tin trade. The raising of this capital could not be shifted on to the Pewterers' Company as a whole, because by no means all the members were rich enough to contribute considerable sums. The only remaining alternative was for the rich members to find the necessary funds. In 1615 twelve members of the company subscribed £7000, to be used, together with £800 contributed by the company as a body, to take over the monopoly for five years. Part of the tin thus acquired was divided (at cost price, plus a certain surcharge) among the working members; the remainder was used for the trade purposes of the richer members.[5] Thus the finishers belonged at that time for the moment to those whom the monopoly profited instead of to its victims. Their power was shown in the fixing of prices. It seems to have been

[1] Lewis, 'Stannaries,' p. 147.
[2] 'Tinners' Grievances,' pp. 5 and 6
[3] Cf. *infra*.
[4] Lewis, 'Stannaries,' p. 45.
[5] Unwin, 'Industrial Organisation,' pp. 152-156.

the policy of the monopolists to offer the tinners economically dependent on them a fixed price, and to screw up the market price on the contrary as high as possible.[1] The hold which they, as the financiers of the trade, had over the actual working masters enabled them to limit the profits of the latter to the minimum. The effect of this policy on the mining industry itself we shall have to describe later.

While the Crown was able to create a monopoly in tin mining by its right of pre-emption, in the mines of the famous Forest of Dean where no such right existed it adopted another course.

The district, like the stannaries of Devonshire and Cornwall, was one of the few so-called " free mining " regions, in which by virtue of the royal rights of the Crown freedom of mining was the settled tradition. Every " free miner," that is to say, every member of the mining community, was allowed to pursue the occupation of mining, so long as he complied with the conditions fixed by the community. Under James I. this state of affairs was replaced by a special grant of the Crown rights. The Earl of Pembroke obtained in 1612 the exclusive right to extract iron ore and coal in the Forest of Dean. The free miners would not recognise this grant, and were allowed by the Attorney-General to continue their occupation " as an act of grace and clemency, and not of legal right " ; the monopolist receiving a right of pre-emption over their output, and no further increase in the number of free miners being allowed. This monopoly was several times renewed. Under Charles I. it was held by Sir John Winter, whose privileges were later confirmed by Charles II. Between 1660 and 1670 the earlier rights of the free miners seem to have once more flourished.[2]

[1] Lewis, p. 146 and *seq.*, pp. 218-19. " General prices continued to rise while that given them for their tin by the monopolists was kept stationary."

[2] For the expression " free miners " cf. ' Fourth and Fifth Reports of the Dean Forest Commissioners (House of Lords),' Sept. 9, 1835, pp. 4-6 ; also the ' Award of the Dean Forest Mining Commissioners,' London 1841, pp. 12-14. For the monopolies cf. H. G. Nicholls, ' The Forest of

Other minerals, the production of which was organised in a monopolist fashion, were alum and salt. In contradistinction to coal and tin, these commodities were not yet generally used in England, and required protection from foreign competition. The output of salt in England was limited until 1670,[1] in which year salt mines were for the first time worked, to the production of sea salt works. Attempts to develop the trade in the time of Elizabeth had been frustrated by the importation of much better and cheaper salt from Scotland, France, and Spain, which stifled English production. Since the end of the sixteenth century monopolies for salt mining had been granted to particular individuals.[2] They were among the most unpopular of monopolists, and in the Anti-Monopoly Debate of 1601 it was asserted that they had in some places increased the price of a bushel more than tenfold.[3] Elizabeth had to annul the grant, and James I. dared not renew it. It did not appear again until the time of Charles I. Political reasons had in the years following 1620 reduced the imports of salt to the advantage of the English producers, and when imports again commenced they naturally sought to retain by artificial means the advantages which the Spanish war had given them.[4]

On the ground that " it would be a great benefit for the Kingdome of England and that of Scotland to erect workes for the making of a sufficient quantity of salt and at a certaine moderate price," [5] the petitioners obtained (i) the prohibition of the importation of salt from the continent, (ii) the incorporation of a company to conduct the salt

Dean,' London 1858, pp. 24-6, p. 29, pp. 143 and 231 ; also 'Report Dean Forest,' 1874, p. 3. For the later development cf. the description of the Mine Law Courts in Nicholls, p. 45, and following.

[1] 'Social England,' vol. iv. p. 620.

[2] Price, 'Patents of Monopoly,' pp. 112-113.

[3] 'Parliamentary History.'

[4] Price, p. 113.

[5] J. Davies, 'An Answer to those Printed Papers published in March last by the late Patentees of Salt,' London 1641, p. 5.

manufacture of the east coast from Southampton to Newcastle. Scotch competition the Government sought to defeat by commanding producers in that country to join the new company (Company of Saltmakers of South and North Shields), on the ground that "a work of this nature should be under one rule and government."[1] The complaints of the consumers were loud. One of them in 1641 said: "A free trade that is now so much desired of the subject and a settled price desired by the Patentee cannot consist, for a constant price forced upon a native manufacture as a principall part of monopoly."[2] According to Rogers' calculation the price of salt, about 13s. 4d. between 1630 and 1635, rose by 1640 to 27s. 4d.; in particular a great difference in price existed between the sphere of the Salt Company and places west of Southampton.[3] The trade was artificially retained by protection and monopoly, although the conditions of production were immeasurably inferior to those obtaining abroad; but it was only when rock salt was discovered that the English salt trade really began to expand successfully.

In its general organisation the alum monopoly, which flourished from 1607 to 1648, resembled very closely the salt monopoly. For our present purposes it will be enough to give its results as they are shown by the excellent investigations of Mr. Price. Here again the industry was most unfavourably placed in England, and could only be built up by the prohibition of imports and the grant of monopolies. As has already been mentioned, very considerable sums, drawn from the pockets of speculative monopolists, who followed one another in fairly quick succession, were spent on its introduction.

The financial results of the "Alum Company" were extremely unsatisfactory, at least for those who would not stoop to underhand practices. The supply sufficed neither for the demand, which had to be met in part by smuggling,

[1] Price, p. 114. [2] Davies, pp. 21-23.

[3] Rogers, 'History of Agriculture and Prices,' vol. vi. p. 408 ff.

nor to cover the costs of working. The average output of alum only amounted, for instance, between 1619 and 1624, to 313 tons a year, whereas to make the enterprise pay a production of 2000 tons was required. Naturally in these circumstances prices were high, and aroused discontent among the clothiers and dyers. The quality of the native product was also considered lower.[1] None of all the monopolies of the seventeenth century, whose nature and peculiarities are known to us, seem to have been more disappointing, alike for producers, for consumers, and for the Crown, though its effects from the economic point of view are not so serious as those of the monopolies in more important commodities.

Glass was another of the monopolies existing in little developed branches of early industrial capitalism. It lasted from 1574, when the Italian Versalini obtained a patent for the production of drinking glasses, to 1642. From 1615 on it was in the possession of a capitalist courtier, Sir Robert Mansell. As the main condition of his patent was that coal was to be used for the furnaces and not wood, the existing glass manufacturers, who, unlike him, worked with wood, were for Mansell troublesome "outsiders." On the ground that trees must be protected, he succeeded in securing the prohibition of the use of wood in glass-making, in addition to getting various obstructions and prohibitions imposed upon the importation of foreign goods. The original patent thereby became practically a monopoly of the entire glass industry of the country, and Mansell's influence was so powerful that he even extorted the exclusion of his monopoly from the provisions of the statute of 1624. The support of the law was given to his privileges by the Privy Council with rigorous severity, and the suppression of all outsiders who did not respect his rights was energetically carried out. Mansell began glass-making on a grand scale at Newcastle, imported many foreign workmen, and certainly put large sums of money into his enter-

[1] Price, pp. 82-101 for details.

prise. But in 1642 the opponents of his monopoly, who accused it of producing high prices and inferior goods, succeeded by the aid of Parliament in overthrowing it.[1]

The history of the salt, alum and glass monopolies, so far as their organisation and growth are concerned, is very simple. In all three we find a new branch of industry of an obviously risky nature, and therefore not particularly likely to arouse lively competition. But in trades long known in the country, in which the power of the monopolists could only be attained after hard struggles with the original producers or afterwards with newly arisen "outsiders," the history of the monopoly is very different, and shows a series of dramatic catastrophes favouring now one side and now the other. This is most clearly seen in the development of the soap monopoly.

Like so many other monopolies it started with the grant of a patent for a particular process of manufacture. Such a patent was conceded as early as 1622 by James I. to two manufacturers, who were the protegés of a courtier. In 1631 several courtiers took over this patent. They swore[2] among other things "to make cheaper and better soap than the soap makers of London" (about twenty citizens up till now the chief manufacturers of soap). By promising the king a high royalty on their output they obtained permission to establish themselves as "The Society of Soapmakers of Westminster," and further, the right of view of all soap not made by them. This privilege enabled them to cheat the London Soapmakers, but not to overcome them. They next tried to amalgamate with them, "but finding that notwithstanding all endeavours their white soap would not vent according to their expectations, they laboured to draw the Soap Makers of London to joyne with them, using many persuasions and promises of great

[1] Price, pp. 68-9, 72-3; 74 and 77-80.

[2] 'A short and true Relation concerning the Soap Business,' London 1641, pp. 3-5.

profit."[1] When this attempted Cartel failed, another way was suggested, and efforts were made to gain the aid of the civic authorities and the state.

In the presence of highly placed persons and of the Lord Mayor of London an exhibition of washing was given, in which the Society's soap was found to be better than that of the old London Soapmakers. In vain the latter begged with promises exceeding those of the Society for incorporation and the privileges of the monopolists.[2] The influence of the monopolists was stronger. Besides the right of search, they had obtained the prohibition of the importation of potash, thereby cutting off their competitors from their supply of raw material, intending themselves, in accordance with their process, to use only native material. A further royal proclamation, forbidding the making of soap from anything but vegetable fats, dealt a mortal blow to the London soap manufacturers who used train oil.[3] The rise of new competitors was made subject to the discretion of the Star Chamber, and a special ordinance passed " that outside a circle of one mile round London, Westminster and Bristol " no soap might be made, and that the whole trade should follow the regulations of the Westminster Company.[4]

As the opponents of the monopolists did not scruple to break these regulations, prosecutions and lawsuits followed. The result is described later in 1641 by a somewhat partial author in these words:[5] " Many Citizens of London were put out of an old trade in which they had been bred all their time and which was their only livelihood, by Knights, Squires and Gentlemen, never bred up to the trade, upon pretence of a Project and New Invention, which in truth was not so, their persecutions of the Soap makers of London in the Star Chamber being beyond example in respect of the

[1] 'Relation,' p. 6.

[2] F. C. Montague, 'History of England,' London 1907, vol. vii. p. 181.

[3] 'Relation' and Price, p. 120. [4] Price (following Rushworth), p. 120.

[5] 'Relation,' p. 27.

manner of proceedings and of the sentence itselfe, who for using fish oyle and not obeying their searchers, were fined at great summes, imprisoned at three several times about twenty months, their goods extended, their Pannes, Fats etc. broken and destroyed, their houses of a great yearly value made unuseful, their families dispersed and necessitated and their estates almost ruined."

The manufacture of soap by private persons for their own use was also forbidden. But the most important concession gained by the monopolists was acquired in 1634. Their soap was not favoured by the chief consumers, the dyers and wool-combers, and they accordingly obtained the right to use train oil and to apply the old process,[1] so that the original patent grew into a monopolist usurpation of the whole trade. A mad policy of increasing prices resulted from this ever-growing monopoly, and kindled the resentment of all consumers. Even the Crown joined in their complaints, perhaps chiefly because the Company neglected to pay the promised royalties. A proclamation of 1634 stated that soap formerly costing 2d. a pound had now risen to from 6d. to 12d. a pound.[2]

By 1640, however, the position was changed. The old soap-makers succeeded " in buying their trade and their freedom " by promising the Crown larger yearly subsidies than the " Projectors." [3] They in their turn became a corporation, on the condition that they would buy up the Westminster Company.[4] The original " outsiders " succeeded, accordingly, to the rights of the adversaries they had so often fought. They appear to have industriously studied the Company's monopoly system in order to be able to make use of it themselves. We hear that they petitioned for protection, because " many persons did use the making of soap privately and secretly, carrying the same to sale,

[1] Price, p. 121. [2] 'Relation,' p. 17 ff. and p. 23.

[3] R. Wilkins, 'The Sope Patentees of London's Petition opened and explained,' London 1646, p. 8.

[4] Price, pp. 123, 127.

even to the ruin of the Petitioners," and that they eventually obtained not only the exclusive right to sell soap, but also the exclusive right to purchase potash, in order to paralyse the " outsiders " who were springing up against them.[1] The complaints once so loud against the Westminster monopolists were now re-echoed against those of London.[2] " These men will have no competitors in their gains, they well knowing by experience how to taste a greater sweetnesse of gain than the other sope-projectors, having for twenty years together gained much riches by monopolising the Sope boyling mystery into 8 or 10 men's hands, to the ruine of many a family."

Although the soap monopoly was one of the most unpopular, it succeeded, as Mr. Price has shown,[3] in maintaining itself even in the anti-monopolist days of the Commonwealth. The monopolists controlled, besides the district in which their operations had commenced, the much contested market of London and Westminster, also other important outlets like Bristol and York. When they were finally abolished is unknown, but it is certain that they were still firmly established in 1657.

The monopolies so far described were created in industries whose capitalist development had already commenced. Another not less important group is to be found in the union of domestic producers of the artisan class with capitalist entrepreneurs. We have already explained that after the end of the sixteenth century a number of crafts had experienced a great need for capital, which led to a division of the industrial producers into on the one side capitalist masters and entrepreneurs and, on the other, independent producers without capital either economically dependent on capitalists or gradually sinking to the position of paid workmen. For about a century monopolies exercised an important influence on this development.

[1] Wilkins, p. 21; also, 'A Looking Glasse for Sope Patentees,' London, 1646, p. 5.

[2] Wilkins, p. 13.

[3] Price, pp. 125-127.

It is easy to understand that all who possessed sufficient capital to commence a monopolist undertaking turned towards the craft corporations of the "small masters." They were already a monopoly, if at first only of a local kind, and the companies of the then centre of trade, London, exercised an extensive influence on all the markets of the country, or could attempt to obtain such an influence by royal ordinance. The incorporation of crafts, though advocated and carried out in the interests of the "small masters," was also a means by which the capitalist could exploit trade on monopolist lines. The poor craftsman was eager for incorporation, in which he saw protection from further competition; though in fact it only gave the capitalists greater power and control over his interests.[1]

It was, of course, also possible for the members of a corporation themselves to raise capital by means of common contributions, with the assistance of the public and by special calls on the richer gildsmen. This was, as we saw, in fact done by the pewterers to secure a supply of raw material when the raw tin monopoly was bought. The felt-makers of London adopted a similar system in 1611 to assist poor members of the gild to purchase wool. Such measures, however, appear never to have had a lasting success, owing to financial weakness. A far more successful device was for one or two capitalists to finance the gild, and use the weight of their political influence to obtain the grant of monopolist privileges.

A typical example of this form of organisation is to be found in the pin monopoly. In 1605 the pin-makers became

[1] Unwin, 'Industrial Organisation,' p. 145, speaks of "the tendency of industrial privileges vested in bodies of craftsmen to fall into the hands of speculating capitalists, who could attempt to exploit the industry somewhat on the lines of the modern trust. Failure in these enterprises was quite as frequent as success, and the breakdown of one projector afforded the Government the opportunity of issuing another patent covering the same privilege. In this way one monopolist took the field against another monopolist, and the interests of the craftsmen, which were the supposed motive of the grant, so far from being forwarded, were not even considered."

a special corporation. They had not sufficient capital to meet the costs of incorporation, and accordingly they contracted with a courtier to undertake the matter for them in return for a forty years' subsidy on every 1200 finished pins. As a large number of pins were imported from Holland, the gild's monopoly was not yet complete. It was necessary to secure protection from foreign competition. Once again capital was required. To obtain from the Government exclusion of foreign pins was costly, and the craftsmen who wished, after obtaining such exclusion, to extend their production, required considerable sums of money at their command to provide themselves with raw material. A second courtier, Sir Thomas Bartlett, promised to supply the necessary resources out of his own pocket, and he became much more closely connected with the pin-makers than his predecessor. In November 1616 he bought the latter out for £8000, and took over his claims on the company. He then made an agreement with them, binding himself to deliver to them the necessary raw material, wire, provided that they made over to him at a fixed price all the pins they manufactured. Having thus taken to himself the monopoly of pins, so far as London and the surrounding country was concerned, Sir Thomas attempted to complete it by obtaining the sole right of import. This he acquired in October 1618, though with limitations, which only secured him the monopoly in London and its suburbs, and compelled him to promise a conservative price policy—to use a modern expression. Owing, however, to the lax enforcement of the prohibition of import, an important condition at the base of the agreement between Bartlett and the pin-makers remained unfulfilled. The undertaking failed, and after Bartlett's death pin-making remained free from such schemes until 1635.[1]

In that year the pin monopoly arose in a new form. The Company of Pin-makers was re-incorporated and received two important privileges. Imports were strictly forbidden

[1] Unwin, 'Industrial Organisation,' pp. 165-168.

in their favour, and all pin-makers throughout the kingdom were put under the London Company.[1] The monopoly thus spread beyond local boundaries and was secured in its operation by the company's right of viewing, sealing, and regulating. Its financial organisation was this time undertaken by a Mr. Lydsey, who attempted in the interests of Bartlett's heirs to regain the capital he had lost in the undertaking.[2]

A scheme prepared in 1639 and 1640 in connection with the pin monopoly gives a good example of the operations which the monopolists were prepared to undertake. An attempt was made to amalgamate the pin and the wire monopolies. The wire industry, the introduction and capitalist development of which since 1500 has already been mentioned, had become increasingly monopolist. Fiscal protection, suppression of new enterprises by law, and partial monopolisation of locally limited raw materials (iron, wood, calamin) had for decades given the monopolists a secure position in the industry. Just before 1640 the aforesaid Lydsey had acquired a monopoly in the production of brass wire from the Royal Battery Company, the privileged wire-makers. This monopoly it was now intended to strengthen by amalgamation with the pin-makers, and no less a person than Charles I. himself figured as the "promoter." He promised to place £10,000 at the disposal of the pin-makers, in return for which his agent was to buy all their output at a fixed rate agreed to in a list of prices. The pin-makers on their side were to use only Lydsey's wire, and no iron wire. With Lydsey the king had made a similar fixed agreement. The king, therefore, was attempting to amalgamate in one single monopoly two hitherto separate industries; and the monopolisation of the finished product, in order to obtain a more secure and more profitable market for the raw material, brings to mind exactly the modern trust organisation. When the king gave up the scheme, a capitalist called Halstead is said to have undertaken all his

[1] Price, p. 40. [2] Unwin, p. 168.

liabilities towards the pin-makers on the one side and Mr. Lydsey on the other. Lydsey, we are told, got back from the profits of the new enterprise part of the capital, according to his own account £7000, which he had put into the pin monopoly. The king failed in his attempt to play the part of financier, because he was himself in want of money. His sole aim was to secure for himself a share in the profits of what seemed a well-conceived undertaking. The outbreak of the Civil War, however, prevented the realisation of the complete scheme.[1]

This perhaps in the best illustration of the relations between craft corporations and capitalist monopolists. But similar cases occurred in various other trades, for instance in the manufacture of finished cloth. The monopoly organised in that trade by the well-known Alderman Cockayne has been recently described in detail by Mr Price.[2] Mr. Unwin, whom we have to thank for much light on these events, has shown that a similar development took place in the production of beaver hats. The use of beaver in opposition to felt attracted the attention of several capitalists to the fact that a separate industry distinct from that of felt-makers could be made in corporate form out of it and organised as a monopoly. This scheme was realised in 1638, when the Company of Beaver Makers received the sole right to manufacture beaver hats. As the monopoly grew it was soon seen that the poorer members of the company, who had formerly made either felt or beaver hats, had fallen on evil days, now that they might only produce the latter. As in other cases we have mentioned, they had not sufficient capital to supply themselves with the large amount of costly raw material that was necessary, if they were to limit themselves exclusively to the manufacture of beaver hats. Accordingly complaints soon arose that the eight capitalists who had been the lead-

[1] Unwin, pp. 166-168. For the agreement between Charles I., Lydsey, and Halstead, *ibid.* pp. 236-240.

[2] Price, 'Patents of Monopoly,' pp. 102-6.

ing spirits in the matter had, by their economic preponderance, acquired the monopoly of beaver hat making. [1]

Many inferences might be made from the general bearing of the facts so far considered. But the outstanding and fundamental conclusion is that industrial capitalism in England was cradled in monopoly, not in competition. Early industrial capitalism tended to expand on national lines and similarly its monopolies differ from the monopolist organisation of the craft gilds in not being limited to special areas. There are many reasons for this. Many merely local seats of production owing to natural or economic causes or on account of transport facilities supplied distant parts of the country, so that a monopoly in such a district immediately became a national monopoly, as in the instance of the coal industry of the north, the Cornish tin mines, or such trades as for some reason or other were concentrated in London. Secondly, the expansion of a monopoly over the whole country arose where there was a new industry whose founder had obtained by law, or could acquire by lawful means, the privilege of sole manufacture throughout the whole country, as in the glass monopoly, the salt monopoly, or the wire industry. Finally, the "nationalisation" of monopoly might result from the affiliation of several local monopolies, especially of craft gilds, or from the control acquired by a particular corporation over other gilds. It was by this method that the London Soap and Pin Makers extended their monopolies over production and markets in all the most important parts of the country.

The essential foundation of all these early national monopolies was the grant of privileges by law to particular persons or corporations and the legal suppression of the unwelcome competition of other producers. Where these means were not sufficient, private agreements could of course also be made. As we saw, the Coal Gild of Newcastle created a system of division of production to restrict competition within the privileged corporation itself. Other

[1] Unwin, pp. 145-6.

forms of association must also be mentioned. In some gilds, as with the Beaver Hat Makers, economic advantage enabled the capitalist masters to gain for themselves a monopoly over the heads of their poorer brethren. In the pin trade, on the contrary, the gild monopoly was carried on by an agreement between the corporation and a courtier till it fell into the hands of a single capitalist. Another kind of association attempted to give the copper wire monopoly the entire manufacture of pins from wire. Private agreements, therefore, played a not inconsiderable part in the formation of monopolies, though secondary to the foundation on privilege. Lastly, foreign trade policy served to increase monopolies. Wherever foreign competition appeared, restrictions of import for the protection of the monopolists, as we have seen, commenced. The importation of such goods as competed with the products of monopolies was hindered by customs duties and prohibitions, and special attempts were made to restrict the importation of raw material, so as to make competition by any outsiders who might in spite of the prohibitions of the law have arisen, as difficult as possible ; witness the prohibition of the import of potash in the case of the soap trade.

Monopoly arose, therefore, in the early days of English industrial capitalism on the support of three chief buttresses, privileges from the Crown, suppression of internal competion by law, and a protective trade policy ; it developed further by the aid of private agreements between persons seeking to profit by those privileges, and it was distinguished from the monopolies of the craft gild by the national sphere of its activities. To give an account of the various forms of this organisation was our first duty. The question of the importance to be attributed to these monopolies from the point of view of the industrial and economic development of England during this period leads to the examination of their various effects.

CHAPTER III

EFFECTS OF MONOPOLIES: THEIR FALL

THE monopolies of the seventeenth century have been generally condemned by almost all the economic writers who from the time of David Hume to the present day have dealt with them.[1] Mr. Unwin has recently added to the number of such verdicts, though Mr. Hyde Price endeavours to find some favourable results at least in the indirect effects of monopolies.[2] Possibly it is the general condemnation which these monopolies have met with that has made certain writers find something to praise in the system itself, and to consider only its application and its accidental concomitants disastrous. For instance, the author who describes them in 'Social England' says: [3] "The system of monopolies cannot be regarded simply as a means of raising money without parliamentary sanction, nor merely as a means of enriching favourites, nor as wholly based upon mistaken ideas upon the subject of what we now call Political Economy. It was all these and something more—a provision against real as well as fancied dangers, and in some cases a praiseworthy encouragement of business enterprise and invention. But the British public did not make the needful distinctions."

[1] Cf. especially Hume, 'History of England,' vol. v. p. 458; also Ch. Fisk Beach, 'Monopolies and Industrial Trusts,' St. Louis 1898; Hirst, 'Monopolies and Trusts'; Palgrave's 'Dictionary,' vol. ii. p. 802; F. C. Montague, 'History of England,' London 1907, vol. vii.

[2] Unwin, 'Industrial Organisation,' *passim*; Price, p. 129 and ff.

[3] 'Social England,' vol. iv., London 1903, p. 192.

Professor Cunningham also, though by no means, as Mr. Price seems to believe, a defender of the monopolies, adds to his description of them some remarks on the good intentions and economic ideals of the Stuarts, in which he represents the monopolist system of industry to some extent as a well-meant but unsuccessful experiment.[1] This point of view seems to me, however, a dangerous one. It is extremely difficult, if not impossible, to decide what in fact the motives of the Crown in granting patents were. It is inconceivable that hidden motives like the enrichment of the king and his favourites were not as weighty as the openly proclaimed aims of engrafting new industries, cheapening production, and improving quality. Which of these motives was the most present in the grant of monopolies, how far the personal wishes of the king where they conflicted with economic reasons gained the victory, and which of the alleged objects were from the beginning only pretexts, it is quite impossible to say. Secondly, even if it could be established that the grant of monopolies was "well meant" on the part of the ruler, and represented an attempt at a national organisation on broad lines, that fact would not help us to an objective verdict on its practical working. And the elucidation of these practical results is the more necessary, because they almost always turned out differently to what the granters of the monopolies expected, or professed to expect.

It was this discrepancy between actual and expected results which was the constant excuse of the Crown when the wave of popular anti-monopoly movements rose high. Just as to-day many persons regard Cartels and Trusts as a system of organising industry just as advantageous economically if moderately managed, as it is harmful when fully exploited, so in 1601 Queen Elizabeth expressly maintained

[1] Cunningham, pp. 285-6. Later, especially on pp. 287-8 and 307-9 there are a number of remarks in condemnation of the monopolies, so that the author can hardly be said, as Price thinks, to sympathise with them, although he has tried to say something (p. 248) in favour of the Crown's motives in granting monopolies.

that she had never given privileges which had in her judgment been "*malum in se*."[1] In her "golden speech" on November 30, 1601, she represented herself as the victim of deception, and thanked the Commons for showing her the truth about the monopolies which without their intervention she would never have heard. About forty years later Charles I. used exactly similar words when compelled to promise restriction of the monopolies. He explained in 1639 that the privileges which had been given "on pretences that the same would serve the common good and profits of his subjects" had proved themselves "to be prejudicial and inconvenient to the people,"[2] the main cause of which had been that the privileges were "notoriously abused."

The result found most intolerable was the increase in prices, especially when inferior quality went together with higher cost. Nearly all the monopolists had, as we have seen, promised to supply a better quality more cheaply. In no single case was this promise fulfilled. Coal, soap, salt, copper wire, glass and similar articles rose considerably in price under the sway of monopoly. The charter of the Coal Gild of Newcastle set forth the "better disposing of sea coals" as one of the objects of the incorporation, but the essence of the later complaints in Cromwell's time, put forward in the form of a Bill, was that the Coal Gild with the help of the town authorities had greatly obstructed "the free and quick trade of these staple commodities, had made the River [the Tyne] dangerous, and often in many places almost unnavigable," in order to limit the coal trade to the town of Newcastle alone.[3] The rise in coal prices during the first half of the seventeenth century must be regarded as proved, although the especially alarming increase about 1640 was due to the political crisis.[4] Complaints against

[1] 'Parliamentary History,' p. 933.

[2] Price (Appendix), pp. 160 and 173.

[3] Gardiner, 'England's Grievance,' pp. 32, 64, 98 ff., 121.

[4] Dunn, 'View of the Coal Trade,' pp. 14-15.

the sale by the monopolists of bad and unusable coal, already rife at the end of James I.'s reign, found renewed expression before the Council of Trade about 1650.[1] That the rise in the price of soap shortly after the incorporation of the monopolists led to a petition to the Crown itself has already been related. How bad the soap of the Westminster Company soon became can be seen from the fact that they had to abandon their new process and adopt the old method of manufacture to find a market for their goods.[2] In 1637 the Lords of the Privy Council warned the head of the glass monopoly that " they had found that glass was not so fair, so clear, nor so strong as it used to be." [3] In 1601 Parliament was informed by Sir E. Hobby that the price of salt had risen in certain places from 16 pence to 15s. or 16s. a bushel.[4] Between 1630 and 1640 an equal amount of salt cost £4 15s. to £6 in the area of the monopoly, in other parts of England only £3 or less.[5]

Prices of this kind, though made possible by protection and the grant of monopolies, were often the premium necessary for the introduction of new trades. As such they are often defended, or at least lightly judged. But there is room also for scepticism. Historical investigations show that a number of the " new created " or " improved " branches of industry were of very doubtful importance. Professor Cunningham, for instance, finds such an industry in salt mining, begun in England in 1565, for which he thinks " England was very well adapted." [6] But the history of English salt mining in the seventeenth century shows that it could only exist at all under continuous and very extensive protection. When Cromwell removed this protection, it was faced with complete ruin. " The ambition to develop salt and native manufactures by means of monopoly and prohibition of imports resulted only in dis-

[1] Gardiner, pp. 50, 98. Further evidence in Cunningham, p. 300.

[2] *Supra*, p. 36.

[3] Price, ' Patents of Monopoly,' p. 77.

[4] ' Parliamentary History,' p. 930.

[5] Price, p. 114.

[6] Cunningham, pp. 77, 309, 310.

appointment," says Mr. Price.[1] Only when the rock salt deposits were discovered in 1670 did the industry become lasting and successful, while the produce of the sea salt industry, so long nurtured by monopoly, was unable to withstand such competition.[2] Alum is a further example, as we have already explained, of the negative results of an artificially fostered industry.[3] There are, further, among these monopolies many enterprises which were merely of the nature of passing but expensive experiments. The best instance is the dyed cloth monopoly granted to Alderman Cockayne in 1615. By the aid of a prohibition of the export of "whites," and the possession of the sole right to trade in coloured cloths, he hoped to transfer the dyed cloth trade to England, an object which had attracted the attention of Sir Walter Raleigh at the beginning of the century. But Cockayne's cloths were apparently not so good or so cheap as those dyed in Holland, and found no market; and Cockayne was not in a position to carry out his obligations as to the purchase of white cloth.[4] It was clear even in those days that an industry could not be created by merely obtaining an embargo on the export of raw material to other countries. The Dutch not only forbade and obstructed the importation of dyed cloth from England, but also made attempts to manufacture white cloth themselves by favouring weavers. This in turn limited the market for such white cloth as could not be utilised and sold in England, which the monopolists had received permission to export, while on the other hand he could not look for a larger export trade in his goods because of their inferior value.[5] As a result the whole monopoly was a complete fiasco, and one of the chief industries of England suffered considerable disturbance both in its home market and in its foreign

[1] Price, p. 117. [2] 'Social England,' vol. iv. p. 620. [3] *Supra*, p. 32.

[4] A. Anderson, 'Geschichte des Handels,' Riga 1776, part iv. pp. 361, 372, 409.

[5] Anderson, part iv. pp. 409, 410; Price, pp. 105, 106; Cunningham, p. 294; Unwin, pp. 191, 192.

connections. As early as 1617 the privileged company had to abandon its undertaking. A royal proclamation shortly afterwards says:

"We declare our desires to have brought to passe as a principal work of our times the manufactures of dying and dressing of broad cloth within this realm . . . but finding that time discovereth many inabilities which cannot at first be seen . . . we intend not to insist and stay longer upon specious and faire shows which produce not the fruit our actions do aim at . . . perceiving that the former grounds proposed to us by the Undertakers of the worke consisted more in hopes than in effects and finding the work itself to bee too great to bee brought to pass in a very short time."[1] Thus ended the attempt to transfer an industry all the conditions of which were obviously wanting by the grant of a monopoly and by a fiscal policy.

The most essential presupposition to the introduction of finer textile industries, the existence of a qualified class of workmen, was not fulfilled in England at the beginning of the seventeenth century,[2] and this need was only supplied by the later immigration of foreign workers.[3] It was not till fifty years later, and then with far less external stimulus, that this long-desired and afterwards so famous branch of English textiles was successfully introduced as a permanent industry.[4] The cotton industry also, which had already commenced about 1640 in Manchester,[5] has to thank no monopoly for its creation, a fact not to be

[1] Unwin, p. 193.

[2] Ashley, p. 249.

[3] The facts here given essentially reduce the importance of the results formerly deduced by Friedrich List from the protective policy of James I. and Charles I. (F. List, 'Der internationale Handel,' Stuttgart 1841, pp. 79-80).

[4] Anderson, vol. v. p. 538.

[5] E. Baines, 'History of the Cotton Manufacture,' London 1835, pp. 100-101; L. Roberts, 'The Treasure of Traffike,' London 1641, pp. 32 ff.; also J. R. M'Culloch, 'Treatises and Essays,' Edinburgh 1859, p. 471.

forgotten as evidence against the alleged "educational" effects of the Stuart economic policy.

James I.'s failure in the textile industry was closely paralleled, except that its effect was less widely felt, by Charles I.'s attempt to introduce by aid of monopoly a new process in the manufacture of soap, which being in reality less valuable than the existing method was unable to make its way in spite of its monopoly.

The results known to us, therefore, hardly warrant the conclusion that the grant of monopolies was an effective instrument for the introduction of new industries, or that it was the necessary condition for the formation of economically important productive power, and to a certain extent the needful and successful premium against risk for men embarking on doubtful undertakings. It was not undeveloped but easily fostered branches of production that clamoured for monopoly, but on the contrary the possibility of obtaining protection of this kind which often led to attempts to carry on trades condemned to failure from the beginning by unfavourable economic conditions.

In trades which did not require fostering but were already firmly established, monopoly could not even outwardly profess to be a mere "encouragement." In such cases it was nothing but a check to a process of development already begun. Nowhere is this more clearly seen than in mining. The Coal Gild in Newcastle with its trade rules hindered the expansion of the production of coal for decades. Many owners, says Gardiner in 1655,[1] preferred to let their mines fall into decay rather than make themselves dependent in selling their coal on the gild and the town magistrates. But the best example is in tin mining. As we saw, it was the policy of the monopolists to put down the price as far as they possibly could against the real producers, whom they financed. In 1636 the Cornish tin miners complained to the king that the mines were falling into neglect, as the expenses were continually increasing, while the price they

[1] Gardiner, 'England's Grievance,' p. 205.

received for their tin remained stationary.[1] The heavy fall in the figures of production between 1625 and 1646 gives some support to these complaints.[2] When under Cromwell the monopolist right of pre-emption, which belonged to the Crown, together with the regulation of sales which so hampered the producers, were for about ten years in abeyance, a hitherto unknown spirit of enterprise appeared in tin mining. The producers now had "the freedom to sell at all times and at the best price." [3] Traders, so we are told,[4] left their profession in large numbers and began to mine tin. "Then it was that the old works which were turned idle many years, before paying the wages of perhaps a hundred men, were now wrought again with advantage, and employed three or four times as many." [5] In the days of the monopoly the profits of the mine owners and smelters were so regulated by the monopolists, that they were insufficient to attract anyone to devote himself to such a trade. And capitalists above all would be shy of putting their money in a branch of production of whose profits they could only receive a share fixed by a third party.

Even in later days reference was frequently made to the paralysing influence of the monopolists' policy on mining enterprise.[6] It was even declared that the feeling of insecurity for many years later predominant in mining was a kind of traditional relic of the bitter experiences gained in the time of the monopoly continuing into the days of free mining[7]:—a singular instance of the irony of fate, when we remember that the special aim of the Stuarts

[1] Lewis, 'Stannaries,' p. 219, also p. 41. [2] *Ibid.* p. 255.

[3] *Ibid.* p. 152. [4] 'Tinners' Grievances,' p. 2. [5] *Ibid.* p. 5.

[6] G. Abbott, 'Essay on the Mines of England,' London 1833. He describes how the monopoly rights of the concessionaires led the owners to conceal the richness of the ore-bearing land (pp. 266-7), how the monopolists themselves were not in a position to develop the mines to the extent warranted by their mineral wealth (pp. 207-8 and 210), and how, lastly, the monopoly checked the advance of mineralogical investigation (p. 211 ff.).

[7] Abbott, p. 225.

was to guide fresh capital into tin mining by means of the monopoly.[1]

The glass industry, so long as it used wood as a firing material, was scattered over all England, and developed rapidly without the protection of monopoly. In 1589 fifteen glass factories are said to have existed, and seven years earlier the Chancellor of the Exchequer had attempted to put a tax on glass factories to counterbalance the waning receipts of the import duties. The desire to produce finer glasses, drinking and cut glasses led to the grant of a monopoly, which ultimately, as we saw, brought with it the suppression of the old wood-burning factories in favour of those that used coal. In consequence the advance of the glass industry was slight, because the monopolists progressed but slowly with their new process. The patent granted in 1574 for the manufacture of Venetian glass became within seventy years, step by step, a monopoly embracing the entire glass production of England. As the monopolists had had continual difficulties in obtaining skilled foreign workmen, or in training English workmen, the families they had suppressed, who were closely connected with the glass makers of Normandy and Lorraine, again entered the trade, and had, in some cases down to the early years of the nineteenth century, a considerable share in its prosperity. The rapid rise of competition after the abolition of the monopoly was typical. In Newcastle a new undertaking sprang up at once in spite of the Civil War. Glass-making spread to other regions, and a writer of the Restoration says that the advance of the glass trade before the Civil War was unimportant compared with its progress during and after the war. At the end of the seventeenth century there were ninety glass

[1] So Lewis recently, p. 220 : " To this period of monopoly alternating with usury followed in the years 1650 to 1660 a policy on the part of the Commonwealth of complete *laissez faire* as regards the stannaries, and certainly it must be admitted that in this respect, where the Stuart nostrums had failed, Cromwellian non-interference was accompanied by a return in the stannaries to a condition of abounding prosperity."

works in England, twenty-three of which made the finer kinds of glass. The greater number of these works arose after the Restoration.[1]

If to decide how far English industry in fact developed under the régime of protective monopoly during the sixteenth and seventeenth centuries is difficult and at times impossible, to throw out the question how might it have developed without that protection seems at first audacious in the extreme. Yet curiosity is continually posing that question. When one keeps before one's eyes the inglorious history of the industries created by monopolies, how, on the contrary, without monopolies, either after their abolition or even during their existence, trades arose and continued to live, and how lastly the development of flourishing manufactures was hampered by the monopolies and acquired new life at their fall, the greatest caution cannot blind one to the conclusion that the expansion of England's industrial productivity can only have suffered by the system of monopolies, and that if that system had not been adopted the growth of industrial wealth might certainly have been greater.

In the first place, monopolies led to the promotion of trades which had no possible prospect of being able to exist without them and without all sorts of privileges from the State, for which the monopoly could at no time be regarded as protection during the initial stages only, and which in many directions were a dangerous burden to general economic progress. Secondly, as the system was not limited to new industries, but equally applied to developed industries, the general spirit of enterprise was thereby checked for the advantage of a few monopoly owners, and the development of many industries for which England even then possessed great facilities hampered.[2]

[1] Price, pp. 67, 68, 79 ff.

[2] On the first point (New Industries), Price, pp. 129-130, comes to the same conclusion, with which I gladly agree. The second point I have specially emphasised and illustrated by examples (Coal, Tin, etc.) because it is not mentioned by Price.

But even this is not the final condemnation of the effects of monopoly. So far we have considered only the expansion and development of industrial production and the finding of a market for its manufactures. The evil effects of monopoly are most clearly seen in the creation of a particular type of industrial undertaking, which has given a special impress to the original organisation of early industrial capitalism in England as compared with that of later times.

In later days the development of industrial capitalism in all branches of production led to the springing up of numerous competing capitalist manufacturers. But the grant of monopolies caused a concentration of capitalist ascendency in the hands of a single individual or group of individuals. Take the case of tin mining. The tinners and smelters had become capitalist " masters " as early as the end of the sixteenth century. This process was interrupted by tin mining becoming the monopoly of a few capitalists. The entire control over the tin market rested in the hands of the monopolists, and a further capitalist development followed. Competition among the buyers of the raw product from the independent producers was suppressed, and the mass of sellers found themselves faced by a single buyer who could economically oppress them. Thus it happened that during the first two-thirds of the seventeenth century the only period of comparative affluence for the tin miners was the time of the Commonwealth, from 1650 to 1660, when the right of pre-emption and the limitation of sales to two dates in the year were in abeyance. Once more after a long interval there arose, we are told, a great number of independent miners. The abolition of the monopoly caused a reversal of the process by which owing to a single individual becoming the financier of the entire tin mining trade, capitalism had been carried to a high stage of development. The old movement however soon recommenced, and gradually the capitalist smelters became the economic masters of tin mining, a fact still to be traced to-day according to Lewis in the "apparently unjust business relations between smelter and tinner."[1]

The intention of the Crown in granting the tin monopoly had been, in addition to many other motives, to secure a fixed price for the producers and thereby to improve their position by freeing them from the capitalist tin merchants.[2] The opposite happened. The dependence of the tin miners on external capital, already for various reasons considerable, was necessarily accentuated by giving capitalists the monopoly. They used their economic vantage-ground over the penniless miners to keep the price steady, it is true, but so low as to leave the smallest possible surplus for their dependents.

A similar position arose when capitalists became the monopolist financiers of a gild. In pin-making financial control during the days of the monopoly was concentrated in the hands of a single capitalist, and the craft had at once to buy raw material at a fixed price and to deliver pins to the monopolist at a given price. As in several similar cases, the capitalist ascendency either of the richer masters or of particular traders over the poor craftsmen was succeeded by the exclusive power of the single concessionaire, who did not hesitate, having once acquired the means, to use his position to the utmost in every way. At the beginning of the seventeenth century all limitations on the number of trade apprentices were removed, and in 1617 it was proposed to give every master thirty apprentices, and further, a great number of women and children were employed who had never been apprenticed. "The organisations," says Mr. Unwin,[3] "which in other cases furnished through their handicraft traditions a protection to the workmen, were dominated in the case of the monopolist companies by the speculative capitalist, who was as little inclined to maintain

1 Lewis, 'Stannaries,' pp. 218, 219 for the position of the monopolists; pp. 223, 229-230 for the position of the smelters.

2 *Ibid.* p. 218.

3 'Industrial Organisation,' pp. 170, 171.

the best industrial conditions as is the modern shareholder when dealing with unorganised labour." In the manufacture of beaver hats, too, as we related, the monopoly resulted in the repression of the poorer masters by the eight capitalists who financed it.

In the case of newly introduced industries never organised as handicrafts monopoly from the beginning implied the rise of gigantic undertakings, as the monopolists were by the help of protective duties to supply the needs of the whole country. In these capitalistically organised industries the sphere of the enterprise was much further expanded by monopoly than on technical and economic grounds was possible for a single manufacturer. While, for instance, after the abolition of the glass monopoly there arose many separate factories scattered all through England, in the days of Mansell all factories were united in one undertaking. Further, as we have seen, factories using wood had been suppressed at the instigation of the monopolists. England being poor in wood must naturally have lost the small wood-using factories far more rapidly than the forest regions of the Continent, but this suppression all the same gave a further artificial advantage to the large coal-using factory. While in Germany the demands of technical progress for greater capital expenditure led till the end of the eighteenth century in many cases to co-operation in glass founding, leaving the individual glass-makers their independence,[1] in England already at the time of the monopoly a single large capitalist undertaking was omnipotent.

Starch-making, a new industry introduced at the time of Elizabeth, remained, so long as it was a monopoly in the hands of certain patentees, confined to four plants which manufactured for the needs of London and neighbourhood, although these concerns had to replace the entire former imports. When the monopoly of the patentee and of the later company incorporated under James I. was abolished, numerous small undertakings sprang up in a very short

[1] Grossmann, 'Glasindustrie,' Leipzig 1908, pp. 70, 71.

time, the process of manufacture being obviously well suited to small craftsmen.[1]

In the wire trade the works at Tintern in Monmouthshire dominated the national production. About 1600 one Steere opened a new works at Chilworth in Surrey with workmen he had enticed from Tintern. A stormy dispute arose, and finally the monopolists had to buy up Steere's works and materials, and find employment for him himself at "reasonable wages." [2]

No doubt there were circumstances in mining, in handicrafts and in the new industries which made the growth of capitalistic enterprise necessary; but it was due to monopolies that the functions of the numerous capitalists that arose or might have arisen—for instance, capitalist smelters, capitalist masters, capitalist factory owners—were united in single individuals, who were able by their financial importance to gain control of an entire industry. If Prof. Sombart [3] is right in seeing in the transmutation in our own times of the industrial organisation of large undertakings into a purely financial administration one of the highest stages of capitalist organisation, that stage was already reached by the old monopolies. The possessor of large capital resources was in a position to finance whole industries, either by himself entering into the manufacture, building works and trying new processes, or by merely undertaking the purely financial organisation and management or the placing of the goods on the market.

This possibility of uniting in one hand the financial control of particular industries by obtaining monopolies made early English capitalist industry the happy hunting-ground of all who wished to lay out large capital sums to advantage. Such undertakings were in strong contrast to the hazardous ventures of charlatans which sprang up at the end of the seventeenth century in every sphere of English

[1] Cunningham, pp. 77, 78, and 93; Price, pp. 15, 16, and 38.

[2] Price, pp. 79, and 56, 57.

[3] 'Die Deutsche Volkswirtschaft,' Berlin 1903, p. 373.

industrial life. These were mere fradulent " Projects " for the deception of a readily speculative public, but the monopolist companies of the Stuart days were either due to the union of interested traders (coalowners, tin founders) or to the commercial activities of rich and politically influential persons, who hoped to increase their wealth by financing large branches of industry and accordingly bore the risk themselves. That these " large business men " belonged to court circles, and used their political influence and their accumulated wealth for one and the same purpose appears to us by no means remarkable, though it at times struck their contemporaries as peculiar. When Sir Robert Mansell, hitherto an admiral, renewed his patent for glass-making the king was amazed [1] " that Robin Mansell, being a seaman, whereby he had won much honour, should fall from water to tamper with fire, which are two contrary elements." Sir Walter Raleigh was, as we have seen, for a time the owner of the tin monopoly. Sir Thomas Bartlett had gained £40,000 in the service of the queen, with which he financed the pin monopoly.[2] A great number of monopolies were given by the Crown " as special favours in place of hard cash " to favourites, retired officials and officers who hoped thereby to increase their wealth or to make use of their privileges to gain riches by the help of capitalists.[3] The monopolies in alum, soap, starch, wire, and many other commodities were financed by wealthy courtiers. It is often difficult to recognise the real personality of the " Promoter." The beaver hat monopoly, as we saw, was due to eight capitalists, who decided the great mass of craftsmen to form a separate corporation. But the actual charter was obtained for them by the Earl of Stirling, who spent " a considerable capital " on this company-promoting business, and was to receive therefor a fixed payment out of the tax collected by the company on the sale of every beaver hat.[4]

[1] Galloway, ' History of Coal Mining,' p. 38.

[2] Unwin, ' Industrial Organisation,' p. 166.

[3] Price, p. 17 ; Unwin, ' Gilds of London,' p. 307.

[4] Unwin, ' Industrial Organisation,' pp. 145, 146, and ' Gilds,' p. 320.

The type of monopolist varied accordingly in the different industries. In the coal trade, where the monopoly approximated more to a Cartel, it was the mine-owners who united to organise the monopoly. The soap monopoly of the London manufacturers was similar. But in the majority of cases the monopoly was in the hands of one or more big capitalists. Their functions again varied. Some of them appear only as the source of money or political influence, standing behind the scenes of the organisation itself, or interested in it only as shareholders. Others took an active part in the industrial and technical growth and the commercial management of the enterprise, like Sir Thomas Bartlett and Alderman Cockayne. They appear as the directors of new industries or processes, conduct lawsuits and prosecutions, regulate prices, are at pains to influence the commercial policy of the government in their favour, and engage workmen from abroad, uniting in their persons the functions of the large manufacturer and those of the organising financier. It was against this kind of monopolist, in whose hands a more or less considerable political power lay and who without regard for the interests of the thousands he injured changed the social, industrial, and fiscal conditions of the country and brought his dominating influence to bear on the most diverse fields of economic life, against the capitalist financier of large industrial monopolies who made himself unequivocally a dictator of national industry, that the anger of the people and of Parliament was chiefly directed in the anti-monopoly movement. Mr. Price [1] is therefore certainly justified in explaining the continuance of the London soap monopoly even under the Commonwealth by the fact that this monopoly embraced all the original London makers, and so was from the point of view of a democratic government less easily assailable than the monopolies owned in contrast by particular individuals. With a little goodwill the monopoly in this case could be defended as the systematic organisation of the

[1] 'English Patents of Monopoly,' p. 125.

trade; whereas if it had been in the hands of a single individual who through his wealth and political influence had gained control over a trade with which he had no natural connection, that line of argument would from the first carry but little weight.[1]

Monopolies had a very decided influence on the early growth of capitalism in English industry, for they increased the power of capital in those industries in which it had gained a footing, and concentrated it in a few hands. In this sense the opposition to monopolies was a movement against the ascendency of a capitalist rule artificially stimulated by privilege. In the last few centuries England has several times gone through periods of economic agitation unparalleled in intensity in any other land. Not unfrequently this phenomenon has been due to the exceptional degree attained in England by the economic grievances which caused the conflict, the result being a very heated agitation for their removal. Never was a battle against an existing commercial policy fought with so much bitterness, enthusiasm, and energy as in England in the 'forties, for the very reason that never had a one-sided class policy so threatened the general weal as did the prevailing system of high corn duties. The same is true in the history of English monopolies. In Germany there was no similar agitation against them, or, at least, owing to the division of the country into numerous small states, it never acquired a single, clearly recognisable character. Generally speaking the German monopolies, whatever may be the reason for it, did not tend to such intense economic consequences as the English, and they did not become important as the

[1] About 1650 a judgment was given as follows: "Certainly upon a serious consideration all such patents and bye-laws as tend most to the well regulating and ordering of trades and the better management of them, so that the benefits of them may be derived to the greater part of the people, though with a prejudice to some particular persons, have always been allowed by the law, but patents which tend to the engrossing of trade, merchandise and manufacture, into one or a few hands only, have always been held unreasonable and unwarrantable."

instrument of a system of government hated in domestic politics.

In England the system of monopolies was from the beginning the expression of a definite and independent royal policy, pursued with ever-growing eagerness in spite of statutory opposition from the days of Queen Elizabeth, and in a few decades so successfully developed that in almost every important trade national monopolies arose. At first doubtfully, and then ever louder rose the opposition to this policy from the most diverse quarters. At one time enmity was kindled by purely economic results, such as the increased price to consumers, or the restriction of competition which crippled enterprise; at another by the ascendency of courtiers, the arbitrary evasion of the law by the Crown, or financial mismanagement. As monopolies steadily increased all these streams of opposition met in a single movement, which succeeded in extirpating in England, after a comparatively short but exceptionally effective existence, the monopoly system which in other countries continue to flourish in one form or another for over a century more.

The main centre of the anti-monopoly movement was the House of Commons, which "found the whole nation behind it" [1] on this question. Ever after the days of the great monopoly debates in 1597 and 1601 the House made continual angry protests against monopolies and monopolists. Even in the debate of 1601 the majority of the speakers showed such determined and energetic hostility to monopolies that their defenders, Cecil and Bacon, could not obtain a hearing, and the queen had to soothe the discontent by formal promises. The Statute of Monopoly in 1624, though in practice ineffective, was a further proof that Parliament desired vigorous measures against the monopolies. When, after the absolute rule of Charles I., Parliament met again in 1640, one of the first things it did was to declare the chief monopolies invalid, and to use its

[1] Macaulay, vol. viii. pp. 12, 13.

growing power over the Crown for an energetic attack on all industrial privileges. The deep hatred of the Long Parliament for all monopolies is seen in the drastically worded resolution which decisively refused any monopolist a seat in Parliament.[1] On January 21, 1641, four "monopolists" were, in fact, expelled from the House.[2]

The speeches delivered on the various occasions on which the Commons occupied themselves with the question show sufficiently clearly the severity with which individuals condemned the monopoly system, and the ardour with which they attacked it.[3] The speeches of 1640 were fomented by an extensive popular movement against monopolies. From all parts of the country petitions reached Parliament for the removal of "grievances," especially of monopolies.[4] At the end of his fine and impressive description of the monopolies Colepepper could with truth say: [5] "I have echoed to you the cries of the kingdom." But these oratorical displays are not by any means the only evidence from which we can picture the anti-monopoly movement of the seventeenth century. They are supported by an abundant literature of pamphlets.

The growth of this literature in the seventeenth century is very largely due to the lively discussions on the monopoly question.[6] The characters of the numerous pamphlets vary widely. A great number are purely inflammatory. At times they are satirical, intended to put before the people in grotesque shape the evil effects of the monopolies.[7] Just as at the present time the anti-trust agitation in America

[1] 'Parliamentary History,' vol. ii. p. 653. [2] *Ibid.* p. 207.

[3] Cf. especially the speech of Colepepper cited above, 'Parliamentary History,' vol. ii. pp. 654, 655; *ibid.* pp. 641, 650, speeches of Pym and Bogshaws; *ibid.* vol. i., speech of Sir E. Coke on March 1, 1620, of Sir E. Hobby on November 20, 1601 (p. 930), and of Mr. Martin, p. 927 and *passim.*

[4] 'Parl. Hist.' vol. ii. p. 542. [5] *Ibid.* p. 656.

[6] 'Social England,' p. 621.

[7] *E.g.* 'The Projector's Downfall,' London 1642.

represents the industrial monopolies in all kinds of humorous allegorical shapes, so we find pictures of the seventeenth century monopolists with the products of the various monopolies as symbols of their activity and with such legends as :

> "If any aske, what things these monsters be,
> 'Tis a Projector and a Patentee." [1]

Many of the pamphlets are concerned with the conditions of a single trade alone, and are the appeals to public opinion of consumers or producers oppressed by the monopoly in the industry in question. Instances of this are to be found in the cases of the wine, soap, and salt monopolies of 1640 to 1650,[2] and especially in the pamphlet on the coal monopoly written in 1655,[3] the importance of which has hitherto been unfortunately not recognised.

The author of this work, Ralph Gardiner of Chirton, was for many years mistakenly identified by posterity with a coiner of the same name, and was only rehabilitated by the investigations of Dr. D. Ross Lietch in 1849.[4] His pamphlet, whose contents we have already had frequent occasion to quote, attacked the monopolist policy of the town of Newcastle, whose bye-laws under its charter were, according to the writer, contrary both to common and statute law. The special object of his attack was, however, the coal monopoly. This, he in one place states,[5] would most certainly have been declared invalid by Parliament in 1640 " if any public spirit had arisen and denounced this great

[1] 'Social England,' p. 624, illustration ; Unwin, 'Gilds,' p. 298.

[2] 'A True Discovery of the Projectors' Wine Project,' London 1641 ; 'A short and true relation concerning the Soap Business,' London 1841 ; R. Wilkins, 'The Sope Patentees' petition opened,' London 1646 ; J. Davies, 'An Answer to those Printed Papers, etc.,' London 1641.

[3] R. Gardiner, 'England's Grievance Discovered in relation to the Coal Trade,' London 1655.

[4] Dr. Lietch published Gardiner's pamphlet in 1849 without the author's name. The preface gives the events of Gardiner's life. His rehabilitation is on pp. xiii-xv.

[5] R. Gardiner, p. 193.

pest which more than any other affects the life of men." Gardiner hoped himself to kindle in 1653 the agitation which was wanting in 1640.

He had suffered as a brewer in North Shields from the privileges and monopolist control of the town, and became finally a bitter opponent of all monopolies and restrictions on trade. Whether he undertook the fight against Newcastle's monopolies in revenge for the long time he had lain in prison there, or from unselfish motives, we cannot say. If Parliament had not been dissolved by Cromwell on December 12, 1653, Gardiner's agitation, which had already led to an important enquiry by the Committee of Trade and Corporations, would certainly have been successful. As it was, Newcastle remained unmolested. But Gardiner's tireless and heroic zeal in attacking the coal monopoly contributed largely to a clearer knowledge of the effect of the coal gilds, and his vehement but well-informed polemic strengthened the movement against monopolies, even though his immediate object, the abolition of the gild, was only in fact realised about 1660.

The agitation, of which pamphlets and Parliamentary reports give us such a lively picture, exercised an influence on public opinion which extended to days in which monopolies had long been abolished. It is a curious thing that down to the present day the English consumer is especially opposed to any kind of industrial monopoly or monopolist amalgamation, and the main origin of this anti-monopolist national conscience is to be found in the anti-monopoly agitation of the seventeenth century. Until the Elizabethan policy of monopolies began, the expression "monopoly" had always been connected with the acute commercial monopoly which we nowadays call a "corner," and the chief monopolists were merchants who bought up corn and food supplies. Against such persons the statutes passed by Henry III.[1] and again under Edward VI. against "regraters," "engrossers," and "forestallers" were sufficient

[1] 'Annual Register,' 1766, p. 224.

protection.[1] The condemnation of monopoly in the case of exchange of goods expressed in these statutes was transferred to industrial production when at the end of the sixteenth century it began to show an inclination to such a system. It seemed a matter of course that monopolies were harmful.

Henry Parker states in 1648:[2] "That which seizes too great matters in the hands of too few, and so is in the nature of a monopoly, has been always condemned as preventing trade, and held to be injurious to the major part of mankind." The lawyers tried to define more accurately the effects of monopolies. In a famous lawsuit tried in 1602 the Court found "the evil of the monopoly" to lie chiefly in the fact that "the price of the same wares has increased"; that after the grant of the monopoly "the wares were not so good and serviceable" as before; and that other producers had, through the monopoly, become unable to find work and so put out of the trade.[3] This opinion was shared by writers like Misselden and Malynes, who may be called the forerunners of the political economists.[4] Misselden starts that part of his book written in 1622 which deals with trade monopolies with the words: "The parts of a monopoly are twaine. The restraint of the liberty of commerce to some one or few, and the setting of the price at the pleasure of the monopolist to his private benefit and the prejudice of the publicke."[5] Other writings of the time also use the expression that the monopolist regulates the price at "his pleasure," or "as he pleases,"[6] a phrase which Adam Smith appropriated in this connection about 150 years later.[7]

[1] Cf. the essay of S. Browne, a Judge, 'The laws against Engrossing,' London 1767, *passim*.

[2] Henry Parker, 'Of a Free Trade,' London 1648, p. 21.

[3] Fisk Beach, 'Monopolies and Industrial Trusts,' St. Louis 1898, pp. 11-13.

[4] Raffel, 'Englische Freihändler vor A. Smith,' Tubingen 1905, pp. 9 and 11.

[5] Misselden, 'Free Trade,' London 1622, pp. 57-58.

[6] Malynes' 'Lex Mercatoria,' quoted by Raffel, *supra* p. 12; and later, 'Britannia Languens,' p. 73.

[7] A. Smith, 'Lectures on Justice and Police,' ed. by Dr. E. Cannan, 1896; cf. Hirst, 'Monopolies, Trusts, and Cartels,' London 1903, p. 21.

Only, Adam Smith had in his mind merely local gild monopolies, and applied to their conduct words used a century earlier for much more extensive trade organisations. The writings of Misselden and Malynes, though as much concerned in attacking privileges of trade and commerce as those of purely industrial monopolies and patents, are important evidence for estimating the anti-monopolist movement of the time. The expression "free trade," which first appears at the end of the sixteenth century, came to be used indifferently as the watchword against artificial restrictions of trade and commerce by joint-stock companies, colonial companies and municipal corporations, and against the real trade monopolies of the Stuarts. The writings of Parker, Roberts, and Brent, all between 1640-50, show how in the most diverse fields of economic life as it then existed the beginnings of a movement for the abolition of monopolist fetters and the development of free competition were present.[1] It cannot be doubted that this economic tendency was strongly influenced by experience of the Stuart trade monopolies. On the other hand, writings which attempted to introduce into other fields a freer economic system may in their time have added vigour to the agitation against industrial monopoly.

That agitation can at any rate be regarded as an independent movement by the side of the general tendency to economic freedom if such a tendency is to be regarded in the first half of the seventeenth century as a single entity at all. For economic Liberalism, with its systematic opposition to all restrictions on free competition—whether by the mercantile system or by the trade regulations—was a far later development. The early outburst in particular trades, and the popular character of such a free trade movement as the anti-monopoly agitation, was due to the

[1] Parker, p. 29, against Cockayne's monopoly; L. Roberts, 'The Treasure of Traffike,' London 1641, deals with monopolies as a merchant and exporter; cf. p. 47 and *passim*; Nath. Brent, 'A Discourse of Free Trade,' London 1645, the Cloth Trade. For monopolist 'Joint Stock Companies,' see Misselden, p. 69 ff.

growing bitterness among the people against the manner in which particular individuals enriched themselves by monopolies. Doubts might exist as to the economic value of a monopolist organisation in industry, just as to-day in America the position of the people with regard to the chief questions of trust building is still undecided. But against individuals who openly exploited the system, unlimited hatred reigned, just as in the United States it is the struggle against the trust magnates, against Rockefeller, Armour, Havemeyer, and similar persons that attracts the populace towards the anti-trust movement. In the seventeenth century the monopolist was in England the publican of the Bible. " Bloodsucker " and " monster " were the popular names for him. And this hatred was deep-rooted among Englishmen even in later days. When, in the second half of the eighteenth century, small farms were concentrated into larger ones, certain opponents of that agricultural development thought the easiest way to discredit it among the people was to compare a large farmer to a monopolist.[1]

The popular character which marked the movement against monopolies led to the rapid fall of that special form of industrial organisation in early capitalist England. We have seen that the growing power of Parliament brought about the abolition of many monopolies after 1640, and that the legal foundations on which monopolies had arisen were destroyed in 1689 by the repeal of the royal power of prerogative and by an important alteration in mining law. It was thereafter impossible in principle to obtain exclusive rights from the Crown, as monopolies, even for foreign trade, could only exist if authorised by Act of Parliament.[2] Internal monopolies Parliament would not be persuaded to grant: it held fast by the anti-monopolist principle of common law and by the provisions of the Statute of Monopolies.

[1] Cf. authorities cited in the author's 'Large and Small Holdings,' Cambridge 1911.

[2] Cox, 'Staatseinrichtungen Englands,' Berlin 1867, p. 548.

As early as 1690 Parliament gave certain projectors a proof of the hopelessness of their wishes by refusing to grant recognition to a plan for renewing the pin monopoly.[1] Not content with preventing the growth of monopoly by royal privilege, they also expressly opposed private understandings of a monopolist kind between merchants; for instance, in 1711 an Act was passed, especially aimed at all contracts and agreements between coalowners and others for the monopolisation of coal.[2]

In the treatment of the newer industries a similar difference is found between the trade policy of Queen Anne and that of the greater part of the seventeenth century. Monopolies were absolutely forbidden. A close student of English economic history of that time writes: [3] "The whole tendency, both of legislation and parliamentary practice, was to afford stringent protection to infant industries by prohibiting competitive imports from abroad, and at the same time to trust that the founding of several factories of the same kind would provide sufficient safeguards for the consumer by keeping prices low through the resulting competition."

Important new industries arose in the eighteenth century, in spite of the unwillingness of Parliament to grant their promoters any monopoly protection beyond the usual inventor's patent. In the still youthful silk industry a certain John Lambe, who had studied the throwing of silk in Italy, received a fourteen years' patent in 1717. When this ran out in 1732 his successor strove in vain to obtain its renewal. Instead he received compensation to the tune of £14,000 and a peerage! [4] The tinplate trade, to this day such an important industry in England, arose in the same way at the beginning of the eighteenth century without any protective monopoly.[5] And Parliament, even if

[1] Unwin, 'Industrial Organisation,' p. 170. [2] 9 Anne, c. 28.

[3] W. R. Scott, 'Records of a Scottish Cloth Manufactory,' Edinburgh 1905, p. 21.

[4] Th. Wardle, 'Report on the English Silk Industry,' 1884, p. xlvi. (Blue book).

[5] Ph. W. Flower, 'A History of the Trade in Tin,' London 1880, *passim*.

it abstained from any grants of monopolies, had other Colbertian means, especially bounties, by which it could encourage and support an industry.[1]

So far as our knowledge of industrial England in the eighteenth century goes, no national monopoly based on legal privilege any longer existed at the time in any industry. Tucker, in his first essay, and later Adam Smith, whose detestation of monopoly was all-embracing, would certainly have noticed any such abomination. They know, however, only colonial trade monopolies and a few town monopolies, as a special object-lesson in which they both choose the privileges of Butchers.[2] To illustrate the attempts of manufacturers to obtain monopolies by law, Adam Smith could find no other example than a Dutch clothier in Abbéville.[3]

Undoubtedly the continued existence of craft corporations with exclusive rights in many ways restricted competition. Adam Smith himself experienced its effect in Glasgow when Watt came there to build and sell his steam engines. The corporation of Hammermen refused to allow him to do so, and his projects could only be carried out within the bounds of the University.[4] But the case can hardly be characteristic of the general influence of town corporations at that time. This had, at least in the eighteenth century, considerably diminished.[5] While at the beginning of the eighteenth century Lord Molesworth still complained of their harmful influence, Tucker could write in 1782:[6] "The exclusive Corporations and Companies of Trades in Towns and Cities have at present very little Power of doing mischief compared with that which

[1] Cunningham, p. 409, also pp. 515, 516.

[2] Tucker, 'A Brief Essay,' etc., London 1753, pp. 41, 42; Adam Smith Lecture quoted in Hirst, 'Trusts, Cartels, etc.,' p. 21.

[3] 'Wealth of Nations,' 1817, vol. ii. p. 196.

[4] Toynbee, 'Industrial Revolution,' p. 188.

[5] Details in Cunningham, pp. 321, 322.

[6] Tucker, 'Cui Bono?' London 1782, 3rd ed. p. 53.

they formerly had." More recent investigations have shown that the attenuated rights of these corporations had mostly fallen into abeyance, and that in many trades " the freedom of the corporation need no longer be bought, and the right of view and other means of gild control had entirely ceased at the end of the eighteenth century." [1] Authorities on English economic history, like J. E. Thorold Rogers, have expressly insisted that " the old system of gild and freeman production and trade . . . was by no means universal, for the great industries of the north were not shackled by these limitations." [2]

Whatever may have been the functions of these monopolist town corporations in the eighteenth century they are essentially distinguished from the monopolies we have hitherto considered by their limitation to a single locality. While the latter could create a national system of capitalistic industry, the town gilds, so far as they were active at all, could only impose monopolist regulations on small masters in a local market, whilst capitalist trades organised on the commission,[3] or even on the factory system, could settle in towns where gilds were unknown, or in the country.[4] The growth of transport facilities and the rise of so many centres of industry destroyed, after the end of the seventeenth century, the monopolist position held in certain goods by the chief towns, and especially London, and accordingly the national importance of local monopolist organisations also disappeared. When the London Company of Frame Work Knitters tried to extend their rights beyond their own local sphere of influence to Nottingham, their attempt was not supported by Parliament. They had to allow the ten masters and operatives of Nottingham to

[1] Unwin, ' Gilds,' pp. 344, 345.

[2] Rogers, ' The Industrial and Commercial History of England,' London 1892, p. 374.

[3] Cf. note on p. 12.

[4] Brentano, ' Arbeitsverhältnis gemäss dem heutigen Recht,' Leipzig 1877, p. 49.

escape their tyranny and continue their trade in independence.[1] So very different were the monopolist trade regulations of these corporations from the industrial monopolies of the Stuarts that a High Court Judge, in a celebrated judgment in 1711, denied altogether the monopolist character of such local restrictions on trade.[2] Though wrong in the abstract, this legal distinction was clearly based on the obvious but far-reaching difference in the economic importance of two systems of trade organisation both clearly forms of monopoly. In any case, no gild regulation could lead to the concentration in the hands of a few privileged persons of the control over capitalist industries working for a national market or even for exportation on a large scale, as would have happened with the Stuart monopoly system.

By the end of the seventeenth century, therefore, the most essential half of Free Trade had been won for English industry. Even though, as Prof. Brentano has excellently shown,[3] the coming of the modern " industry " as opposed to the handicraft was delayed by antiquated gild regulations, and especially by the Law of Apprentices, this fact only affected the competition between the old and new forms of trade. Within the bounds of industrial capitalism the way was open for competition. No man who wished to put capital into a rising industry found himself hampered by the prior rights of others or by legal decisions restricting competition.

This freedom of trade was won at a time in which English industry and industrial capitalism were in their infancy. Had not the monopoly system so quickly fallen through its excesses and become a standing abomination to the English people, who knows that Parliament in the eighteenth century, in its ardour for the Mercantile System, would not have tried that method of State interference in commercial

[1] F. Moy Thomas, 'J. and R. Morley,' London 1900, p. 12.

[2] Hirst, pp. 98, 99. [3] Brentano, p. 47 ff., pp. 70, 71.

matters also? It was the part played by Parliament itself in the battle against industrial monopoly which made this impossible. The mighty growth of industrial capitalism in England which began in the eighteenth century and reached its climax in the Industrial Revolution, followed in the train of a previously won freedom of trade.

The difference between capitalist organisation in the seventeenth and eighteenth centuries, as regards liberty of trade, comes out very clearly in the history of industrial monopoly in England. A comparison with the country that has longest known legal restrictions of competition in capitalist industry shows for what a long time the freedom won so early in England was in striking contrast to the organisation of other industrially advancing nations. A short digression on the growth and duration of German monopolist restrictions shall therefore conclude this subject.

CHAPTER IV

COMPARISON WITH GERMAN DEVELOPMENT

A FEW preliminary observations are necessary. In the first place, Germany has never had so uniform a system of monopoly as that existing in England under Elizabeth, James I., and Charles I. The peculiarities of particular trade privileges alone made that impossible. The phenomenon of a prince attempting systematically to unite industry wherever possible in great national monopolies was unknown. The movement towards monopoly started amongst capitalists, and found support partly in the administration of trade by a bureaucracy imbued with " mercantile " principles, partly in the craft gilds, and partly in the mining regulations. The princes did not play the part of eagerly speculative " Promoters " of capitalist undertakings, while personal enrichment and the trade interests of courtiers, so widespread in England, never had a decided influence on the monopolist organisation of German industry. Perhaps just for the reason that these shady sides of the system were unknown, it remained longer in existence than in England and was abolished without leaving such general hatred behind it.

It is hardly necessary to say that in speaking of the monopolist organisation of early capitalism in German industry it is not implied that this organisation always appeared in concrete form. Certain forms of trade monopolies existed, like the privileged companies or the creation of a " staple " of capitalist merchants. But very often the monopolist organisation of industry was only seen in restrictions of some kind set on new enterprises by law, which accordingly put particular merchants in the position of monopolists. When in spite of such provisions competition between existing factories arose, such works might still have a monopoly against subsequent fresh competitors. If in any such cases special organisation further improved the monopolists' position, the importance of their prior rights increased. In any case, however, legal limitations on fresh competition gave monopolist protection to the existing concerns. We must, therefore, take into consideration all laws which introduced such restrictions, even if they did not lead to the grosser forms of English monopolies.

An enquiry into the effect and importance of monopolist organisation on the growth of German economic life would be outside the scope of our present discussion. We are only concerned to develop a descriptive comparison between the growth of industrial organisation in Germany and England, and to answer the question to what extent the monopolist organisation of early industrial capitalism, the rise and fall of which in England we have described, lasted longer in Germany. To criticise this system would necessitate a very different examination of details than is required for the purpose of this book. It will be enough for the present to give a sufficiently detailed picture of German industrial monopolies to enable us to institute a comparison between their history and the early disappearance of monopoly in England.

In Germany, as in England, mining is an important industry for trade monopolies. Owing to transport advantages certain areas of production had down to the nineteenth century and retain in part even to-day a "natural" monopoly in markets at some distance from them. In such cases restrictions imposed by law on competition were much more effective in creating monopolies than where producers had to compete for a market with other industrial regions. From the latter part of the eighteenth century up to about 1865 mining was especially subject to monopoly where the so-called "Direktionsprinzip" or system of State administration, a characteristic instance of the mercantile theory in mining, obtained. When freedom of mining had been declared by virtue of the rights of the Crown, every person who found specified deposits in any place was entitled to permission to occupy that place as a miner. This grant was regarded as the consequence of the share in mining rights assured him by private law.

This freedom, which could only be limited by the reserved rights of the State, gave considerably greater facilities than had formerly existed for the continued growth of new undertakings. The Prussian Government regarded the threatened competition of many new mines as by no means desirable. Accordingly the royal share of the mining rights was used to retain for the State the power to make regulations which might allow or refuse the creation of new enterprises. A distinction was drawn between the grant of the royal rights, the grant of a mining area, and the exercise of those rights [1] (in other words, the commencement of an enterprise) and by decisions concerning the last, the competition allowed by the declaration of free mining could again be restricted at will. That was the case in coal mining in Rhenish Westphalia, which, after being up till the end of the eighteenth century of only local importance, became thenceforward a leading branch of German mining. The rich coal deposits in the neighbourhood of the Ruhr, originally only used by coal-digging peasants, were first systematically mined in the time of Frederick the Great, when the trade was regulated by a mining ordinance, and put under the control of the State department of mines. In the area of the Cleve-Mark mining ordinance the working of coal seams was dependent on the permission of the royal

[1] C. F. Gerber, 'System des Deutschen Privatrechts,' Jena 1852, p. 144.

officials. The probability of obtaining such permission could be estimated from instructions issued in May 1783, at the instigation of the Minister von Heinitz to the department of mines in Cleve-Mörs and Mark,[1] which insist that "No new coal mines shall be opened until the need of them is proved." The general intention of these instructions, as the wording clearly shows, is to assure a monopoly to the existing mines. "Owing to the many seams which are being worked coal has fallen in price, and one mine takes away the market of the next," and the object is to secure that "each of the mines can count on a comparatively safe market." These regulations were renewed in 1821, and continued in principle until the reform of the mining laws in 1865.

How this principle in practice, even as late as the middle of the nineteenth century, hampered the growth of fresh competition is seen in the history of the origin of the "Kölner Bergverein," which had to wait two and a half years for the formal sanction of its statutes, and finally received it only in 1849, after numerous "doubts" of the authorities about the statutes in their original form had disappeared.[2] Till after 1860 the authorities clung to the belief, as the explanatory memorandum to the 1865 mining law shows, that a co-operative mining association (Gewerkschaft), and not a limited company, was the most suitable form of mining undertaking.[3] The difficulties put in the way of every new company are therefore intelligible. But they meant neither more nor less than the artificial restriction of just that form of undertaking to which the future of mining belonged.

While on the left bank of the Rhine, where French mining law obtained, the firm of Haniel acquired, in face

[1] 'Entwicklung des niederrheinisch-westfälisch Kohlenbergbaues,' Breslau, x. Teil, p. 48 ff.

[2] O. Stillich, 'Steinkohlenindustrie,' Leipzig 1906, pp. 201-204.

[3] Uhde, 'Produktionsbedingungen des deutschen und englischen Steinkohlenbergbaues,' Jena 1907, p. 85.

of the protests of their competitors, the enormous area of 10 million square metres, official administration on the right bank aimed at maintaining as far as possible equality between the various mines and the continuance of small masters.[1]

Monopoly in coal mining did not rest, therefore, on an agreement between producers, who enjoyed and sought to develop special monopolist prerogatives. Its supporters and directors were the government and the administration. They protected existing concerns as far as might be from fresh competitors, and they saved individual mines from the possibility of mutual competition in the market by fixing a single price for the whole district.[2] They even granted a bounty on export in bad times.[3] The aim of the State in organising the monopolist system was no doubt partly to put the miners in a position to bear the heavy taxes laid until 1865 on mining,[4] and therefore here, as in England, the connection between the grant of monopoly and the interests of public finance can be traced, though naturally in less gross forms.

A similar system of royal right and official administration prevailed since the enactment of the mining regulations of 1769 in the coal mines of Upper Silesia. But the landowners received as compensation a previous, or, as it was later, a coincident right of mining (Vorbau-Mitbaurecht) in the case of grants on their land. Some of them received the *jus excludendi alios*.[5] Till 1854 the expression "landowner" was interpreted by the authorities to mean only the few remaining "Dominialherren," in the district of

[1] Eberhard Gothein, 'Konzentration in Kohlenbergbau,' Archiv für Sozialwissenschaft, 1904, pp. 426-427.

[2] Gothein, p. 425.

[3] Bosenick, 'Der Steinkohlenbergbau in Preussen,' Tubingen 1909, p. 81.

[4] Klostermann, 'Das allgemeine Berggesetz,' Berlin 1884, 4th ed. p. 48.

[5] Heymann, 'Die gemischten Werke im deutschen Grosseisengewerbe,' Stuttgart 1904, p. 179, and Uhde, *op. cit. supra*, p. 95.

Beuthen the nineteen owners of estates in knights fee (Rittergut).[1] Finally, the State had the power, as always where royal rights obtained, to reserve for itself any area it desired by a mere declaration of the mines department. In Silesia, too, royal rights, official administration, privilege of landowners, and reservations by the State tended to restrict new competition, though monopoly did not outwardly appear in so uniform a shape as in Rhenish Westphalia, where the principle of official administration was adopted with greater logical thoroughness.[2] And the extensive speculations in the exploitation of mining land which occurred when in 1854 every landowner received the Mitbaurecht [3] shows clearly how the limitation till that date of such rights to owners of " Dominium " had checked the expansion of mining.

In iron mining, which must be considered in close connection with iron smelting, the circumstances were mostly different. Though the latter had been from early times a separate industry, not legally subject to the principle of the Mining Royalties, the unavoidable economic dependence of smelting and forging works on iron ore and wood enabled the owners of land and of mining rights (except where, as in Upper Franconia and Siegerland, they were pushed into the background by the manufacturers), gradually to subject the smelters to their own conditions and provisos.[4] Usually the owner granted a speculator a concession, in return for payment in iron or later money, to dig for iron in a given radius, to build smelting works, or to take a given amount of wood from the forests.[5] Both

[1] H. Solger, ' Der Kreis Beuthen,' Breslau 1860, pp. 216 and 276-77.

[2] For the effects of the Direktionsprinzip in Silesia cf. Fechner, ' Zeitschrift für Berg-Hütten und S.-Wesen,' vol. 48, pp. 318, 319 (1900) ; vol. 50, pp. 493, 494 (1902). In the zinc industry this influence was less. Cf. von Wiese, ' Entwicklung der Rohzinkfabrikation,' Jena 1903, pp. 36, 37.

[3] Solger, pp. 217, 218.

[4] von Inama-Sternegg, ' Deutsche Wirtschaftsgeschichte,' Leipzig 1901, vol. iii. part 2, p. 191 ff.

[5] Heymann, ' Gemischte Werke,' p. 273.

in this case and where princely owners of mining rights owned smelting works, fresh competitors found a barrier erected against them from the first. It was imperative, for the sake of securing a fitting income from dues, to save the concessionaire from any new enterprise which might by competition lower his prices.

The connection of landownership with smelting might result in the protection of existing works even where free mining had been declared, as is shown by the history of the Mansfeld copper mines. They received "a patent of freedom" as early as 1671, and in consequence several works sprang up, apparently in complete independence of one another. From time immemorial miners and smelters had enjoyed the right of getting their supplies of coal and wood at very moderate prices from the forests of the Counts of Mansfeld. Production increased, and as the fuel at their disposal became more and more insufficient, the various works made mutual arrangements as to the exact extent to which each might share in the available coal; in fact, the whole smelting industry and its kindred trades was conditioned and regulated in extent by the fixing of the so-called "Firing shares" (Feueranteile). Any new producer had to attempt to secure a share in this fixed amount of fuel, or in other words, to come to an agreement with the "cartel" of existing works. Naturally this fact put very considerable difficulties in the way of fresh competition.[1]

Where special grants of mining rights prevailed, competition was entirely out of the question. This system of special grants was chiefly used by princes where mining was considered a particularly hazardous business, entitling those engaged in it to the continuous protection of a monopoly. An instance are the mines at Ilmenau, which the Duke of Weimar attempted about 1780 to rescue from their entirely neglected condition and to restore to prosperity.

[1] Cf. Kupferbergbau und Hüttenbetrieb in den beiden Mansfelder Kreisen,' 1881, p. 33 ff.

A new mining association was formed and received the privilege of " taking over at its pleasure, subject to customary notice and sanction, all seams and borders which might thereafter be discovered in that part of the Henneberg mountains belonging to Weimar." It also received the right of pre-emption over " all wood and coal necessary for mining." [1] In the Rothenburg district and in the Saale region, contrary to the practice in Mansfeld, similar privileges were granted to a single association by the owner of the royalty. Their exclusive right of copper mining was renewed in 1691, and lasted till their indebtedness led about 1670 to the concession being taken over by the State.[2]

In Siegerland the position was very curious until well on in the nineteenth century, though there, too, the law gave protection by monopoly. Mining and smelting were influenced not by landowners or princes, but by the craft (Zunft).[3] Abolished in 1806 on the conquest of the principality by the French the craft gild was reformed in 1813, and in 1830 the gild of " smelting and forging works " received anew the royal sanction to the " Smelting and Forging Regulations for Iron and Steel Smelting and Forging in Siegerland." These regulations show the way in which the transfer to an increasingly capitalistic industry of the monopolist institutions of the craft gild was attempted.[4] The law first lays down that no new wood-consuming smelting works shall be set up within the bounds of the principality of Siegen.[5] After this restriction on new works the law goes on to deal with the limitation of smelting days, which had existed for many years to economise coal and water supplies, and now becomes a means of dividing production between the then new blast furnaces. Excesses over the limit were punished by fines, but smelting or forg-

[1] Schlözer's ' Staatsanzeigen,' 1784, vol. iv. pp. 425-433.

[2] Kupferbergbau cited above, pp. 25 ff., 30 and 48 ff.

[3] Heymann, pp. 55, 56. [4] The ' Berggeist,' July 29, 1856, p. 39.

[5] Special attention is drawn to this, because Heymann (*op. cit. supra*, p. 61) represents this fact merely as the pious wish of an interested party. Possibly the writer he quotes was the first to suggest it.

ing days not used could be sold to another works in the same district. "This provision," it is stated in the 'Berggeist' as late as 1856,[1] "is so often made use of that there exist to-day smelting works that may be in activity the whole year, and forges that are entirely shut down. . . . Though the forges are temporarily closed, the works receive their regular income by the regularly repeated sale of their forging days." The possibility of transferring to another the quota of production represented by the number of smelting days opened the way for concentration of the production of each works in this cartel, in fact to a kind of trust organisation. Apart from this fact, these regulations, like official administration in coal mining, were simply the means of protecting small masters against concentration, and naturally delayed the development of large capitalist undertakings. The growing facilities for coal transport (Ruhr-Sieg Railway, 1861) shattered the monopolist position of charcoal-burning works, as the Smelting and Forging Regulations did not apply to coal-burners. But this artificially maintained monopoly did not cease to be effective in practice until about 1860, and was only abolished formally in 1865.[2] The English economist, Banfield, travelling in Germany in the forties, was greatly astonished at these trade regulations. "The principle of competition," he says,[3] "by which so much has been done in Cornwall, is . . . altogether rejected."

It is clear from what has been said that in German mining and smelting in the eighteenth and in some cases till late in the nineteenth century the law hampered competition and led to the monopolist dominion of existing undertakings. The facts that led to this result are various. Official administration produced the most extreme mono-

[1] Cf. 'Berggeist' quoted on previous page.

[2] Even at the end of the 'fifties the smelting works at Eisefeld were punished for exceeding their smelting days. 'Berggeist,' November 11, 1859, p. 178.

[3] T. C. Banfield, 'Industry of the Rhine,' London 1848, series ii. pp. 89-94.

polist organisation, more especially when it was combined with a dislike on the part of the authorities to the new form of undertaking represented by the limited company. Before the declaration of free mining, special grants of State mining rights[1] had had a decidedly monopolist effect, and officialism substituted for a single monopolist a compulsory Cartel of many members. The influence of landowners and the gild organisation of the legally recognised craft corporations combined with the monopolist tendency of the mining rights to restrict the development of competition. The reform of the mining laws between 1850 and 1870 was expected to lead to a general encouragement of capital, and of the hitherto suppressed spirit of enterprise,[2] and nowadays it would be admitted that no slight share in the resulting expansion of mining was due to the era of free trade then inaugurated.[3]

In trades where there were no craft associations, monopoly depended on the grant of privileges to special factories and manufacturers, a custom which continued till about 1800. Wherever the system of concessions prevailed, the government was guided by the principle that there must be "a demand" for a new undertaking before it could be sanctioned.[4] As the government itself decided whether such a demand existed or not, this criterion frequently acted as a check to competition. The history of the numerous privileged factories [5] offers very many examples

[1] Gerber, *op. cit.* p. 217, note 5. [2] Gothein, p. 458.

[3] Cf. *e.g.* v. Schmoller, 'Grundriss der allgemeinen Volkswirtschaftslehre,' Teil i. 1908, p. 479 : "The watchword of the period from 1840-70 was free, speculative trading by private persons, a new independent form of industrial unit, the limited company, freedom of mining and the waiver by the State of its mining rights and of the direction of the industry."

[4] Horster, 'Die Entwicklung der sächsischen Gewerbefassung,' Krefeld 1908, p. 67.

[5] Cf. *e.g.* Schütz, 'Die alt-württembergische Gewerbefassung,' Zeitschrift für die gesamte Staatswissenschaft, 1850, p.297 ff. A number of remarkable examples of factory monopolies are given by Eberhard Gothein, 'Wirtschaftsgeschichte des Schwarzwaldess,' Strassburg 1891, *passim,* and esp. pp. 718-722 and 804. Some lasted till the nineteenth

of this. The Calw Cloth Company, for instance, had owned since 1774 a factory which rejoiced in the most complete monopolist protection. In 1775 a clothier at Nagold sought permission to start a second cloth factory. His petition was, however, refused, as the company succeeded in persuading the Chamber of Commerce and the government that a factory of this kind would narrow its sphere of business.[1] As in England in the seventeenth century, infant industries especially received protection, and by exactly the same methods. An excellent instance is to be found in pottery. In Bavaria the heirs of Pfeiffer were granted in 1770 a monopoly by the Markgraf of Ansbach. Forty years later an inventor named Leers petitioned for "the sole privilege of manufacturing china and stoneware, and the prohibition or heavy taxation of all imports from abroad of his wares." Apparently Leers had not anticipated that official views on the grant of monopolies had changed since 1770, or had hoped to move the government to sanction so extreme a measure of protection by his financial promises. And in fact he obtained quite a sufficiently monopolist position by the promise "that no privilege of setting up a similar factory would be granted without consultation with the owner (of the monopoly), and without detailed investigation."[2] Equally instructive is the history of the famous porcelain manufacture in the Frankenthal. The founder of the industry, Paul Anton Hannong, had wished to make porcelain in Strassburg, but had been hampered by the monopolist privileges of Vincennes, and, when threatened with the demolition of his furnaces if he continued his trade, had sought salvation in the Palatinate. There he received in 1755 the monopolist advantages he was seeking, the right of exclusive manufacture of porcelain in

century. A. Thun, 'Industrie am Niederrhein,' Teil i., Leipzig 1879, pp. 88-90, describes a monopoly in the silk industry of the Rhine owned by the family v. d. Leyen from 1759 to 1794.

[1] W. Troeltsch, 'Die Calwer Zeughandelscompagnie,' Jena 1897, p. 130.

[2] W. Steida, "Die keramische Industrie in Bayern,' Leipzig 1906, pp. 25-28, also pp. 231-232.

the Palatinate, the prohibition of the importation of foreign porcelain with temporary provisions as to foreign wares in stock, the right to acquire under compulsory powers land containing porcelain earth, and cheap supplies of wood from public forests.[1]

As regards early capitalist trades not organised on the factory system, such monopolies as existed were far less uniform and much more complicated. Capitalist financiers (Verleger) mostly traders, capitalist masters, and craftsmen sunk to working for financiers (Verlagsarbeiter) are all to be found. Just as we have seen was the case in England, the State in sanctioning such monopolies aimed at protecing small masters, to secure for whom steady and profitable prices it was thought necessary to protect capitalists by the grant of monopolies.

In the Solingen cutlery trade, which in the sixteenth and especially in the seventeenth century had become a domestic industry financed by capitalists,[2] the struggle for monopoly became at the end of the eighteenth century increasingly severe. A remarkable book written in 1777 describes this struggle in detail and with inside knowledge.[3] The privileged traders who, in spite of all attempts at legal protection, had degraded the small masters to the position of " slavish day labourers," [4] attempted to paralyse the outsiders by aid of the law. The " outsiders " consisted of first the unprivileged traders, and secondly the so-called " finishing " small masters, who possessed sufficient capital to buy raw material and, in contradistinction to the dependent craftsmen who only carried out certain processes, delivered their knives to the traders completely manufactured, or sold them directly themselves.[5]

[1] E. Heuser, ' Pfälzisches Porzellan,' Speyer 1907, pp. 20, 21.

[2] Thun, ' Die Industrie am Niederrhein,' Leipzig 1879, p. 23 ff.

[3] " Wahrhafte Beschreibung des Zustandes, worin die Sohlinger Fabriken durch die neue Ordnung versetzt worden," Schlözer's ' Staatsanzeigen,' Göttingen 1783, ii. Heft 8. The author is supposed to have been Hofkammerrat Windscheid.

[4] Thun, *op. cit.* p. 31.

[5] *Ibid.* p. 24.

In 1777 the privileged traders tried to shake off this troublesome competition by new trade regulations, which forbade (i) the combination of retail trade and manufacture, (ii) the admission of new unprivileged traders, (iii) the giving out by unprivileged traders of raw material to craftsmen, and (iv) the purchase of knives by unprivileged traders from the "finishers," except at a higher price than that paid by their privileged brethren. In other words, the "finishers" were to a certain extent compelled to sell to the privileged traders, inasmuch as they were forbidden to trade themselves, and difficulties were put in the way of sale to unprivileged persons. There was worse to come. The privileged traders ceased to buy finished knives. They found it more profitable to have their goods made in separate stages; for finished goods there was a price fixed by law, whereas where each process was separately paid there was no normal rate.[1]

"The palpable result," writes the author of the above-quoted book,[2] "is that if a finisher cannot sell the goods which he has made with his own materials either to privileged or unprivileged merchants or abroad, he must either close his works or become dependent on the privileged merchants who secured the exclusion of the unprivileged from manufacturing under the New Regulations, and accept from them the raw materials which he formerly bought himself considerably cheaper, and, like every other downtrodden day labourer, gain his scanty daily bread by piece-work. This way lies slavery, as certain a concomitant of the monopoly gained by the privileged traders under the New Regulations as light is of fire."

The argument that by reducing ruinous competition prices can be kept, to the advantage of the dependent craftsman, from a "fall,"[3] was again and again used by the privileged traders in support of their monopolist aspirations. A similar motive was alleged in another early capitalist industry, the iron wire trade of Altena, where the

[1] (Windscheid), pp. 456-8. [2] *Ibid.* p. 459. [3] *Ibid.* pp. 456, 465.

traders and the capitalist "Reidemeister" (wiremasters) formed a monopolist organisation. Unlike Solingen, capital and trading were not actually united in the hands of one class, but the capitalist (and mutually competing) "Reidemeister" were closely dependent on the merchants.

Early in 1662 the Elector's Vice-Chancellor Diest suggested a recipe for alleviating the depressed producers, which was often used in similar cases :—that the retailers should be given a monopoly, and be obliged in return to take all wire at fixed prices. At the time this scheme proved impracticable, but after 1700 it was fully realised in the so-called "staple." Just as about 1700 the London felt-makers had engineered a project of making themselves more independent of the middlemen haberdashers by establishing a common place of sale with monopolist privileges,[1] so the "Carding Wire Staple of Iserlohn," "the Iron Wire Staple of Altena," and the "Steel Wire Staple" united the interests of the merchant and the maker by means of a single market. Contrary to what happened at Solingen, a well-established monopoly organisation arose. The details of the organisation changed, but its constant fundamental principle was that the staple company should be in a position to pay producers a higher price by the deliberate suppression of over-production and mutual competition and by the possession of a monopoly. The organisations based on this principle, which have been recently described in detail by Knapmann, could, however, only exist by means of trade privileges, and all such staple companies are accordingly of the compulsory type. For instance, even in the first carding wire staple of 1720, any person who did not sell his entire produce to the staple was threatened with imprisonment, and similar provisions were also usual later. Further, once formed the staple companies became the only legal source of supply for native merchants. These coercive powers were essential for the successful regulation of prices and division of production,

[1] Unwin, 'Industrial Organisation,' pp. 157-162.

and for the assurance that the provisions relating to individual production, most clearly expressed after 1773 in the Repartitions or allotted quotas, were duly observed. In 1779 the evasion of the Repartitions by means of outside labour was made punishable by heavy penalties and removal from the trade. Further considerable restrictions were set on the rise of fresh competition by trade regulations. In 1767 entry into the iron wire staple was made more difficult, and an ordinance of 1754 limited by statute the number of forges in the steel wire trade to 36, a provision which chiefly benefited the rich "Reidemeister," four of whom controlled more than hålf the total output.

A clear proof of the importance of these and many similar official measures to the existence of the staple organisation is to be found in the fact that when legal compulsion ceased monopolist associations were unsuccessful. For instance, in 1810 a projected combination in the steel wire trade could not be carried out because, since freedom of trade had been introduced in 1809, newly risen makers could not be forced to join. Similarly, after 1809 many manufacturers and "Reidemeister" in the iron wire trade no longer regarded themselves as bound by the staple, so that here too, after much litigation, the combination was dissolved. State protection of monopoly had become a thing of the past. When in 1810 an attempt was made to re-found the steel wire combination, the government refused sanction and asked: "Is it right to favour an organisation which extorts from its fellow-citizens prices above those which the trade would command naturally?"[1]

The history of the wire industry in Altena and Iserlohn shows how State limitation of competition could lead to

[1] Cf. Dr. Karl Knapmann's excellent book, 'Das Eisen- und Stahlgewerbe in Altena,' Leipzig 1907: Motives of the Association, pp. 40, 68, 69, and 104; Compulsion, pp. 44, 45, 46, 49, 50, 53, 66 and 95; Limitation of Production and Repartitions, pp. 48, 51, 56, 62, 77-9, 95 and 100; Fixing of Prices, pp. 55 and 83; Influence of Freedom of Trade, pp. 86, 88, 89, 100, 101 and 105.

monopolist combination of capitalists employing small craftsmen, and therein differs from that of the Solingen industry in which the privileged retailers were unable to formulate in the concrete form of a single union based on common interests the advantages they obtained as employers. Besides the staple, *i.e.* the compulsory cartel or officially regulated association, the monopolist organisation in a handicraft controlled by capitalists might take the form of a capitalist company, differing from a staple much as a trust differs from a cartel. Such an undertaking was the Calw Cloth Trade Company (Zeughandelscompagnie) founded in 1650 as a public trading company. In return for loans of money it had obtained various monopolist privileges from the government, for instance, dyeing privileges (Färberrechte), as they are called in the Clothiers' Regulations of 1686. These privileges restricted the freedom of independent clothiers, *i.e.* those not employed by the company, and assured it thereby a firmer control over production by making competition in finished goods from this side impossible. They were also aimed against the competition of outside dyers, whose markets were similarly limited by various regulations to the company's advantage. Like the English patentees, the company succeeded in obtaining the exclusive right to supply a number of goods, whose manufacture they introduced from France, and taught to the clothiers dependent on them, claiming on this account the right of a "new discovery." No new trader could enter the district. Within the region affected by the trade regulations the rise of clothiers who might seek to employ their poorer brethren ceased. No member of the company could leave it and set up an independent business. Outside the above region the company tried by means of rights of view and pre-emption to restrict the markets of independent clothiers. Free goods, that is goods not bought from the company, were stamped by them, and this stamp, popularly called a "Voulez-Vous," whether rightly or wrongly, depreciated the value of the goods by the implication that the company had rejected them. Between 1674-1688 attempts were also made in the cloth trade to establish, by means of the "Knappenhaus," a monopolist mart for both buying and selling, for the protection of producers. Clothiers had to bind themselves to deliver all their goods to the "Knappenhaus," which was bound in turn to take them all. Private sale to foreign traders being thus intercepted, the Knappenhaus, in which the company played the chief part, could, by regulating production, balance supply and demand, and at the same time prevent the sale of raw material at low rates to foreign outsiders. Just as the wire interests in Altena created a staple to control the production of raw material, the Calw Cloth Company found in the Knappenhaus a means of imposing their own conditions on its delivery. When the market ceased to develop after 1686, and the company's influence was directed towards an increasingly heavy reduction in the amount of goods produced, the general opposition of the clothiers brought the Knappenhaus to an end. But other trade regulations remained, which tended to reduce to the company's advantage the production of raw material; for instance, the gild regulations which tried to check over-production of cloth by putting restrictions on the younger men, by making it hard to become a master, and by decreasing the number of apprentices.

Nevertheless, all this mass of privileges failed to uphold the monopoly for long. The State had tried to assure the Calw company a monopoly over as large a field as possible in the so-called "Moderations Bezirk"; but it could not protect the company from the rise of the cotton industry, which began after 1750 to spread all over Germany, and whose products entered into close and successful competition with those of Calw. Just as the use of coarse cloth had given the Calw traders certain safe markets, so now Calw in its turn was threatened by cotton goods. The changing circumstances of the market necessarily brought about the fall of the State-supported monopolist organisation. Such an organisation ceased to have any sense from the capitalists' point of view when it could no longer, by suppressing competition, help to exploit the monopoly their goods enjoyed in a market. Though the trade system which gave the Calw company its monopoly had not altered in principle, the company dissolved in 1797. Contrary to what happened in many other cases, the system of " moderations " and the monopolist trade rights came to an end because the interference of the State in matters of production was found unnecessary and even burdensome by the manufacturers just at the moment when their predominance in the market began to wane.[1]

The examples quoted will serve to show the existence in the eighteenth century, in some cases till late in the nineteenth century, of a monopolist system in the early industrial capitalism of Germany, mainly in mining, smelting, newly founded factories, and in handicrafts controlled by capitalists. The monopolies differ greatly among themselves. Some owe their existence to a system of direct official administration or to mining laws of a monopolist tendency ; others to survivals of feudal or trade gild organisation ; others again to all kinds of exceptional rights and privileges granted them by the State. In form, too, they vary from the mere monopolist position of one or more competing traders to the compulsory cartel or the single monopolist undertaking resembling a trust. But the universal characteristic in all cases is the limitation of competition by trade regulation. The history of their rise and fall is no more uniform than was their legal basis. By no means in every case was it reorganisation on free trade lines which led to the downfall of the monopoly ; as in the case

[1] Cf. for this account Troeltsch, pp. 73-76, 84, 113 ff., 130, 323 ff., and 327. That the rise of the factory system must shatter the old form of trade organisation on the domestic system is clear. But a monopoly might continue under the former system, and the Calw company's factory actually possessed a monopoly (*supra*, p. 83). The dissolution of the company was, however, primarily due to changing markets, which necessarily led to reduced profits even with such a monopoly.

of the Calw clothiers, a change in the economic foundation of the undertaking might make the continued existence of a monopolist trade system superfluous. The general causes of the decay were the introduction of freedom of trade, the abolition of the privileges of landowners, the repeal of regulations framed by gilds but favouring capitalist employers of craftsmen, the growing distaste of the government for monopolist concessions to particular factories, and the increasing success of the movement for the reform of the mining laws. The gradual union of the German States in a single trade area, which made it impossible to favour producers in the markets of a single State by prohibitive duties, vetoes on imports, export duties or bounties, was likewise opposed to State-protected monopolies; and the development of transport facilities brought to an end the dominant position long held by given areas of production for supplying large markets. It was just in the case where this predominance continued longest, as in mining and in some instances in smelting, that the old trade system of monopoly rights lasted latest.

The great difference between the beginning of freedom of trade in German early capitalism and the abolition of monopolies in England lies in their dates, and in the contrast between a consolidated England and the separate States of Germany. While in the German States the trade regulations restricting free competition continued to a great extent to exist in the eighteenth and nineteenth centuries, and only came to an end by degrees—sometimes quickly, sometimes slowly—England abolished industrial monopolies at a blow at the end of the seventeenth century. In 1775 the Calw Cloth Factory received in Germany a monopoly; the large New Mills Company in Scotland found itself exposed soon after 1700 to the competition of other undertakings, and tried to come to "a good understanding"[1] with them. Throughout the first half of the nineteenth century State administration was still hampering

[1] W. R. Scott, 'Records of a Scotch Cloth Manufactory,' p. lxxi.

the growth of new concerns in Rhenish Westphalian coal mining, and regulating on a uniform plan the competition of the existing collieries. In the north of England, after the downfall of the Coal Gild, coal mining was completely free from all official interference; in fact, the creation of even an entirely private combination of colliery owners was expressly forbidden in 1711 and 1730.[1]

There remains the important question of the economic effect of these monopolist systems on the growth of early capitalist industry in Germany. That we cannot here answer. Was the protective trade monopoly necessary for the creation of certain industries or of modern forms of industry, or not? Did it, on the contrary, delay development by preventing capitalist competition? If a general answer can be given to these questions, it requires much more extensive examination of facts than we can here undertake. For our purpose, the answer is also not essential. Our object is merely to contrast the history of a specific form of trade organisation, which was abolished in England by the end of the seventeenth century, with that of a similar system in Germany. The contrast is certainly not unimportant, if we desire to form an opinion of the trade system under which the powerful English industries of the eighteenth century arose.

It is remarkable that English political economy at the end of the eighteenth century was not aware of the contrast between the form assumed by capitalist industry in England throughout the eighteenth century, and both that which it had taken in the seventeenth century and that which it was then taking on the Continent. Neither Sir James Steuart nor, as we saw, Adam Smith dealt with the abolition of the former industrial monopolies in England, or in any way drew attention to its importance for the industrial development of their own day and country. Both know

[1] Dunn, ' View of the Coal Trade,' p. 25.

only trading monopolies or monopolist civic corporations.[1] In the case of Adam Smith this is partly to be explained by the fact that in his observations on industry he mostly has the handicraft system in mind. When he is thinking of wholesale capitalist production no special explanation of competitive trade seems to him necessary. What he says of the introduction of new industries shows this.[2] He who introduces such an industry, "the projector," expects "extraordinary profits," and, if the project is successful, his gains are in fact at first very great, but "when the trade or practice becomes thoroughly established and well known, the competition reduces them to the level of other trades." These words were written about the time that the projector, or entrepreneur, was being most vigorously attacked as a monopolist in Germany. Von Justi, for instance, writes: [3] "When in a given kind of manufacture or factory there exists only one entrepreneur, the competition and rivalry of many men in one thing, to which the goodness of commodities and the cheapness of prices is due, is wanting. The lack of good and cheap goods is not only harmful at home, but makes it impossible to gain credit abroad. . . . Entrepreneurs are therefore, from every point of view, contrary to good principles." While von Justi hurls the bitterest attacks at privileged entrepreneurs,[4] and in Germany the organisation of wholesale industry on the basis of free competition was regarded as a much desired reform, to English economists the existence of such a system seemed something quite natural, and they regarded it neither as the remarkable result of a struggle which raged a century before, nor as a special form of industrial organisation, unknown at that time in any other land. They had

[1] Steuart, 'Principles of Political Economy,' London 1767, vol. i. p. 200 ff.; A. Smith, 'Wealth of Nations,' Edinburgh 1817, vol. i. pp. 99-100.

[2] 'Wealth of Nations,' vol. i. pp. 188-9.

[3] Von Justi, 'Polizeiwissenschaft,' 1760, vol. i. p. 447.

[4] *Ibid.* pp. 489 and 755.

not the least idea what a rare form of organisation it was.[1]

[1] No comparison has been made here with the monopolist organisation of early industrial capitalism in France, advisedly. It may, however, be remarked that Chaptal, unlike English writers, was very well aware of the importance of the monopolies which French industry had had, especially that of the privileged factories, and of the contrast between these monopolies and the later freedom of trade. *Vide* 'De l'Industrie Française,' Paris 1819, vol. ii. pp. 372 and 379, 380. For the monopolies of the eighteenth century *vide* G. Martin, 'La Grande Industrie en France,' Paris 1900, pp. 224-232.

PART II

FREE TRADE AND THE EARLIEST MONOPOLIST COMBINATIONS

CHAPTER V

THE DOCTRINE OF FREE COMPETITION

After the seventeenth century prolonged competitive struggles between numerous manufacturers arose wherever legal monopolies had been abolished, and were regarded as a natural consequence of freedom of trade.[1] On such competition the English Parliament, which in its admiration for Colbert on the one hand opposed all industrial monopolies, and on the other tried to aid industrial progress by bounties, prohibitions of imports, export duties, etc., or by the artificial stimulus of consumption, counted. The same protective measures which had enriched particular individuals or companies under Elizabeth and the early Stuarts were now under the magic influence of competition to benefit whole branches of industry, and, inasmuch as they favoured numerous mutually competing manufacturers, even consumers also. Accordingly the inevitability of competition was always the argument with which the fears of the consumer were soothed whenever, in consequence of the high protection given to an infant industry,[2] he thought himself delivered over to the arbitrary dictation of a few monopolist manufacturers.

[1] Cf. von Justi, 'Abhandlung von den Manufakturen,' Copenhagen 1767, pp. 149, 150.

[2] For an instance see 'A Brief Essay on the Copper and Brass Manufacture of England,' London 1712, p. 20. The author defends high duties thus: "Whoever lives a few years will probably see many more undertakers of these works, who, by striving to undermine one another, will always keep prices low."

These views, generally accepted in England after the end of the seventeenth century, prevailed also among the founders of classical political economy at the end of the eighteenth and the beginning of the nineteenth centuries. Very similar terms to those which we have already found in Adam Smith were used later by Malthus: "If a machine was invented in a particular country by the aid of which one man can do the work of ten the possessors of it will of course at first make very unusual profits; but, as soon as the invention is generally known, so much capital will be brought into this new and profitable employment as to make its products greatly exceed both the foreign and domestic demand at the old prices. These prices, therefore, will continue to fall till the stock and labour employed in this direction cease to yield unusual profits." [1]

Except for legal restrictions on competition by gild regulations and for certain special peculiarities in particular occupations, Adam Smith knew of no circumstances which could prevent the tendency of manufacturers' profits to equalise. Starting from the proposition that industrial production could be increased at will at the same cost, he concluded that when for any reason the profits of a particular industry rose above the normal level in a country, an immediate increase in undertakings would take place. From this it necessarily followed that agreements between manufacturers to keep up profits must in the end prove ineffective, and that the interest of each manufacturer was best served by free competition. If, on the other hand, profits were reduced to beneath the normal level, Adam Smith assumed that the weaker were crushed out, either losing their capital or investing it elsewhere; so that here again the interest of the stronger was in the competitive struggle.[2]

[1] T. R. Malthus, 'Essay on the Principle of Population,' 5th ed. London 1817, vol. ii. p. 404.

[2] Compare chap. ix. of vol. i. and vol. ii. p. 50. In coal mining also Adam Smith holds that the closing of pits worked at a high price was a necessary consequence of the competitive struggle, vol. i. p. 279.

It is to be noticed that Adam Smith only identifies the interest of the individual manufacturer with competition where he assumes elasticity of production. Where a restriction of already existing undertakings seems probable, he fully recognises the possibility and the appropriateness of a coalition. As he explains in his lectures: "When a number of butchers have the sole privilege of selling meat, they may agree to make the price what they please."[1] In another place he says that "The trades which employ but a small number of hands run most easily into such combinations. Half-a-dozen wool-combers, perhaps, are necessary to keep a thousand spinners and weavers at work. By combining not to take apprentices, they can not only engross the employment, but . . . raise the price of their labour much above what is due to the nature of the work."[2] Another time he contrasts two competing trades with twenty traders, and says:[3] "In the latter case competition would be the greater, and the likelihood of their combining to rise the price the less." It would therefore be wrong to assume that Adam Smith identified competition with the interest of the individual unconditionally. Where he had in mind a limited number of sellers the substitution of combination for competition seemed to him both possible and also in the interests of the traders.[4] His later editor, D. Buchanan, vigorously attacked this opinion, seeing in all such remarks of Smith's a desertion of his own doctrine of enlightened selfishness, and failing to notice that to make use of coalition instead of competition in Smith's hypothetical case was simply the result of the desire for the greatest possible profit which animated the trader. Against Smith's wise reservation in the case of competition among few traders, Buchanan argued that competition was the strongest of all motives animating traders, and would therefore even in such cases

[1] Hirst, 'Monopolies, Trusts and Cartels,' p. 21.

[2] Adam Smith, 'Wealth of Nations,' vol. i. p. 209-210.

[3] *Ibid.* vol. ii. p. 50.

[4] *Ibid.* vol. i. p. 206.

be the only consideration in their minds. He disputes Smith's example of the wool-combers thus:[1] "Dr. Smith is not aware that if the principle of combination be once admitted it may be turned against the most valuable of his doctrines. But a combination of rival traders is a phenomenon which, until human nature is changed, will never be exhibited." In other places[2] Buchanan, again in polemic against Adam Smith, formulates more closely the peculiar and invincible desire of "human nature" for competition: "No body of traders ever can frame an effectual combination against the public; as all such engagements are broken by the partial interest of the individual concerned. No trader will keep up his prices for the profit of others; he will always sell when it suits his own convenience, and upon this principle accordingly is founded all this rivalship of trade." Even where official interference makes the original rise of competition difficult or impossible, as among gilds, Buchanan will not hear of the possibility of the private combination of such privileged workers.

"The same principle of selfishness which prompts them to form the league, prompts them also to break it. Rival traders have no confidence in each other; not two of them will ever act in concert."[3] M'Culloch was of quite the same opinion. While he, in support of Adam Smith, deduces the impossibility of increasing prices from the law that profits tend to equalise,[4] he is, on the other hand, convinced[5] that the principle of competition must prove effective even where the number of sellers is limited and no fresh competitors are added. For as soon as a number of traders in combination raise the price above "what is due to the nature of their work," it would be "in the interest of a large body of the combiners to secede from the combination and throw their goods on the market."

[1] Buchanan on A. Smith, vol. i. p. 210. [2] *Ibid.* p. 100. [3] *Ibid.* p. 207.

[4] J. R. M'Culloch, 'Principles of Political Economy,' Edinburgh 1825, p. 246.

[5] M'Culloch, 'An Essay on the Rate of Wages,' Edinburgh 1826, p. 190.

Therefore one can trust the supply of the most necessary articles to the unfettered competition of a comparatively small body of masters.

While Adam Smith admits combination in the case of a limited number of competitors, his immediate pupils were convinced of the unconditional value of the law of competition and of its necessary application even in such a case. To them competition is the necessary consequence of individual desire for gain, which will sooner or later break down every monopolist combination, even if to the common advantage of the interests concerned.

Not till John Stuart Mill do we find a doubt as to this opinion and a rehabilitation of Smith's reservations. Mill quotes the experience of municipal gas and water works in the thirties and forties and of the railway companies to show that undertakings may be so large that a very few of them can satisfy the entire demand. To think prices can be kept low by competition between such companies is a mistake.[1] "Where competitors are so few, they always agree not to compete. They may run a race of cheapness to ruin a new candidate, but as soon as he has established his footing they come to terms with him." He is further of opinion that manufacturers often succeed by all manner of chicanery in compelling new competitors to follow the fixed custom of the trade, and that, similarly, they compel its observation within their own ranks.

It is typical of Mill's scrupulous treatment of the subject that, in view of the few exceptions that he finds to the law of competition, he disowns the doctrines of individualist economy which assume its ubiquity. The effects of excluding competition had just been exhibited to all beholders in a new field of industrial life, in the erection of large municipal gas and water works and in railways. Combination had conquered one whole sphere of industrial activity. But it was very different with the large manu-

[1] J. S. Mill, 'Principles of Political Economy,' London 1849, 2nd ed. vol. i. pp. 176 and 301; vol. ii. p. 499.

facturing trades, which had continued after 1800 to develop on former lines. In this sphere of industry competition ruled, as before, without exception. More especially is this true of the most important finished goods of the period. In these trades we find in ever-increasing degree the continually growing number of undertakings and the multiplicity of existing factories, which are nowadays also a general sign of the prevalence of competition.

In 1835, 1313 establishments existed in the wool and worsted spinning trade, an increase of 10 per cent, in four years.[1] In 1787 cotton mills numbered 143, in 1835 they were 1070.[2] The silk industry, though a late offspring of English textile trades, also showed a rapid increase in the twenties and thirties. Silk factories increased in Manchester and Salford alone from 5 in 1820 to 16 in 1832, and in 1835 the total number of them in England was 231. The total number of wool, cotton, flax, and silk factories increased in the short period from 1835 to 1839 by 1016, 98 of which were not working in the latter year.[3] The iron trade had as early as 1791 73 coal-burning furnaces; [4] as prices rose their number increased in five years to 121, and in 1806 Great Britain already contained 233 such furnaces.[5] The number of furnaces is no very safe guide to the number of undertakings, as even at the end of the eighteenth century many ironmasters owned more than one.[6] The large number of undertakings is seen, however, from the fact that in 1806 233 furnaces were divided among 133 works. In 1791 Scotland had possessed only 16 modern (coal) furnaces; in 1850 it had 113, and in England the number had risen to 405.[7] Paper factories numbered several hundreds between

[1] G. R. Porter, 'The Progress of the Nation,' London 1851, p. 173.

[2] E. Baines, 'History of the Cotton Manufacture,' London (1835), p. 219.

[3] Porter, pp. 192, 219, 220 and 233.

[4] E. T. Warner in 'Social England,' vol. v. p. 635 ff.

[5] H. Scrivener, 'History of the Iron Trade,' 1841, p. 92.

[6] *E.g.* the Carron Company had 5; cf. Warner, p. 635.

[7] Porter, *ibid.* pp. 574 and 268.

1820-30.[1] Copper and brass had become divided, since the eighteenth century, among numerous mutually competing manufacturers, and where the consumers once feared the monopoly of a few works we have the Birmingham makers complaining in 1799 that, owing to the "numerous competitors," they could not sell at profitable rates.[2] About 1820 these industries, both in Wolverhampton, Birmingham and other places, were given over to an unceasing competitive struggle. Comparatively little capital was required to start a new business, and hundreds of small competitors sprang up beside the big works.[3] A similar development took place in other industries—for instance in the glass trade.[4]

In 1833 a Parliamentary Committee enquired into the state of manufactures, commerce and shipping, and the extensive evidence taken showed that in the manufacturing of finished goods—which alone were, in fact, considered—a vigorous competitive struggle was going on.[5] This had produced in the bad years which preceded 1820 such a lowering of prices[6] that the profits of most undertakings were exceptionally small, and in some cases no longer covered the cost of production.[7] The opinions of the experts heard by the Committee were characteristically expressed by a textile worker:[8] "We have long considered that part of our grievances was caused by the steam looms and by the competition of foreign manufacturers; but we consider that a very trifling matter in comparison with the home competition that exists among our masters, and till there is some remedy for that we shall never be better." Employers and workers seemed equally

[1] A. Dykes Spicer, 'The Paper Trade.'

[2] 'Report on Copper Mines, May 7, 1799,' p. 4, also p. 47 and *passim*.

[3] 'Report on Manufactures, Commerce, and Shipping, August 19, 1833'; questions 4369-4371, 4377 and 4385.

[4] Porter, pp. 256, 257. [5] Evidence: questions 1903, 4678 and *passim*.

[6] Tooke and Newmarch, 'History of Prices.'

[7] 'Report,' p. 774. Evidence: question 9971, 3 d.

[8] *Ibid.* question 11724.

convinced of the oppressive results of competition; but there is no trace throughout the evidence of any united action to restrict or abolish it. Rather, in all branches of industry competition was regarded as an evil, as inevitable as it was harmful, and the survivors regarded it as little more than a natural consequence of the struggle for existence that the weaker gradually became entirely submerged. Adam Smith had taken the ruin of such men as a completely natural fact, unimportant compared with all the advantages of the competition he championed. He had in mind the condition of affairs which an expert stated in 1833 to be prevalent in England when he said:[1] "I should ascribe to increased competition the misfortunes of many people in England. If too many people run into one line of business, of course the weaker portion must give way."

The general characteristic of this great industrial expansion in England was, therefore, ever-growing competition. All the variations which close observers like Mill noticed appeared necessarily not as a refutation but at most as a passing exception to the rule. They were important enough to refute the current deduction of competitive trade from the individualist spirit of the manufacturer, but they were not sufficient to alter essentially the general complexion of industrial organisation. They were in consequence neither fully recognised nor thoroughly investigated.

This is especially true of the monopolist combinations which existed in the various branches of English mining in the eighteenth and the first half of the nineteenth centuries, sometimes for long, sometimes for short periods. It is only recently that these first variations from the competitive type since the establishment of industrial freedom have begun to attract the attention of economists as early examples of the monopolist organisation which is at present gaining increasing control over industry. In their own day they were hardly noticeable exceptions to the

[1] 'Report on Manufactures,' question 2004.

general tendencies of contemporary commerce, but we can now see that though they themselves have long since passed away they were the forerunners of modern cartels and trusts. The most important were the combinations in the north of England coal trade.

CHAPTER VI

MONOPOLIST COMBINATIONS IN ENGLISH MINING

(a) ENGLISH COAL CARTELS IN THEIR PRIME

AFTER the official coal gild of Newcastle was broken up coalowners continued to regulate the sale of coal by private arrangements. In 1665 " a meeting of the several principal traders in coal " was held and came to an agreement as regards production and prices ; [1] though, as we have seen, the most vigorous attempts were made by legislation in the next few years to strangle any agreement between mine-owners which might result in a monopolist control over the coal trade. The first prohibition of this kind dates from 1711.[2] If one may deduce from its contents the state of affairs which it was intended to meet, the agreement of 1665 was not unique, but a common phenomenon in the northern coal trade. The Act, for instance, declares to be " void and illegal " all contracts and agreements, written or oral, between coalowners, etc., aiming at the monopolisation of coal, or the prevention or hindering of any person from buying, loading, shipping, or selling coal. This provision was to come into operation as from June 1, 1711,[3] and any person who after that date maintained, continued or called into existence an agreement of the aforesaid kind is threatened with heavy penalties.

[1] 'Report relating to Coal,' London 1874, Committee E, p. 9.

[2] 9 Anne, cap. 28.

[3] 'The General Shop Book,' London 1755, under 'Coal.'

It is clear, therefore, that at that time agreements among the Newcastle mineowners were everyday matters. Of the succeeding years we know little. The last known cartel of the earlier eighteenth century dates from 1725.[1] It may be assumed that Queen Anne's Act, renewed in 1730 by George II., did something to hinder the rise of cartels, though Rogers doubts this,[2] and is of opinion that the experts who stated in evidence given in 1800 that 1771 was the year in which the cartels began, had forgotten the existence of the earlier ones. This assumption is, however, improbable, because there appeared before the Committee of 1800, persons who had been engaged in the northern coal trade, in one case ever since 1755.[3] There seems little justification for accusing their memories when we know of no facts, apart from an attempt in 1768,[4] which prove the existence of combinations in the years before 1771.

The theory that a combination existed at that time rests on assumptions and probabilities, and against it there is one important fact. The combination of 1771, the so-called "Limitation of Vends," was the result of certain competition which had for some considerable time troubled the coalowners. This competition, due to newly discovered mines in the north of England, must have contributed more to prevent the rise of a single organisation of owners than the prohibitions of the law, which, though drastic, could not touch private agreement.

It must also be remembered that the Sunderland coal trade, which only began in 1654, had reached considerable dimensions by 1750. Between 1755 and 1770 a great number of new mines began to be worked, among others

[1] M. Dunn, 'The Coal Trade of the North of England,' Newcastle 1844, p. 23.

[2] Rogers, 'Industrial and Commercial History of England,' p. 616 A.

[3] Cf. evidence of Mr. Thompson, 'Report on Coal Trade, 1800,' p. 13.

[4] Rogers, 'Industrial and Commercial History of England,' p. 615 B, and 'Report of 1871 relating to Coal Report E,' Appendix ix. p. 3.

the famous Denton and Tanfield Moor collieries.[1] Finally, the use of steam in mines greatly increased production. After 1756 steam engines, chiefly owing to the efforts of Brown of Throkley, became more and more common in the northern collieries. The technical advances due to them and other innovations of that time "produced a new era, paving the way to the opening of those extensive and valuable collieries below Newcastle in the Wallsend seam, and the deeper collieries upon the river Wear." This development was regarded with dismay by those who, on the advice of "far-seeing" agents, had acquired mining property, then considered extremely profitable, but now of decreased value. The Ravensworth, Strathmore, and Wortley families had leased such districts as offered in the existing state of technical knowledge a profitable return, hoping thereby to acquire a monopoly, whereas owing to technical progress since 1750 entirely new mining districts now sprang up producing the most excellent coal and more favourably situated for transport. The overproduction caused by these mines seemed bound to lead to a fall in prices, and thereby to the ruin of the older coalowners, who "in their great eagerness to monopolise those districts," had burdened themselves with "long and costly leases."[2] Technical progress had increased production on the one hand and the discovery of larger quantities of coal on the other led to the sudden suspension of the law of diminishing returns in various districts of the northern coal trade—a severe blow to those who, like the old owners, could not profit by its suspension, the more so as the new owners, to gain all they could from the law of increasing returns, worked their mines at the highest pressure.[3]

[1] Dunn, 'Coal Trade,' pp. 17 and 23. [2] *Ibid.* p. 43.

[3] Dunn, 'Coal Trade,' p. 45: "The steam engine had become directly applicable to the drawing of the coals from the mine, which enabled an extraordinary increase in quantity to be realised, and that, too, of a quality greatly superior to the produce of many of the old districts." For names of the new mines on the Tyne and Weir besides the above-mentioned, cf. Dunn, 'Coal Trade,' p. 44.

A later writer[1] gives the following description of the competition which long raged between the various mines and which finally led to the cartel:—

"As more collieries were opened below the Tyne bridge, adjacent to the river and the sea, every facility of exportation was increased, both by situation and cheapness. Hence a rivalry took place between the ancient and the new and improved collieries. The contention between them was long, arduous and mischievous. It was which of them should by whatever means engage and keep possession of the market and the public supply. The superiority of the new collieries in quality and adjacency to the river was naturally and by the aid of steam engines so great, that the inferior collieries were obliged, in order to keep up competition, to resort to a practice so blameable that nothing can justify it except the plea of self-preservation. It was this, to pass their coals through a screen or sieve, and so separate the round and the large from the small, that they might meet in the market. This practice was a sacrifice of labour and of materials, so that the smallest coals passing through the screen were made worse than useless. The waste was so immense that the labourers were directed from time to time to set fire to the heaps accumulated, in order to rid the ground of an encumbrance. Thus with a known loss they were enabled to meet in the market the superior article. But of this contention, after lasting some years, both parties became weary; they found it prudentially wise to unite in interest, to equalise the price, to regulate the transmission from each colliery and to feed the public at their own prices and according to their own convenience; hence their union became a direct monopoly; it was agreed that the market should be fed, and not glutted."

The answers of Mr. Thompson to the Committee of 1800 corroborate this description.[2] He became in 1768 manager of one of the most important new mines. After

[1] R. Edington, 'A Treatise of the Coal Trade,' p. 57.

[2] 'Report on Coal,' p. 14.

some years the profits of the mine were not satisfactory, and he informed the chief coalowners that he "thought it highly expedient that a certain price should be fixed." The exclusion of competition seemed to him a necessary preliminary to an increase in profits.

At his instigation representatives of the coalowners of Sunderland—who had only ceased to sell their coal through Newcastle in 1704[1]—met the coalowners of Newcastle. Meetings were summoned and agreements as to prices and other matters made, and these measures were repeated at regular intervals, until in 1771 a permanent union arose, which, though in no way a direct successor to the old gild, must be regarded as a renewal of the organisation which formerly existed in a different industrial system.

For the existence of this association of owners, which lasted with certain interruptions from 1771 to 1844, two preliminary conditions were essential. First, the area of production had to be such that it could be worked on a uniform plan by the association, without allowing outsiders to develop effective competition, underbid prices and make its decisions useless. Secondly, it was necessary to find a market in which Newcastle was cock of the walk; a market which could be controlled, and in which prices could be dictated because other producers or groups of producers, whether at home or abroad, could not develop any considerable competition. In short, the combine rested on the monopolisation of production and the monopolisation of the market. This latter it achieved in London and its neighbourhood.

As late as 1800 it was shown that no other English coal district could in any way effectively compete in the London market with Newcastle. Besides Durham and Northumberland, Yorkshire, Lancashire, Cumberland and Westmorland in the north, Nottingham and Derby in the midlands, Shropshire, Somerset and Wales in the west had been important producers of coal[2] since 1750, yet

[1] Rogers, 'Industrial and Commercial History of England,' p. 616.

[2] 'General Shop Book,' *cit. supra*, 'Minerals.'

even at the end of the century it was only as a makeshift in times of great emergency that the metropolis drew on them for its supplies. The great cost of transport prevented the growth of real competition with the Newcastle trade. The Committee of 1800 declared [1] that a great number of coal deposits existed in the midlands and the western counties, " an aid . . . against which no legislative Prohibition at present exists, but which nevertheless has been very seldom called to the supply of the London market." Welsh coal was practically unknown in London. Since 1780 it had been exported in rapidly increasing amounts,[2] but only very exceptionally to London, freights from Swansea to London being far higher than those from Newcastle.[3] Inland coal was in no better position to compete in the London market. Neither Yorkshire, nor Warwick, nor Derby, nor any of the districts dependent on inland navigation for transport could rival Newcastle. Attempts to bring inland coal to London proved only too often unprofitable.[4] Though the building of canals had greatly advanced since 1770, it was in no way capable of coping with the regular transport of large quantities of coal. On such canals as existed the water supply was so deficient that frequent interruptions in carriage were necessary,[5] the dues were heavy and appreciably restricted competition with coal transported by sea,[6] and, finally, inland coal did not at first enjoy in London the repute of the northern coast coal.[7] As a result, at the beginning of the nineteenth century it was only when prices were very high that coal came to London by inland transport. We hear for instance in 1801, when coal was exceptionally dear, of a "growing feeling" in favour of bringing

[1] 'Report,' Dec. 1800, p. 16.

[2] *Ibid.* June 1800, p. 186. 13,319 tons in 1799 against 86 tons in 1770.

[3] *Ibid.* June 1800, p. 77.

[4] *Ibid.* Dec. 1800, p. 34.

[5] *Ibid.* June 1800, pp. 79 and 85.

[6] *Ibid.* p. 80.

[7] The Report (Dec. 1800, p. 16) states the coal of all English districts was " inferior " compared with that of Newcastle and Sunderland.

coal from the midlands, whereat the northern coalowners were much concerned.[1]

Their fears were, however, superfluous. For some decades their monopoly in the London market remained safe, though about 1820 the limits within which they could extort monopoly profits without attracting a rush of coal from other districts became narrower. The owners in the north attempted, according to an expert's account in 1830, to keep their price always a little under that at which it would pay other districts to compete. Sometimes, however, they miscalculated. In 1828, for instance, a syndicate price was fixed which was apparently too high, for the supply from Scotland, Wales and Yorkshire immediately increased, and the cartel had to lower its price again.[2] The fact that under certain circumstances competition existed was brought forward by the defenders of the coal cartel to prove that it was not a monopoly [3]—a somewhat thin argument, but used to-day by supporters of cartels and trusts who point to the number of outsiders and so on. An absolute monopoly the English coal cartel did not possess. But the fact remains that it was, up to a certain point, in a monopolist position; that is to say, so long as it did not screw up the price so high that it became profitable to get supplies from other sources. Up to that price limit (which was rather high) the northern collieries retained their monopoly in London even in the thirties, owing to the far greater cheapness of bringing coal to the market from the north coast. When prices were low inland coal never reached London.[4] In 1833 and 1834, when coal was exceptionally

[1] 'Report on Coal, 1871.' 'Report of Committee E,' p. 12.

[2] 'Report on Coal, 1830,' p. 255.

[3] 'Report on the State of the Coal Trade, 1836,' p. 12: "I do not consider the present agreement can by any possibility be called a monopoly." The proof being: "I understand a monopoly to mean where the sale of the article is in your own hand. If we were in possession of the whole of the market and if we had no competitors, either in Scotland, Yorkshire, or from inland coals or in Wales, we might become monopolists."

[4] 'Report on the Coal Trade, 1830' (House of Lords Committee), p. 67.

cheap, only about 6000 tons of inland coal in all were sold, as against over 4,000,000 of "sea" coal in the same two years. How great, even at this time, the share of the northern mines in the London supply was, can be seen from the following table: [1]

Place of Origin.		1832 (Tons)	1833 (Tons)	1834 (Tons)	1835 (Tons)
Newcastle, -	Sphere of the Coal Cartel.	456,880	460,848	774,835	534,000
Newcastle Wallsend, -		708,998	599,299	667,538	732,210
Sunderland, -		59,235	74,209	55,959	28,152
Sunderland Wallsend, -		559,363	590,174	501,321	601,402
Stockton, -		169,247	170,187	221,711	229,885
Blyth, - - -		49,927	48,649	64,268	65,046
Yorkshire, - -		48,938	16,050	17,139	27,394
Scotland, - -		49,579	15,138	39,487	40,955
Wales, - - -		38,644	28,416	31,025	35,420
Various, - -		1,195	60	446	367
Small Coal, - -		10,174	3,583	2,487	744
Total by Sea, - -		2,139,078	2,010,409	2,078,625	2,298,812
Total from Inland Districts, - -		10,742	4,395	1,826	1,004

These figures sufficiently show the predominance of the northern coal districts on the Wear, Tyne and Tees in London. Of about 2,300,000 tons of coal transported to London in 1835 they claimed about 2,150,000, while only the very trifling amount of about 1000 tons came from inland.

The peculiar relations of northern coal with the London market thus satisfied one of the necessary conditions for the creation of a mineowners' cartel. The second condition was that the possibility of using these special advantages should not be snatched from their grasp by mutual rivalry. If the northern owners were to turn to advantage the monopoly assured to them, subject to a certain high price limit, by the exclusion through natural causes of outside competition, it must not be made value-

[1] Compiled from the 'Report on the Coal Trade of 1836,' pp. 225, 231-238.

less by unceasing competition among themselves. To regulate the price of coal to the greatest conceivable profit of the mineowners, no under-bidding and a systematic plan of common control over sales were essential. Without that the attainment of a "fair price," naïvely defined by an interested witness in 1830,[1] as "a price a little below what the consumer can get the same article for elsewhere," was impossible. The experience of the years between 1770 and 1840 pointed to the same moral. Where competition between the various mines prevailed, prices showed a tendency to sink to the cost of production. When there was common regulation, prices rose independently of the cost of production to the limit at which considerable importations from other coal districts became probable.

All the numerous cartel agreements made in the northern coal trade after 1771 had therefore one aim, to keep prices in the London market high. For this purpose various measures were adopted at different times. The reasons which prompted the first important agreement, in 1771, we have just seen. In that year for the first time the Tyne and Wear owners consented, after a prolonged period of competition, to a cartel. The agreement was made in secret and its terms were not published, for fear that the existing prohibitions of monopolist "combinations" might be set in motion against it and its members fined.[2] One phenomenon which runs through the history of all later coal cartels appears already in this very first combination. Special care was taken to ensure, by fixing the price, that mines whose coal was inferior in quality and more expensive to work should obtain profits. In other words, the weaker and the stronger were to be united for their common development. Experience had shown that all mines suffered from competition, but that the chief sufferers, even to the extent of complete ruin, were those who produced the less valuable kinds of coal.[3] As the Committee of 1800 found,

[1] 'Report of 1830' (House of Commons), p. 254.

[2] 'Report of June 1800,' p. 14. [3] *Ibid.* p. 15, also p. 31.

the mines which had the worst coal often showed the highest working expenses.[1] New shafts cost more to sink, and their situation with regard to the river was less favourable than that of the good mines. The mines with the lowest working costs had also adopted newer machinery and "so reduced the work of men and horses." [2] Further, they had better appliances for loading.[3] In the circumstances it is clear that competition between good and bad mines meant a short shrift for the latter. In proportion as it reduced the price of the best coal, it attracted buyers to the kinds which thus became considering their quality the cheapest, and left the poorer kinds to fetch prices which did not cover the high cost of their extraction and transport.[4] To assure profits to the owners of mines worked on less favourable conditions, it was therefore absolutely necessary to restrict the production of the best mines so that it covered only part of the demand. The owners of the better mines could be compensated for this restriction of their production by driving up as high as possible the price of their coal—which in turn profited the poorer owners, for the outlet and price for the inferior coals depended mostly on whether the market was overladen with good coals or could only get them at famine prices. Gardiner already had complained [5] that it was the policy of the Coal Gild to sell bad or even "unmerchantable" coal together with good coal, and nearly 150 years later the same desire to ensure a market and favourable prices for the inferior coal again led to combination in a cartel. The desired object could, in the circumstances we have described, only be attained by fixing a scale of prices graduated according to quality,

[1] *Ibid.* (December), p. 4; June, pp. 18 and 29.

[2] R. Edington, pp. 56, 57. [3] *Ibid.* p. 55.

[4] 'Report of June 1800,' pp. 30, 31: "Shipowners so much prefer the better coals, that the poorer mines would not be in a position to sell their coal, so long as the better mines could cope with the demand." Compare also p. 15.

[5] Gardiner, 'England's Grievance,' pp. 50, 205: Discoveries in relation to the Coal Trade.

of course with the highest possible price for each quality. In this way the poorer mines were assured the position given according to the theory of profits to those who produce in the most expensive way, but whose goods are necessary to meet the demand.

An expert who had himself been secretary to the first cartel gave the Committee of 1800 some details of the organisation of the 1771 combination. The mines were classified by the quality of coal they produced, and their sales regulated accordingly. Five of the best mines received the main share of the total sales for a given time. Two further groups were given a smaller share at lower prices. Usually the prices of the different qualities differed by one shilling a chaldron.[1]

Of the cartel of 1786, which was the continuation of the above, we know rather more. The 1771 cartel had collapsed about 1780, and for a few weeks the markets had been open.[2] The price of coal sank, as might be expected, when regulation of production ceased. In Rochester harbour it fell from an average of 27s. in 1780 to an average of 23s. in 1785.[3] Whether it were so low that, as was alleged,[4] a number of mines did not cover their working expenses, can of course not be proved. But it is beyond doubt that about 1785 the northern mines were suffering from over-production and sinking profits.[5] This state of affairs led to a renewal of the cartels. They were defended on all sides [6] as the means of saving " many of the Persons interested in Collieries from ruin," and preventing a further fall of prices and closing down of mines. A cartel was formed in 1786 and 1787, and lasted, with the exception of a few months, for a great number of years. Its organisation was retained by all later coal cartels. Its inner managing committee was called " the Committee of the Coal

[1] 'Report,' December 1800, p. 14.
[2] 'Report of 1836,' p. viii.
[3] 'Report of 1800,' p. 187.
[4] *Ibid.* p. 20.
[5] Dunn, 'Coal Trade,' p. 26.
[6] 'Report,' June 1800, p. 21; Dec. 1800, p. 7.

Trade,"[1] and the special agreement as to production and prices "the Limitation of Vend." The terms of this agreement we must now consider.[2]

The main part of the agreement related to the share in the production of coal to be given to the colliery districts on the Tyne and Wear respectively. Of the agreed total output three-fifths were to be allotted to the Tyne and two-fifths to the Wear. The prices were fixed on the same method as that of the 1771 cartel. The restrictions on production were various. First, the entire production was fixed yearly by the cartel committee, and the Tyne and the Wear each given their quota accordingly in the proportion of 3 to 2. Next, the amount to be produced by each mine was laid down, each receiving its due share in the fixed quota of the two districts. This yearly quota was called "the basis"; that of the individual mine "the allotment"—the allotment being "according to the Powers of working and other Circumstances attendant upon each respective Colliery." The yearly basis was fixed according to the results of the previous year's sales, increased by an estimated allowance for expansion, and the total of each district was divided among the individual mines according to their nature and position. If a mine produced more than its allotted share, a special agreed fine was levied on it. For every chaldron of coal in excess of its allotment it had to pay at the end of the cartel year a fixed sum to the cartel. This was considered by the members to be "a Sort of Admission of the Collieries, who have vended less than their quantities, into a Participation of the Profits resulting to the Collieries who have exceeded the vends."[3] But as "the Allowance made . . . is not equal to the profits resulting to the Collieries exceeding their Vend from that Excess" there remained the fear that, despite the fine, individuals might produce more coal than was desirable in the general interests. Therefore, the above-mentioned

[1] *Ibid.* June 1800, p. 43.
[2] *Ibid.* pp. 19, 57; 'Report,' Dec. 1800, pp. 6-7.
[3] 'Report,' June 1800, p. 20.

inner committee decided the exact monthly delivery of each mine. Each colliery had to send a written statement on the first Wednesday of every month of its deliveries; and in many cases the owner's agent had to swear to the statement before a magistrate. The committee then fixed a monthly allotment for each mine according to the state of its yearly share. If a mine had produced more than its share allowed, the excess was subtracted from its next monthly allotment; if less, the deficit was added. The mines received notice every month of the condition of their allotments, and the notice was intended as a guide to owners "how much they should vend upon that Basis till the end of the next month." As the committee exercised great influence on the amounts of fines, the notice must in practice have been a kind of warning, where any considerable irregularity as regards the quota had taken place.[1] Very often also, after 1790, the monthly vend was settled by the committee on consideration of the existing state of the market.[2] This is very clearly seen in some certified copies of letters reprinted by the Parliamentary Committee of 1800. One of them, for instance, says: "The Demand for Coals being much greater than expected, the Committee think it right to give an additional quantity, etc."

Another letter from the Secretary of the Coal Committee runs as follows: [3]

NEWBURN, 24th Nov. 1782.

SIR,

I beg you may vend no more Coals from Flathworth till after the twelfth of next month. As you have already sold above 1000 chaldrons this last Fortnight including Thursday and Friday last, there is no doubt that

[1] 'Report,' June 1800, p. 45.

[2] *Ibid.* p. 48. Mr. Edington, who was an opponent of the cartel, stated on oath in a court of law: "If they find that the London market has had too many coals sent, the market dull and the prices rather falling, they then issue orders for the next month for a lesser quantity to be vented."

[3] *Ibid.* pp. 149-150.

Walbottle [1] will get the Quantity allowed for Five Weeks; if so, you will be a considerable Quantity over your Vend.

I am, Sir,

Your hble. Servt.,

THOS. TAYLOR.

This and similar letters show clearly the active control exercised by the inner committee of the cartel. The annual meeting settled the total amount of the vends; but all individual sales during the year were decided by the committee, which had an office and a secretary at the common expense.[2] The functions of the committee were twofold—first, to regulate the total production according to the position of the market so as to prevent overstocking; and, secondly, to see that the division of production between different mines remained in accordance with the general decision of the annual meeting. The meeting decided the proportion of each mine to the entire produce; the committee saw that that proportion was observed, however much the actual production varied from month to month. Increases or decreases on the total amount were in the same way shared by each mine in proportion to their vend. The division of the total production for the year, and the observance of the fixed ratio throughout the monthly variations of the total, were the most difficult tasks the cartel had to perform.

Inasmuch as the stronger elements, whose coal found at all times a good market, strove to increase their shares, whilst the less favoured opposed such a step, internal conflicts were inevitable. The "superior collieries generally work nearly what the alloted Proportion gives them; but it frequently happens that they are some hundred Chaldrons over such monthly allotted Proportion." [3] We never hear this of the inferior collieries. They had very much less interest in increasing production, especially as the fines fixed for exceeding the vend were a much greater

[1] Another mine owned by the individual to whom the letter is addressed.

[2] 'Report,' June 1800, p. 148.

[3] *Ibid.* p. 137.

burden on their profits than on those of the better mines, a weakness inherent in the joint regulation of the output.

These difficulties often gave occasion to conflicts which threatened the existence of the cartel. In the middle of the nineties the agreement was suspended for some months "owing to some difficulty in the arrangement of Quantities." In December 1799 the agreement was not renewed [1] "in consequence of some collieries which stood on a high basis requesting to be put on a higher."

But they never led to a prolonged suspension of the cartel,[2] which continued down to 1840, in spite of temporary small conflicts during which both the agreement as to prices and the division of the vend were at various times —for instance in 1829 [3]—for some months in abeyance. The fall in prices in such cases soon led to a new combination, usually pressed for with especial eagerness by the less favoured mines.[4]

About 1830 the cartel was faced with a serious danger. Through the opening of the Stockton and Darlington Railway the colliery district on the river Tees had greatly developed in the last few years, and especially since the railway reached the river's mouth its exports of coal by sea had greatly risen. The Tees mines had remained outside the Tyne and Wear cartel, and were regarded by them "as a rival trade." [5] The competition of these important outsiders noticeably depressed prices, especially when the cartel broke up in 1832 and a "fighting trade" began.[6] The market price of the best coal sank from 20s. 3d. in November 1832 to 13s. in June 1833.[7] Whether the

[1] 'Report,' June 1800, p. 44.

[2] The 'Parliamentary Report of 1836,' p. 4, states: "The greatest difficulty the Committee experience is in satisfying the parties that they get their fair proportion of the Vend in the general arrangement."

[3] *Ibid.* p. 8.

[4] 'Report,' 1830, p. 17: "When in the year 1828, competition was increased as the regulations of the Vend were discontinued, the price fell so low that many of the Collieries which are most unfavourably situated were worked to a loss."

[5] *Ibid.* p. 251. [6] 'Report of 1836,' p. 10. [7] *Ibid.* p. 67, also p. 11.

frequently expressed opinion of the 1836 committee that this competition and the fall in prices which accompanied it swallowed up the entire profits of the inferior mines is correct, cannot be decided with certainty. It is beyond doubt that the complaints of the interested persons who represented the position in 1832 and 1833 as entirely ruinous were much exaggerated. We have learnt from experience in our own day that a cartel always depicts the distress in a time of competition in the liveliest colours so as to justify its own existence. But the position of many collieries during the period of open market was clearly much less favourable than it had been under the cartel. Even after 1840, these two years, which had been the only considerable period of competition during seventy years and also the time of the greatest depression known to the coal trade, were remembered with a shudder.[1]

As before, general competition led to renewed attempts at combination. In July 1833 the colliery owners met and passed a resolution [2] "that a general regulation of the coal trade should be entered into." The new cartel, which came into existence in August 1833, was joined on March 1, 1834, by the mines of the Tees district.[3] The cartel was therefore more powerful than any of its predecessors. The number of "outsiders" on the Tyne and Wear was negligible: according to an expert estimate their theoretical productive power in 1836 was about 3,600,000 tons [4] against 8,100,000 tons in the same districts by the cartel, to which must now be added the mines of the Tees, the majority of which, including all those of importance, had now sought admittance.[5] Generally speaking the constitution of the 1833 cartel differed little from that of the previous cartel. It dealt first with the fixing of the yearly basis for the three large districts of Tyne, Wear

[1] Dunn, 'Coal Trade,' p. 236.

[2] 'Report,' 1836, p. 6. [3] *Ibid.* pp. 104 and 145. [4] *Ibid.* p. 118.

[5] *Ibid.* pp. 104-5. Of the total production of 357,000 in 1835 in the Tees district, 299,000 tons was from collieries which belonged to the cartel. Cf. also Dunn, pp. 86 and 88.

and Tees, and for a smaller district which now obtained a basis of its own. The due share of each mine in the total annual production was then decided accordingly. In 1835 the district basis was as follows : [1]

District.	Basis in Newcastle Chaldrons.
Tyne	939,000
Wear	585,000
Tees	160,000
Hartley, Cowper, Netherton	68,750
Total basis,	1,752,750

A fortnightly regulation of production was substituted for the former monthly one. "The basis," so the chairman of the Newcastle Coal Committee declared,[2] "is merely an imaginary quantity; the basis is taken merely to apportion the relative quantities as between the collieries; the coal-owners meet once a fortnight or twenty-six times a year, and, according to the price in the London market, the quantity issued, which is to be divided amongst the collieries, is determined." These meetings, in fact, decided on the amount of coal it was desirable to sell, and each district was then informed that in the coming month they might sell so much coal per thousand of their basis. In 1835 this figure varied in various months from 40 to 85 per thousand of the basis. In the whole year the sum of the monthly amounts, *i.e.* the vend, was to the original basis as 768 to 1000; in other words, the districts were in fact only allowed $76\frac{4}{5}$ per cent. of the basis.[3] The shares of the individual mines were dependent on that of the district, and each mine received monthly its allotted sales in proportion to its share. An exact account was kept, in which excesses and defects were listed as "short" or "over" respectively. Here is an example.[4] The basis for April 1836 was fixed at 65 per thousand. Accordingly, of the annual basis of 969,500 chaldrons fixed for the Tyne district, $62,367\frac{1}{2}$ chaldrons might be sold that month. A certain colliery

[1] 'Report,' 1836, p. 54 ff. [2] *Ibid.* p. 1. [3] *Ibid.* p. 52. [4] *Ibid.* p. 54 ff.

in the district, the Backworth, had been given a yearly vend of 30,000 chaldrons. On the basis of 65 per thousand for April, its share for the month was 1950 chaldrons. As a fact, the 41 cartel mines in the Tyne district showed the following results that month:

	Chaldrons.
Year's basis	959,500
Issue, month of April, 65 per 1000	62,367½
Over	1,265
Short	8,227½
Short of total vend for the month	6,962½

Various steps were taken to secure the observance of the shares of production fixed.[1] Owners had to appoint a representative for each mine, who was required to have exact knowledge of the financial arrangements of the mine and to be responsible for any infringement of the agreement, either in production or in prices. This representative—usually the agent of the mine—must be known to the Coal Committee and correspond with them in matters of dispute. The Committee were empowered by section 16 of the agreement, "to summon the parties to this agreement, or their agents, to answer any interrogatories, and to produce any documents necessary to enable them to give full effect to this agreement." Refusal to give the necessary answers was punishable with a prescribed fine. For the special case of excess on the vend, section 23 provided that "any colliery exceeding the issue beyond 100 chaldrons, or 2 per cent. upon the basis to finish a ship, shall forfeit for every chaldron so exceeding 5s., and such excess shall also be deducted from the issue to the colliery for the next month." To secure the payment of the prescribed penalty, each member of the cartel had to deposit a bill payable at sight to the amount of £20 for every 1000 chaldrons of his basis. This remained in the hands of a Trustee Committee.

To establish this system, which was only a repetition of the former one, was not so difficult. The great difficulty

[1] *Ibid.* pp. 7-9.

of the cartel was to realise its end, defined by the chairman in 1836[1] as " to apportion the vend to the different collieries according to the quality of the coal and the powers of raising that coal." According to him—and he had over thirty years' experience of the trade—that had always been the duty undertaken by cartels. There had been but few differences of opinion as to the suitability of the above system. How to carry out the " Limitation of Vend " when once fixed had rarely been a matter of dispute ; but with the basis of division it was very different. The fixing of prices and the principle which, while duly considering all interests, would give a " fair " division of the output to each, was the debatable and at times very sore point in the cartels.

Prices had to be fixed, first as regards their maximum, as far as this lay within the control of the cartel ; and secondly, as regards the relation between the various qualities of coal. The superior collieries with good coals were less interested in the differences of prices, than in the maximum price for best quality coal. The inferior mines were equally interested in both. All regulation of prices, however, depended on restriction of production. And here, too, there was a double question. To raise the price of all kinds of coal a general limitation of output according to the actual state of the market was necessary ; whereas the relative prices of the different coals depended on the supply of each kind of coal available in the market. Whenever the London market was well stocked with the better coals, inferior coal sold badly at low prices, and *vice versa.* The chief method of regulating the relative prices to the advantage of the poor mines was accordingly to limit, as far as possible, the sale allowed to the good mines.

Within the cartel itself, therefore, individual owners had private interests besides the general interest. The good collieries, always certain of finding buyers, required as large a vend as possible and the mildest penalties for

[1] 'Report,' 1836, p. 1.

exceeding it. The bad mines, which only seldom exceeded their vend, depended for their existence on the greatest possible restriction being placed on the production of the good mines and on high penalties for excesses. Mr. Brandling rightly told the Committee of 1836[1] that "it is the interest of the low-priced collieries to get the high-priced collieries to raise the prices of their coal, because it would enable them to do the same." But by the side of this common interest in general high prices there were conflicts of the bitterest kind with regard to differences of prices and to the shares of production allotted to individual mines.

The 1833 cartel allowed, as far as might be, for these conflicts, and attempted to produce a greater harmony of interests than had formerly existed. Formerly it had been left to the mineowners themselves[2] to estimate the capabilities of their mines and the quality of their coals. In future the Committee named certain persons to act as mine-inspectors, to classify the various mines according to their capacities and to report thereon to the Committee. The Committee thus obtained approximately accurate information as to the working expenses and quality of each mine without compelling each owner to betray the condition of his business.[3] It then fixed the vend of each mine according to the inspectors' reports, with the reservation that the whole matter was a subject of negotiation between the coalowners and their Committee.[4] The owners could oppose an allotment; and special provisions were inserted in the above-quoted agreement to meet such cases. Every difference of opinion came before two neutral "referees," and if they disagreed, a third was named as "umpire."[5] The remarkable effectiveness of this system was seen in a famous dispute between Lord Durham, Lord Londonderry, and the Hetton Company—a dispute

[1] *Ibid.* p. 11.
[2] *Ibid.* p. 43.
[3] *Ibid.* p. 2.
[4] *Ibid.* p. 6.
[5] Cf. §§ 6-11 of the agreement given in the Appendix.

touching three of the most important mines on the Wear.[1]

Besides this important duty of fixing vends, the cartel had to decide on the amount to be produced each month, and to fix the common standard of prices and the actual prices of each quality of coal. The key to all these problems was the state of the coal market in London. The London wholesale dealers in northern coal had formed a ring or pool, and it was therefore extremely easy to calculate the state of London wholesale prices. Further, there was direct connection between the cartel and the ring in London. Every second Thursday the secretary of the latter sent a report to the Newcastle Coal Committee.[2] The Committee, which knew the price of coal at the pit-head and also the cost of freight to London, could at once discover from the London prices the profits derived for the moment by the coal ring from the fluctuating market prices. The price in Newcastle was, however, fixed for a whole year on the basis that the price at the pit-head plus freight to London was just a little under the price at which London could obtain coal from elsewhere. As we have seen, that was the limit within which the cartel could enforce its policy with regard to prices. Having a fixed price, the cartel was not interested in the fluctuations of London prices, so far as their own prices were concerned. But as an expert expressed it:[3] "the price in London" was "the only guide for the quantity issued." As soon as the coal ring's price rose or exceeded the limit regarded by the cartel as the price in open competition, that was a sign that the ring was pocketing "immoderate" profits and that the London market could consume more coal than before at the old price. Then the monthly vend could be increased. If London prices fell, so that it was feared the cartel price could not be maintained, that was a hint immediately to order a restriction of the amount brought to the pit-head. The secretary of the Committee stated frankly in 1836:[4]

[1] 'Report of 1836,' p. 6. [2] *Ibid.* p. 29. [3] *Ibid.* p. 2. [4] *Ibid.* p. 2.

"If we see by the markets in London that the price in the Pool has exceeded the price we consider to be the fair average price, which is a price something below what the coals from other districts can be supplied at, we issue a large supply; if it is below that, we consider the supply is more than the demand requires and we diminish it." In short, the coal cartel was concerned with the fluctuations of price in London, not in order to increase or diminish its own prices, but in order to regulate its production accordingly, and to supply now more now less coal at the same price.

The existence of the London Coal Ring, which dated from about 1770,[1] was of great importance to the northern cartel, of which it was often regarded as an extension.[2] The more the ring succeeded in times of falling demand in keeping prices relatively high, the less the cartel had to vary its monthly quantities of output. A slump in prices, which would have resulted from open competition among wholesale dealers, would have increased the degree of these variations and possibly made the whole system of a uniform price throughout the year unworkable. When, on the other hand, the demand was keen, competition would leave the buyers liable to the danger that prices would be driven up very rapidly and encourage inland rivals, while the existence of an agreement made it possible to delay the rise sufficiently for the northern combination to hasten to meet the greater demand by increasing their shipments. It was therefore in the interests of the cartel to support the ring.

Until 1830 the law helped the ring by ordaining that every sale of coal in the port of London must take place at the coal market and through "factors."[3] As a result, the shipowners sold their cargoes not to the numerous wholesale coal merchants, at this time about 150 in all, but to a small number of factors who had formed a single committee, the so-called Coal Ring. In 1800 there were

[1] 'Report,' Dec. 1800, p. 9. [2] 'Report of 1836,' p. 86.

[3] 'Report of 1830,' p. 132.

only 14 factors as against 28 wholesale merchants. The Parliamentary Committee of that year rightly pointed out [1] that " Monopoly was created . . . by the Exclusion of the Masters and Ship Owners from an Interference in the actual Sale, the Factors dealing only with the Coal Buyers." This state of affairs received legal sanction by an Act passed in 1807,[2] which made the sale of coal in the port of London dependent on sales on the coal exchange and specified the exact procedure to be followed. Wholesale merchants must enter themselves in the exchange register, and must sign at each sale the factor's contract book, which showed the officially certified cargoes of the ships.[3] Although no special conditions were laid down for becoming a factor, there were only 19 in 1830.[4] Each factor made a private bargain with the coal shippers, but they had a common agreement as to the price at which coal was to be offered to the wholesale merchants.[5] In comparison with the enormous increase in sales since 1800, the number of factors, who were in London the first buyers, had risen little. The ships' captains who sold their cargoes at the port found therefore a very small number of buyers—a fact which naturally much increased the power of the ring in its individual bargains. If the shipowners could have bargained direct with the much larger number of wholesale merchants, the greater competition among buyers would certainly have increased their profits. As it was, unless the factors had been set up by them,[6] they had to leave the lion's share of the profit given by the market price over their out-of-pocket expenses (purchase money and freight) more or less to members of the ring.

But in 1831 George IV.'s law granting these privileges

[1] ' Report of 1800,' p. ix.

[2] 47 Geo. III. cap. lxviii.

[3] ' Report of 1830, p. 150.

[4] *Ibid.* p. 170.

[5] *Ibid.* p. 135. The factor Bentley stated : " When the factors have once ascertained the real demand of the market they then proceed to the sale and a price is agreed."

[6] This apparently oftened happened. ' ' Report of 1836,' p. 31.

to factors was repealed. A new law[1] which came into force in 1832 aimed at freeing the coal trade in the port of London from all restrictions, and abolished the obligation to buy shipments through factors. "The trade is open to any parties who choose to attend."[2] Legally factors were abolished, but in practice they long survived. The coal cartel took care that the ring continued. As we have seen, it was greatly interested in its existence, which kept prices steadier than could be expected with unrestricted competition. It was now legally possible for any one who wished to buy coal to get it direct from the shippers, and therefore competition with the factors was not out of the question. But the legal possibility of buying coal directly, to the exclusion of the factor, could only be realised, if mineowners or shippers were ready to sell direct. And this was not the case. In paragraph 27 of the cartel's agreement already quoted the members bound themselves "that all the parties to this agreement shall strictly adhere to such regulations as to the sale of coals in London by the coal factors as the united committees shall from time to time agree upon." The gist of its policy was that no member of the cartel should sell direct to merchants, but solely through factors, whether set up for the purpose by the cartel or merely connected with it by business relations. An expert, the colliery owner, Mr. Brandling, stated clearly in his evidence in 1836 the attitude of the cartel towards requests for the direct delivery of coal. Even if the buyer promised immediate payment, members of the cartel could not be moved to sell without a factor. "If you were to come to my office," he said, in reply to a member of the Committee,[3] "and ask me whether I would sell you coal or not, I should say, Certainly, and my price is so and so, provided that you choose to go to my factor. If you do not choose to go to him, you may buy your coals elsewhere." In such a case there would remain the possibility of buying from an outsider, without employing a factor,

[1] 1 and 2 Geo. IV. cap. 76. [2] 'Report of 1836,' p. 31. [3] *Ibid.* p. 21.

And this way out was suggested by another expert, who defended the behaviour of the cartel with less self-possession than Mr. Brandling.[1] But, as the chairman of the Committee pointed out to him, the number of outsiders was very small, and under severe cross-examination he admitted that most of them had only inferior coal to sell, so that even so the prospects of direct sale were remarkably small. The ring, therefore, with the aid of the cartel, retained its power in London even when its privileges had been abolished. As before a small number of factors, no greater in 1836 than in 1830,[2] ruled the London coal market, each buying cargoes for himself, but offering the coal to the wholesale dealers at a common price.

Even the ring and the resulting restriction of competition among the first buyers does not, however, seem to have produced in all cases the desired degree of steadiness in the London market. A strong east wind or good sea weather might result in a large number of ships reaching London on the same day; and, if their cargoes were immediately delivered to the factors for sale, a fall in price was inevitable.[3] Conversely, unexpected delay might drive prices higher than would be the case with a regular and even supply. As early as 1834 the cartel made an attempt to limit the possibilities of such fluctuations. They appealed to the ring, whose members were partly dependent on the mineowners, to suggest some remedy.[4] The factors accordingly adopted a resolution, with which the cartel heartily agreed,[5] that only a limited number of cargoes should be sold each day in the port of London, the exact number changing with the market price. Incoming ships were entered in a register, and offered for sale by the factors in turn. The first forty cargoes on the register were to be sold, if the market price of the best coal had reached 21s. a ton on the day before; if it rose above 21s. a ton 50, 60, 70 or more cargoes would be put up for sale on the following

[1] 'Report of 1836,' p. 34. [2] *Ibid.* p. 31. [3] *Ibid.* p. 75.
[4] *Ibid.* pp. 31, 32. [5] *Ibid.* pp. 29, 33.

days according to the level the price reached. This decision was carried out with scrupulous care. "The Factors," says a report of 1836, "are very strict in keeping to their regulations; and although a fleet of 300 sail should arrive, no more than 40 ships will be offered on any one day if the prices should be below 21s. the previous market-day. The Factors in reality feed the market, so as to keep the prices as near as possible to those fixed by their regulations."

To carry out these measures, the means which we have already noticed were used. If it appeared that a captain or shipowner had sold more cargoes in one day than the decision of the ring allowed, or that he had not observed the rota decided on by the ring, the secretary of the ring reported the fact to the secretary of the cartel. The cartel then boycotted the offending shipper, and this danger was usually quite sufficient to make shipowners and captains observe the ring's regulations.[1] But occasional transgressions did occur. The Parliamentary Committee of 1836 discussed one such case. It was shown that in 1835 two ships belonging to a London coal merchant, the *Olive Branch* and the *Lavinia* were boycotted by the cartel, on information sent by the secretary of the ring, Mr. Scott, to the secretary of the cartel, Mr. Brandling, that the respective captains had infringed the decision of the factors with regard to the order of sale.

The cartel and the ring worked in organised co-operation. The power of the ring kept down the middlemen's profits, and produced the steady prices which the cartel desired, besides keeping prices at the highest possible level, *i.e.* just under the price of supplies from other sources. The cartel on its side regulated the middlemen's profits of the dealers, by increasing or diminishing the amount of coal offered according to the state of the London market, and so suiting the London price to its own fixed price for the year. The monopoly made this possible.

We see now why the cartel followed the fluctuations of

[1] *Ibid.* pp. 34, 29.

the London demand as regards the quantity it produced only, and did not fix its prices according to those ruling in London. As the London price on the year's average could be regulated so that the middlemen's profits were but moderate, and that considerable fluctuations during the year were avoided, it was far simpler for the managers of the cartel to fix the average price for the year in the north only, and to let the "big" members of the cartel maintain their own London factors if they wished to exclude entirely all middlemen's profits. As far as concerned the cartel as a whole, to fix the price once only meant an important simplification in the functions of the committee; to regulate prices according to those in London would have been more labour than the relatively small loss in middlemen's profits was worth.

The reduction of these profits, whether they went to shippers or factors, was the great advantage which the mineowners gained from the cartel. When competition ruled in the north it was the shipowners and captains who made great profits. Coal was at these times cheap at the mines, and the shippers had the opportunity of buying at a low price and turning to advantage any increase in the London demand. This being so, it is just in periods of competition that we find mineowners themselves owning ships, attracted by the higher profits of transport to take over the vessels in spite of their usual unwillingness to run the risk of carrying freight.[1] When, however, cartels were flourishing, large middleman's profits, either by shippers or by factors, were practically impossible. Both shippers and factors were more or less hangers-on to the cartel, which could remain satisfied with fixing a price for the year,

[1] 'Report of 1830,' p. 7: "When the regulation of the Vend is not established and when an eager competition, or what is called a fighting trade prevails, the Coalowners not unfrequently hire Vessels and send their own Coals to market." Also 'Report of 1836,' p. 16: "The Coalowners are generally desirous to sell their Coals at the staithes and to have no risks afterwards and when the trade is brisk and good they do so; but, in an open trade they have freighted vessels and send them to London, to be sold by the Factors on their account."

and merely used the fluctuations of the London market price to guide it in deciding on its total output.

One last duty remained. To make the poor mines, and especially those which only produced inferior coal, pay, it was not sufficient to maintain a high price for the best coal and to limit the output of the better mines. It was necessary to deal with coals of very differing qualities, the worst of which depended for a market on the difference in price between good and bad coal; and accordingly it was needful to regulate that difference, in other words, to fix the relative position of the prices. The cartel, therefore, regulated on a common plan the year's average price for the various qualities of coal. A similar system had been organised by the cartels of the end of the eighteenth century, and there was no change as regards this in 1830 to 1840. The owners of the best coal fixed their year's price in accordance with the ruling market price, and the remaining owners were asked to conform. Naturally, the influence of the committee as well as that of the impartial umpire was considerable, and the committee's exact knowledge of the mines in the cartel enabled it to see whether the various owners had named a price " corresponding to " the quality of the coal, or whether it required amendment upwards or downwards.[1] As a rule the fixing of prices was a matter of less difficulty than the division of production.[2]

Enough has been said to show that the coal cartel had since 1770 continually tightened the bonds of its organisa-

[1] 'Report of 1836,' p. 3. Mr. Brandling stated : " Before the agreement is signed, the colliery producing the best coal, or the highest-priced coal, is called on to state the price at which they intend to sell ; as soon as they have done that, a colliery of the next best description is called on to state the price at which they intend to sell, with reference to the leading coal at the best colliery, they knowing the price at the best colliery ; if the price that they have fixed is lower according to the rates of the preceding year in proportion to the best coals, than it ought to be in those places where they come in competition, the committee would then call on that colliery to fix their coal at the fair price, that is, at the fair proportionate price."

[2] *Ibid.* p. 2.

tion, and was by 1835 firmly established. It controlled three large mining districts, except for a few outsiders. Shippers and factors were dependent on it, and gained no larger middlemen's profits than the cartel allowed. Wholesale prices were regulated by fortnightly or monthly fixing of production. Its object was the general increase in the profits of the coal trade, all mines, whether working on favourable conditions or not, to share the advantage equally. To that end, increases or decreases in the total production were divided among the various mines on an agreed basis fixed according to the capabilities of each mine, and mutual competition which might have arisen from the rivalry of different qualities was prevented by agreement as to the relative prices of each quality. Such were the essential functions exercised by the northern coal cartel during its continuance from 1770 to 1840.

The origin and organisation of the cartel might provide many suggestive facts for an estimate of the effects of this combination. We see, for instance, that when there was no cartel, prices fell heavily, and that the cartel served to protect weak mines working under unfavourable conditions. But such results, important as they are, can give but little aid in judging the suitability or unsuitability of the system to its object, or its advantages and drawbacks. The high prices for which the cartel was attacked were not denied by those who spoke as interested parties. Then, as now, they were justified on the ground that they were no more than would give a "fair" profit and keep the inferior mines from closing down. So argued the chief witnesses before the Parliamentary Committee of 1800.[1] The same argument was the answer of the secretary in 1836 to the question what would be the result on owners of suppressing the combination. "It would produce a fighting trade; it would increase the competition, and the immediate effect would be a depreciation on prices. How long that would continue would depend entirely on the effect it would

[1] 'Report,' June 1800, p. 17 ff.

produce on those collieries that were raising their coals at the greatest expense. The public, in the meantime, would certainly get their coals cheaper, but there would be a transfer of the labour and capital from one district to another, which would materially affect the value of property within that district." [1]

The rise in price, therefore, which the monopoly made possible, was not only admitted, but defended. To test the real value of the defence would necessitate an exact knowledge of how high coal prices must be to cover the working expenses of the least favoured collieries. As in almost every colliery both these expenses and the quality of coal differed, we cannot of course get this information any more than the Committee could. We can only deduce some general conclusions from the large mass of materials which we have considered. It was certainly true that as early as the end of the eighteenth century the cartel had, by increasing prices, helped to keep alive collieries unfavourably situated, owing to the causes we have related. "The Purpose of these Regulations," says the 'Report of the Committee of 1800,' [2] "was answered, the Evils to which they were avowedly directed were remedied, the Depression of Price complained of was removed, and the Dangers apprehended to the inferior Collieries effectually averted." But even this Committee is driven to the conviction that the level of prices prevailing under the cartel, that is to say, throughout the period from 1771 on, except for a year or so after 1780, had far exceeded the amount justified by the working expenses of the worst mines. Its conclusion [3] was that "the Coals would admit, with just Profit to every Part of the Trade, considerable reduction."

In 1830 and 1835 the position was similar. The Committee of 1830 state: [4] "It is true that the application of Steam Engine and the use of Safety Lamp have enabled the remaining pillars of coal to be worked out of mines

[1] 'Report of 1836,' p. 23.
[2] 'Report of 1800' (December), p. 7.
[3] *Ibid.* pp. 7 and 17.
[4] 'Report of 1830,' p. 17.

which had been heretofore abandoned; and though coal is thus obtained, which would otherwise have been altogether lost, the process by which these workings are conducted is said to be so costly that they could only be carried on under a high market price." The law of diminishing returns made high prices a condition of existence for the inferior mines. But here again the question rises; are not the prices driven up above the limits set by the conditions of production in the least favoured mines? The answer of the Parliamentary Report is: "It is evident that the prices respectively given in by the Coalowners as those which under the regulation of the Vend they are willing to take, are not in all cases the lowest which would afford a compensating return, but are the highest which they think they can maintain under the competition to which they are exposed."

The enquiry of 1836, and indeed the statements of the coalowners themselves, corroborate this view. We have several times already pointed out that it was a principle energetically held and openly admitted by the latter to maintain the price of coal in London as high as was possible without increasing competition from other sources. "That is the point we aim at, and that is the point we consider ourselves justified in aiming at," the secretary of the cartel declared [1] in 1836; and when he was asked, with astonishment, whether that was not the conduct of a monopolist, he replied: "Certainly not. I consider it to be a combination that we are perfectly justified in entering into. It is a combination of the proprietors to keep up the price of their article in the same way as a combination of workmen keep up the price of their property, which is their labour." By which answer he admitted that it was not consideration for a "fair" profit which decided the policy of the cartel

[1] 'Report of 1836,' p. 12; cf. *Ibid.* p. 13. Question: "Am I right in supposing the measure of your power of self-protection is the price at which other coals can be supplied to the London market?" "Decidedly." "While you keep within that, you can control the price in London?" "We can so far control the price in London that we can raise our coals up to that price."

as regards prices, but, on the contrary, consideration for the highest increase in price possible within the bounds of their monopoly.

In view of this fact, it is difficult to defend the cartel's prices on the ground that their sole aim was the protection of the least favoured mines. For the cartel fixed its prices not according to the amount of the cost of production, or at least not only by this amount, but chiefly with a view to the highest possible price which could be obtained without becoming subject to increased competition from other districts. Its policy could not therefore be justified, even on the assumption that it was desirable in the interests of the mines which produced little profits to obtain a relatively higher price than that obtainable by free competition. Even from this point of view, even considering only the interests of such producers whose working expenses were high, we cannot escape the conclusion that the tendency of this monopolist combination was to keep prices at the highest conceivable level, whatever the conditions of production might be. The coal cartel must be judged as regards its prices like many of the cartels which flourished at the present day under protective tariffs. Their representatives also often maintain that the prices aimed at are only sufficient to make the worst factories pay, whereas in fact their policy is entirely governed by import prices, and uses the monopoly given by the tariff to maintain the home price above the world's price by the amount of the customs duty.

Even, therefore, if the conduct of the cartels is regarded solely from the standpoint of its own representatives, it must be admitted that the regulation of prices was far more a policy of self-enrichment than of self-preservation. If, in addition to the producers, the great mass of consumers, who had to pay by increased prices the cost of maintaining mines with high working expenses, are also to be considered, what must then be said of the cartel and its effects? The defenders argued on the point: [1]

[1] 'Report of 1836,' p. 8.

"Consumers also profit by the Cartel; for if prices had sunk owing to general competition, the bad mines would not have continued working, and their cessation would have caused a shortness in coal, which would again have driven up the price, far higher than they have been under the régime of the Cartel."

This argument was but poor comfort for the consumer, as the enquiry of 1836 showed only too clearly. As the price in the time of the cartel usually stood at the level at which it would pay to send coal to London from other districts, and indeed often, for instance in 1828, rose above that level, even if the cartel had not existed it could hardly have risen much higher. The pauses in which a free market existed gave, of course, no opportunity to test the correctness of the expectations which the above argument held out. Competition usually lasted only a few months or at most a year, and therefore no mine closed down during such periods; on the contrary, the rivalry resulted in a great increase in production. How mines with poor coal would in the long run have been affected by the fall in prices cannot be proved, because competition always led in a short time to the renewal of the cartel. But even the opponents of the cartel did not deny that the price prevailing in these periods of competition did not in many mines [1] cover the cost of production.

It remains to consider the position of mines producing good coal. According to Mr. Brandling's statement, the difference in the cost of production varied from 13-14 shillings a chaldron in some mines to 23 shillings a chaldron in others.[2] As in 1836 the best coal sold at 26 shillings on the Tyne, and 28 shillings and 6 pence on the Wear,[3] large profits must clearly have been made by mines producing the best coal cheaply. The owner of one such mine, apparently aggrieved by the restrictions of his output, declared that his gains "had risen above the standard of a reasonable profit." He even protested against the heavy

[1] 'Report of 1836,' p. 11. [2] *Ibid.* question 166.
[3] *Ibid.* questions 821 and 1999.

rise of prices and the accompanying restriction of output, because it seemed to him more profitable for his mine to sell larger quantities of coal at lower prices.[1] Had prices, therefore, fallen to the level at which they stood before the formation of the cartel in 1823, *i.e.* from 22-23 shillings, only such good coal mines as were working at the highest cost would have been appreciably affected. Even mines in which the cost of production was moderate would have made a profit. It is true that the coal of some mines never realised more than 15-18 shillings a chaldron even during the existence of the cartel,[2] and these mines would have been very badly hit by a fall in prices, unless their cost of production was insignificant. But the Commission of 1836 established the fact that the productive power of the mines which supplied good coal cheaply was so great that they alone could have completely satisfied the existing demand in free competition. In other words, the diminished production of poor mines might have been made good by the increased production of good mines had the latter not been artificially checked by the Limitation of Vend.

Mr. Buddle, an inspector of mines and an expert, estimated that the possible annual output of the mines controlled by the cartel had increased enormously in the years 1829-1836, that of the mines on the Tyne and the Wear having risen from 5,887,000 tons in 1829 to 8,123,000 tons in 1835. Technical improvements and the sinking of new mines had contributed to this result. But though the theoretical productivity increased, the actual output was smaller. The total amount sold by the cartel on the Tyne as well as the Wear was less in 1835 than in 1830; on the Tees alone, a far less productive district, it was a little higher. Whilst the possible output on the Tyne and the Wear in 1836 was estimated at 8,123,000 tons, the actual sales of the cartel amounted to 3,495,000.[3] Good quality mines, capable of producing about 150,000 tons annually, received from the cartel an allotment of 110,000 tons.[4]

[1] *Ibid.* questions 2405 and 2431. [2] Cf. detailed table of prices, p. 53, *ibid.*
[3] 'Report of 1836,' p. 15. [4] *Ibid.* q. 2013, p. 15.

Unbiased judges of the conditions of production in the north, such as M. Wood, who had himself been a colliery proprietor, stated [1] before the Committee that the number of productive mines with good coal was so great and their working expenses so low that they alone could have supplied the market at such prices as would have left them a profit, while keeping out the poorer qualities of coal entirely.

The arguments used by those interested to justify the cartel policy therefore became more and more threadbare. It was only possible to preserve those mines which either produced poor coal or worked at great expense by a special reduction of the total output, or else by withholding a large part of the best coal from the market. "The first effect then of the regulation is to force an inferior coal on the market, which in a state of competition evidently could not be sent to pay the producer," said one mineowner,[2] discontented with the price policy of the Committee. The old abuses which Ralph Gardiner had attacked so energetically in the middle of the seventeenth century still existed unchanged nearly two hundred years later. The report of the Select Committee of 1836 seemed merely to repeat his complaints in formulating the results of the enquiry as follows: [3] "The result, therefore, is that at present the great majority of Coal-owners on the Rivers Tyne, Wear and Tees are combined avowedly to limit the supply of Coals to the London Market, so as to raise the Price to the Consumer higher than a Free Trade would command and, also, to force on the Market a larger proportion of inferior Coals at Prices which could not be maintained otherwise than by such a Combination." Whilst, on the one hand, coal was being sold to the English consumer at a higher price to benefit a few mineowners, on the other hand, it was being disposed of abroad at much lower prices. Those pits which were working at a profit, and which were most affected by the limitation of production naturally sought to equalise matters by disposing of some of their surplus abroad. The

[1] 'Report of 1836,' q. 2008, p. 15. [2] *Ibid.* q. 1981, p. 15. [3] *Ibid.* p. 15.

cartel did not regulate export, and every mineowner could export as much as he chose. Although the exporter had to be satisfied with lower prices, mineowners who wished to increase their output considered export business the best means of reducing the inconveniences of a low share of home production. It was stated [1] that coal was often sold for foreign consumption at 4·6 shillings a chaldron less than the price fixed by the cartel for the home trade, and that even at these rates mineowners, whose working expenses were low or moderate, could derive considerable advantage. According to a later Parliamentary report coal from the north of England was actually 40 per cent. cheaper in St. Petersburg than on the Thames.[2]

Consumers were not unnaturally always greatly disturbed whenever a fresh cartel came into being and prices rose again, and naturally the new cartel was often represented as an " illegal monopoly " and so on. The coal cartel in Newcastle was attacked just as the petroleum trust or our coal cartels are attacked at the present day. In the years 1820-30 consumers everywhere regarded the cartel on the Tyne and Wear as an " illegal coalition." [3] Although from 1826 combinations of employers were legal, the common law of England had, from the earliest times, laid down in practice the principle that " contracts in restraint of trade " are illegal. On this ground a suit was provisionally entered in 1793 against the cartel to be tried in York, but in fact it did not ultimately come into court. The enquiries of the Parliamentary Committee of 1836 were partly the result of petitions from the county of Middlesex and the inhabitants of Westminster. The report of the Committee declared that the complaints of the consumers against the existing coal cartel and its monopolist policy

[1] *Ibid.*

[2] 'Report of 1871,' p. 12.

[3] Cf. 'The Coal Trade,' N.D. London, British Museum, 8244, c. 68 (cr. 1830), p. 7: " Of late years it has become popular to accuse the colliery owners on the Tyne and Wear of holding a monopoly, and of being an illegal coalition." Cf. further on the same subject 'The Mining Journal,' Oct. 1, 1836, p. 107.

were not unfounded. "A question may arise," the report says, "whether the Coal proprietors by their combining to prevent Coals being brought cheaper to market, do not subject themselves to penalties." [1] These expressions are cautious enough. No one, in fact, dreamt of prosecuting the cartel for "restraint of trade," or anything of the kind. Without fear of legal consequences the cartel could now openly show the power which it had had to conceal carefully during the period in which cartels were prohibited. The frankness with which the secretary of the cartel explained its position and its policy in matters of price and production showed clearly how secure the cartel felt itself. It stood more firmly than ever. And yet its collapse was approaching more rapidly than any one could have thought possible in the prosperous times of the thirties.

(*b*) MONOPOLIST COMBINATION IN COPPER MINING AT THE END OF THE EIGHTEENTH CENTURY

Before describing the decay of the coal cartel in the north of England another combination must be mentioned which excited much public attention in England at the close of the eighteenth century. In consequence of the increasing number of complaints from merchants and manufacturers in Birmingham concerning the rise in copper, Parliament appointed a Committee in the spring of 1799 to take evidence and to enquire into the existing condition of the copper trade. Tooke's tables of prices [2] show that copper had risen from 84s. a cwt. in 1790 to 109s. in 1795, and to 120s. in 1799. Moreover, in 1799 manufacturers complained that prices for English copper were much lower abroad than at home, and that it was a matter of pressing importance to them to have the customs duty on copper abolished.[3]

The report of the Parliamentary Committee showed not

[1] 'Report of 1836,' p. 8.

[2] Tooke's 'History of Prices,' London 1838, vol. ii. p. 400.

[3] 'Report on the State of Copper Mines,' May 1799, pp. 4 and 5.

only that a cartel had existed in copper mining, but also that after the dissolution of the cartel the concentration of firms interested had been sufficiently powerful to continue a kind of monopolist organisation. The expert evidence given before this Committee is the only witness we possess (a few pamphlets excepted) for the existence of these monopolist conditions. The question of combination played so important a part in the enquiry that the whole history of the movement can be reconstructed.

English copper mining began in the last twenty-five years of the seventeenth century with the discovery of copper ore in Cornwall. It increased rapidly in the eighteenth century, and a large manufacture of copper into finished products of high value developed. England soon produced a large quantity of copper goods which previously had been imported from Germany, especially from Nuremberg and from Holland.[1] One large consumer at the end of the eighteenth century was the Royal Navy, which used copper in increasing quantities for various purposes.[2] In 1784, according to " a German traveller," [3] the production of fine copper in Cornwall amounted to from 3000 to 4000 tons. It was estimated in 1797-98 (June 30 to June 30) at 5427 tons, whilst in 1790 the total output in England was estimated at about 6500 tons annually.[4] Of course these figures must be taken as approximate only. Their importance lies in the fact that England exported copper annually in large quantities. For instance, the amount of copper sold in 1797 to the East India Company alone was 1500 tons.[5] Thus England had far outstripped Sweden, the only other European country which could be seriously considered as an exporter. The output of copper in Sweden was estimated by experts at from 800 to 1000 tons annually, two-thirds of which was exported. The export

[1] 'Report on the State of Copper Mines,' p. 42.

[2] *Ibid.* (plates, nails, bolts, etc.).

[3] Bernoulli's 'Reisebeschreibungen,' 1784, p. 373.

[4] 'Report on the State of Copper Mines,' p. 97.

[5] *Ibid.* p. 56.

trade of several other European copper-producing countries, such as Russia (Siberia), Prussia (Mansfeld), and Hungary, was beneath consideration.[1] In times of unusual demand the copper mines of Armenia and South America could help the importing countries, but the regular supplies were not obtained from these sources.[2]

Although England in the eighteenth century was the largest exporter of copper in the world, yet the English manufacturer had to pay for his material higher prices than those current in the international market. The import price in the continental consuming countries—especially in France in the last decade of the century—was fixed by the competition of the above three exporting regions, especially of Sweden, the most important of them. In England itself competition was restricted by a duty of eleven guineas a ton on copper. But the evidence in 1799 showed clearly that the English price exceeded considerably not only the export price of copper, but the price at which copper could have been obtained from elsewhere under a system of free imports. When in the middle of the nineties the Government required copper for minting, it made the sad discovery that it could not buy copper at the same price which the East India Company had paid. Later it proposed, in order to supply the navy with copper at a cheap rate, to import copper duty free for Government purposes, and to forbid the export of copper by the East India Company—a clear proof of the great discrepancy between the export and the home price. A Birmingham manufacturer stated that he had in 1788 been able to buy copper in Sweden at £98, which cost in England £105. As the English price was no higher than the Swedish plus freight and duty, it did not pay him to import. Even the figures given by Mr. Grenfell—the expert who advocated the retention of the duties—showed that there was great disparity between the English and the Swedish prices. According to him, the price of one ton of copper in Sweden in 1796 was £110

[1] 'Report on the State of Copper Mines,' pp. 41, 77, 53. [2] *Ibid.* pp. 42, 55.

and in England £118. In the same year the East India Company bought English copper at a contract price of £106 a ton, about £12 cheaper than the home buyer.[1]

The remarkable fact that in the largest exporting country of the world prices in the home market were relatively so high in spite of rapidly increasing output began to be noticeable from 1790 onwards. Ten years previously the tendency had been exactly the reverse. With an increase in output prices fell steadily. Copper ore had fallen from £73 2s. 6d. a ton in 1784 to £63 8s. in 1790. Before 1771 the East India Company always paid more than £100 a ton for cake copper. But from this date onwards prices fell steadily, so that in 1781 the company only paid £79. In 1783, in a report, the company expressed its satisfaction that, "notwithstanding the Increase in the demand of Copper for the East India Company and the consumption of his Majesty's Navy and Merchant Ships, and for Manufactures, which have increased in as great a proportion, the Price of Cake Copper has been reduced by £22 5s. per ton, whereby there has been a saving to the Company upon 13,509 tons, which they had purchased from 1774 to 1782 inclusive, of the sum of £300,375."[2] In 1789, according to Mr. Grenfell's statement, copper cost in England £80, whilst in Sweden, as well as in Cadiz, the price was higher. In the same year the East India Company also paid £79-80 —no more than the English consumer. Only in 1790 did the peculiar state of affairs already referred to arise:—concurrently with a constant rise in price a considerable rise in prices in England as compared with those in the international market and a correspondingly marked difference between home and export prices. And from this time the existence of the copper duty was important; earlier it would have been unprofitable at the low rate of prices in

[1] For the statements in this section, cf. 'Report on the State of Copper Mines,' pp. 72-5. For the greater cheapness of copper in Sweden, p. 31; for the year 1792, p. 77; for Mr. Grenfell's price tables, pp. 164 and 165; prices of the East India Company, p. 173.

[2] 'Report on the State of Copper Mines,' pp. 48 and 49.

England to import even duty free, and therefore a duty was superfluous. Now the producer was for the first time able to add to the home price a part of the amount of the duty, and thereby to make a profit from the home trade. The reactionary movement of prices in the English copper market in the last decade of the century had obviously an intimate connection with a concurrent change in the organisation of copper mining. The period of low prices had not contented the producer, however much it had satisfied the East India Company and the home consumer. It was a period of severe competition, which depressed alike prices and profits. It dated from about the year 1773.[1] This same year was marked by the opening up of a new mining district in Derbyshire and Wales—the Anglesea mines. These mines could deliver copper ore at much cheaper rates than the old Cornish mines, and, although the ore cost more to prepare before smelting, still the Anglesea district competed very closely with the old mines. The low price at which the East India Company bought copper in 1781 was directly caused by the determination of the Cornish producers to " keep the Anglesea copper out of the market."

The Cornish producers included both smelters and mine-owners, as the combination of mine and smelting house did not exist in Cornwall as it did in Anglesea. It was probably the lack of this combination which made Cornwall feel competition so much. In 1785 the Cornish mineowners had had enough of the struggle. Addressing themselves to Mr. Thomas Williams, who already occupied a prominent position in the Anglesea district, they begged him to bring about an understanding between the two mining and smelting districts, of which the aim was to be " to bring the metal of both Countries to the Market at a fair stipulated Price." By this means they intended to break with the old system

[1] As the following statements have been taken from the report on the copper trade, I give references to the page number only in such places where they seem to be specially necessary.

of "public ticketing," and to replace the sale of ore to the highest bidder [1] by a system of fixed price agreement. In 1785 influential mineowners in Cornwall formed themselves into the Cornish Metal Company. This syndicate, in its turn, made a contract for seven years with all the Cornish mineowners, binding them to sell to the Metal Company seven-eighths of their total output of ore at a price to be fixed annually, the Metal Company reselling the same quantity to the smelters by virtue of an agreement with them. It was only after the competition among the Cornish mineowners had thus been limited and in part replaced by a single sales organisation that it was possible to come to definite terms with the interests in Anglesea. There it had not been necessary to form a single organisation. Mr. Williams was "acting proprietor" of all the mines; [2] he was the business representative of the whole district and embodied in himself the requisite compact organisation. Now that, on the one hand, the inter-competition of the Cornish mines had been greatly limited since 1785, and that, on the other hand, the copper ore syndicate and the Anglesea district had come to an agreement, there was ground for hoping that the prices of ore and copper would fall no further, and that the mines and smelting houses would become more lucrative again.

The exact nature of the "stipulations" which, according to Mr. Williams, were made with the Cornwall syndicate, is unknown. But from the fact that in 1787 differences arose between the syndicate and Williams as to the respective "Proportion of Sales at Market," it is obvious that there must have been some regulation of the contingent of output to be furnished by each. But their mutual relations did not remain long on the original basis. In 1789 already Mr. Williams had been invited to undertake the general business management of the syndicate. Having on hand

[1] For further details cf. 'Report on the State of Copper Mines,' p. 67.

[2] Williams was joint-owner only in some cases, but he managed all business affairs.

an unusually large stock of ores to get rid of, the promoters were afraid for the safety of the capital they had invested in the concern, if they could not find some capable individual to dispose of the stock at a firm price. They therefore placed the uncontrolled business management in Mr. Williams' hands until the expiration of the agreement of 1785. Thus nearly the whole of the copper output in England and a considerable part of the stock of raw copper was at the disposal of one single individual.

It is difficult to determine how far Williams took advantage of his position to effect a rise in prices. The price of raw copper certainly rose again from 1787.[1] But the reproach subsequently made against him was not so much that he had created an absolute rise in prices as that he had bought ore cheap from the mineowners and sold it dear to the consumers, whether smelters or others. By these means he was said to have forced up artificially the profits of the syndicate. This opinion is confirmed by the official statement of prices before the Parliamentary Committee, which gave the price of copper ore in 1787 at £67 4s. 10d. a ton, whilst the price of raw copper to the East India Company was £69·71. In 1790 the company had to pay £78, when the price of ore was only £63 8s. Apparently the attitude of the syndicate had contributed to increase the disparity between the two prices, and it was therefore not surprising that Mr. Williams should boast subsequently that he had repaid the shareholders their capital plus 5 per cent. interest as long as the contract lasted, and that the obligations of the syndicate had been discharged in full. But while the syndicate was prospering, its policy was damaging two groups of interests. These were, first, the mineowners (who, though not participating financially in the syndicate, had delivery contracts at a fixed price with it), for in spite of the rise in copper prices, the price for ore was no higher than during the time of public sale; and,

[1] 'Report on the State of Copper Mines,' p. 139.

second, the Birmingham manufacturers, who as consumers suffered from the high copper prices.

Individual mineowners first began to move in the matter, and finding that they could get a higher price for the one-eighth of their output which was at their own disposal than the price paid by the syndicate for the remaining seven-eighths, they put on the open market increasing quantities of copper ore in spite of the running contract. Mr. Williams replied by creating a new organisation of copper-sellers. In October 1790 he actually succeeded in securing the total output of Cornish Copper for the Metal Company by means of a contract terminable at first in two years. The mine-owners were to get a higher price for their ore—£76 a ton. For that they contracted to deliver exclusively to the syndicate, but "in case Cornwall produces a greater quantity of Ores, so as to exceed the Consumption, the same shall not be brought to market, but stocked up for the remainder of the term."

The manufacturers of Birmingham saw with alarm that this contract had been the means of making the organisation of the copper trade a much closer one, in fact that it had become a monopoly. Like the tinfounders in the case of the tin monopoly, they proceeded to organise themselves.[1] One of the experts stated before the Commission: "About this time a Company was formed in Birmingham, consisting chiefly of Consumers of Copper, called the Birmingham Mining and Copper Company. They were led to believe that the Advance upon Copper was not owing to the Price received by the miners, but to the expensive medium through which they received it. Their object, therefore, was to bring Copper to supply the Manufacturers of Birmingham as cheap as the nature of the Trade would admit."[2] This company and a second one, the Rose Copper Company, which was founded soon after, strove to outflank the syndicate and its associated smelting

[1] For this and the following statement see the evidence of Williams and Simcox, and Appendix to 'Report.'

[2] 'Report on State of Copper Mines,' p. 7.

houses. They bought mining shares, acquired mines of inferior value, and above all purchased smelting houses. Once their own smelters, they tried to persuade mineowners to sell their ores to the highest bidder by offering better prices than the syndicate price.[1] An expert described the position as it now existed in the following words: "When the Birmingham Mining and Copper Company began to purchase, there was but a small Proportion of the other Ores sold at Public Ticketings; they however would give a better price to the miner than he then received, and yet bring Copper to Market much cheaper than the Consumers could buy it elsewhere. This, I believe, induced some who did not think themselves legally bound, to withdraw from the Contract, and bring the Ores to open Sale." Mr. Williams recognised the fact that there must be an alteration in his sales organisation if it were not to go entirely to pieces. The contract which he brought forward in November 1791 shows that his policy had changed. The syndicate was only to claim delivery of three-fourths of the total output of Cornish ore, and that at a higher price—£82. The smelters were to bind themselves not to buy in the open market, *i.e.* by auction, on pain of forfeiting their share of the contract. The intention clearly was to cripple public sale, as the high prices reached at the auction of such proportion of output as did not belong to the syndicate had always tended to raise the prices paid by the syndicate. At the same time, Williams invited the Birmingham companies to share the contract with him.

But this organisation never came into existence. The companies in Birmingham considered the proportion of the copper output offered them by Williams too small. The Cornish mineowners, on their side, expressed themselves energetically against the proposal in a resolution on January 24, 1792: "To use Arts to obstruct the public Sale of our Ores and to decoy the offerers for them from the Ticketings, are not only manifestly injurious to us as

[1] 'Report on State of Copper Mines,' pp. 6, 7, 50, 94.

Individuals, but prejudicial to the Interests of this Country." So runs the second paragraph of this resolution. Henceforward the main mass of copper ore mined in Cornwall was disposed of by public sale as before.

Although the existence of the syndicate was suspended as far as it represented the union of the Metal Company with the Anglesea miners, the conditions which had given rise to the complaints of the manufacturers still existed.[1] They were intensified at the beginning of the nineties, not only by the further rise in copper prices, but by systematic " dumping " in the export trade. This state of affairs led to the formation of the Parliamentary Committee on the state of the copper trade in 1799. The combinations and the agreements were formally dissolved. But the monopolist organisation of the copper trade, far from disappearing, continued to exist in another form. As a manufacturer said: " Since this Time, the greatest Part of the Ores of Cornwall have been sold by public Ticketings; but even upon this Plan it is not difficult, when Copper is in Demand, for any Purchaser, who has a strong Interest in the high Price of Copper, to advance it as he pleases."

Williams was obviously meant by the word " purchaser." In any case, it was he who, up to 1799, was the most powerful member of the copper trade. In modern terms, he " controlled," as he says himself, the entire output and smelting of Anglesea ore. He rented the mines from the two owners, and the entire management was in his hands. The output of the Anglesea district was about 1700 tons of copper in 1799, about one-eighth of the output in Cornwall. Even after the dissolution of the copper syndicate, Mr. Williams still maintained his relations with Cornwall.

It was shown in the evidence given before the Commission that Williams represented one of the eleven companies who appeared as buyers in the copper ore market. Although the company were not always buyers, they were kept

[1] Cf. evidence: Simcox, Smith, Bolton, etc.

informed by their agent, Mr. Vivian, of the conditions ruling in the Anglesea ore and copper market. The same Mr. Vivian was also agent for another company—the Cheadle Company, which bought every year in large quantities. Thus Vivian was one of the largest buyers in the copper market. In the three months December to February 1799 he bought on account of the above two companies an amount of ore equal to 351 tons of copper. He had himself, in addition, financial interests in some of the mines. It was therefore to his interest to keep prices high both for ore and copper. The interests of the other mine buyers differed widely from one another. The two companies formed by a combination of Birmingham manufacturers had a lively interest in buying copper ore as cheaply as possible, as they worked it up into the finished article, and there would necessarily be a decrease in the consumption of their products if the price rose correspondingly with the increased price of raw material. As a matter of fact, it was stated [1] that in consequence of the high price of raw material since 1793 the consumption of raw copper in Birmingham had decreased by 500 tons annually, and the conditions in the export trade had grown steadily worse. This was an established fact, vouched for unanimously by different witnesses. But the decreased demand from that quarter did not by any means check the movement of prices in the raw copper market. For the decline in the demand of this Birmingham high-grade industry did not hinder the general rise in the consumption of copper. The figures in the appendix to the report of the Committee showed that the consumption of copper bought by the government for the navy had increased very largely in the nineties, in seven years amounting to as much as 1500 tons.[2] In any case, there was beyond doubt an increased general demand for raw copper, further stimulated by the purchases of the government and the East India Company, and in con-

[1] Cf. evidence: Simcox, Smith, Bolton, etc.

[2] 'Report on the State of Copper Mines,' p. 175.

sequence a shortage of copper ore. This shortage led to the mining of much poorer ores than had ever before been put on the market.[1] But who fixed the price of copper? Williams, according to his own statement, followed the quotations for Cornish copper given by Mr. Vivian. But through his agent in Cornwall he was able indirectly to effect a rise in the price of ore, which in its turn naturally caused a rise in the price of copper. The Birmingham companies consumed their own copper. Many manufacturers bought copper in addition in the market. Mr. Vivian represented two companies. The number of smelters in Cornwall who sold copper consisted only of eight individuals. Thus competition among sellers of raw copper was extremely limited. It was therefore quite feasible for the smelters to cause a rise in the price of copper corresponding to the rising price of ore, more especially as they were protected by import duties. Williams, of course, profited most by the high prices. He himself supplied ore, and thus his profits from the sale of raw copper must have been very large. We hear, further, that he owned large works which were mainly busied in working up copper for the navy. Williams thus was the head of a business combination as well organised as any conceivable to-day. The smelting houses pure and simple were obliged to maintain the high price of copper, which was easy enough, as they were few in number and demand was increasing. The manufacturers of fine copper goods in Birmingham were alone in complaining of the high prices for raw copper. To get their stocks on cheaper terms they had broken up the former syndicate, but in so doing they had not rid themselves of the conditions to which they desired to put an end. In spite of the dissolution of the syndicate, several causes prevented a return of that competition which in the

[1] *Ibid.* p. 88 : " Poorer ores have certainly been brought to market in consequence of the high standard of ores." Mr. Vivian recounted that a short time previously he had seen ores in Cornwall which were " the poorest ores that I ever remember in Cornwall."

seventies and eighties had brought about the depression of prices. These were: the demand for copper (which increased rapidly soon after the dissolution of the syndicate), the output of ore which did not increase at a correspondingly rapid rate, and the small number of smelters and consequently of sellers of copper. In a rising market the concentration of the production and the sale of copper in a few hands rendered a joint agreement unnecessary, with one exception.

If the export trade was to be retained in the future, export prices must clearly be lower than those in the home market, now that copper prices in England were extraordinarily high compared with those in other exporting countries. This was the chief consideration in transacting sales with the East India Company, who could easily provide themselves with Armenian copper in Smyrna when high prices ruled for English exports.[1] It was therefore of the first importance to sell to the East India Company for export at lower quotations than those obtaining in the home market. No individual seller could have initiated such a line of policy, which would at best have resulted in a *lucrum cessans*. A general agreement was necessary to the carrying out of a method of exportation which sacrificed the individual in a certain degree for the benefit of the whole smelting industry. Such an agreement was all the more feasible as the East India Company only bought once a year, and then took over a large stock of copper for delivery within a fixed time. As Mr. Williams stated: "It becomes a treaty between the East India Company and the Copper Companies, who always unite on that Occasion. A few Days previous to the sending in of the tenders, the Copper Companies meet, and consider how far all or any of them are inclined to tender, and to what amount. It has been generally agreed amongst them, that they shall furnish the contract when made in proportion to their Stocks on Hand, or rather the Amount of their Stocks purchased within the

[1] 'Report on the State of Copper Mines,' pp. 36 and 42.

last 12 months; the Amount of those Stocks being fixed, the Proportions are made out to be delivered by each Company." We have seen already how such systematic "dumping" led to a marked differentiation between home and export prices, a differentiation made possible in the first place by the import duty.

Thus, even after the dissolution of the principal association, the Cornish Metal Company, an "Export Syndicate," continued to exist in the copper industry; whilst the aim of the earlier monopolist organisation—the keeping up of home prices—was realised without any special general agreement by the concentration of home production in a few hands. This was still more the case when home demand increased, and supply fell off greatly owing to large sales on the Continent whilst output did not increase in a correspondingly equal rate and import was hindered by the duty.

This is, unfortunately, the last that we know of combinations in the English copper industry, though probably a monopolist organisation continued to exist till later. Various writers in later years mention the "consolidations" which took place from time to time in the ownership of copper mines;[1] but no detailed account of the results of such consolidations exists. Copper prices in the first decades of the nineteenth century were on the average hardly lower than at the end of the eighteenth. Certainly they were much higher than in the middle of the eighteenth century. But after 1820 they began to fall.[2] In the following years England lost gradually that supremacy of production which she formerly possessed. New spheres of production were opened up, and after the removal of the duties on copper in 1848 gradually eclipsed England as a copper-producing country. The output of copper in

[1] Cf., for instance, John Taylor, 'Statements respecting the Profits of Mining in England,' London 1825, p. 7; J. R. L., 'Cornwall: its Mines and Miners,' London 1855, pp. 174 and 177.

[2] J. R. L., 'Cornwall: its Mines and Miners,' p. 149. Cf. prices given on p. 230.

England in 1860 amounted to about 16,000 tons; to-day it is not above 500.[1] Thus the conditions under which monopolist combinations can come into existence have long since disappeared.

(c) THE BREAK-UP OF THE COAL CARTEL

Whilst unfortunately but little light can be shed on the later development and decay of the monopolist organisation in the English copper industry, the facts which led to the dissolution of the coal cartel have remained fairly clear. This is the more valuable in that the producers' organisation in the coal trade was much closer and more detailed and of far longer duration than that in the copper trade. The final break-up of the coal cartel meant the destruction of a monopolist organisation which, although it had suffered lapses and alterations of form, had existed close upon 250 years.

The prosperity of the coal cartel in the north of England had had a double basis. It rested on a monopolisation of the sphere of production and on a monopolisation of the export market both in London and on the coast. Production had become even more monopolised after 1830 when the mines on the Tees joined the cartel on the Tyne and Wear, while owing to the expense of bringing coal from other districts, the market was secure up to a fixed high limit of price. But after the close of the thirties both these foundations seemed to be tottering.

In the years 1836-1843, whilst the cartel still existed, difficulties of organisation arose which threatened to lead to a general collapse. From the middle of the thirties in particular both the number of mines and the producing power of the coal districts in the north of England had increased considerably. This increase was due to various causes. As the well-known mineowner, George Elliot, said[2] later, "the high protective price was a temptation

[1] Cf. 'Encyclopædia Britannica,' 1902, vol. xxvii. p. 234; 'Mineral Resources,' Washington 1905, p. 241.

[2] 'Report of 1873'; q. 7521.

to colliery owners to open collieries." The best north-country coal averaged in London in 1832-35 20s. 7¾d. a chaldron. The price rose in 1836-38 to from 22s. to 24s.[1] The "regulation" price for best coal in 1834-6 had been 26s. a Newcastle chaldron on the Tyne, and had then been considered high. In 1844 the cartel price had actually been raised to 30s. 6d. for best coal.[2] These high prices which obtained under the régime of the cartel naturally stimulated fresh enterprise, and thus created fresh competition with the cartel itself. Other circumstances now arose which further increased the tendency.

First and foremost the railway system was making rapid progress and constantly opening up new mining districts. The production of coal increased quickly in the district west of the Wear and the Tyne, which up till then had been unworked, owing to the great expense of transport. As technical progress in railway transport advanced, the cost at which coal could be delivered diminished in a very marked manner. A further factor now appeared. The mineowners formerly had owned railways and means of transport themselves. They paid the ground landlords for the use of the ground "wayleaves," which were sometimes so high as to necessitate a permanent large rise in cost of transport.[3] Then came railway legislation, which empowered the promoters of public railway companies to buy the land required at a reasonable price. As by this means the railway companies found their traffic expenses greatly diminished, the network of railways extended more quickly than before, and a further increase of production in the districts affected took place. Less capital was now requisite for the opening up of a new pit, as the coal districts of the whole north of England were intersected by numerous railway lines, and mineowners whose mines were far from

[1] 'Report of 1836,' p. xviii; Dunn, 'The Coal Trade of the North of England,' p. 205.

[2] 'Report of 1836,' p. 53; Dunn, p. 203.

[3] 'Report of 1836,' p. xxxviii.

river or coast no longer needed to build their own railways, but simply used the nearest public line.[1] By considering how much the cost of transport from the mine to the vessel had added in former times to the cost of production in particular mines, it is possible to gauge the revolution brought about in the paying power of particular mines by the development of this network of communications. It suddenly became clear that the old mines, which lay close to the water and brought forward their own goods on their own lines at high wayleaves, had lost the advantage they had previously enjoyed over the more distant districts, and had become less favourably situated as regards freights than the " new " mines. " The construction of the railway system through the country," said Elliot, " gave facilities for opening out the coalfields extensively and with small capital; because I may mention that previously the large coalowners used to have their own private railways and their private places of shipment, and they had the whole trade very much in their own hand; but after the system of railways was introduced, the difficulties of maintaining the monopoly and high prices became insurmountable." [2]

At first the mineowners fought the new railway system; for they foresaw what it meant for the cartel. As soon as Parliament empowered a railway company to purchase land outright, those mineowners who had to pay wayleaves protested vehemently against the building of any such line. " What we complain of," said the secretary of the cartel in 1830, " is, that the Government should assist the proprietors in inland collieries, to enable them to compete with us in markets we were formerly in possession of." In order to ward off this competition the owners of the old mines petitioned Parliament against the further multiplication of lines in Durham. Each individual member of the cartel was forced to make a money contribution, in proportion to his basis, to cover the expenses of the agitation

[1] Dunn, The Coal Trade of the North of England,' p. 213.

[2] ' Report of 1873,' q. 7521.

against the railways.[1] But this obstructionist policy could not hinder permanently either the extension of the railway system or the opening up of new mines.

According to Dunn, whose long expert experience in the mining districts of the north makes him on the whole a trustworthy guide, the numbers of the mines were as follows: [2]

District.	1830	1836	1844
Tyne - - -	37	47	70
Wear - - -	18	9	28
Tees - - -	0	16	22
Hartley and Blyth -	4	4	6
Total - -	59	76	126

These figures show how much the potential production of the north of England coal area had increased since 1836. But there was no increase in demand equivalent to the increase in supply. Great stress is laid on this fact not only by Dunn in his book, but later on by George Elliot, who had personal experience of these conditions.[3] It was therefore only to be expected that there would be an increased amount of coal exported by the cartel, and, as a matter of fact, the export of coal did increase considerably between 1836 and 1842.[4] But this increase in export, which at its highest at the beginning of the forties amounted to 800,000 tons more per annum than in the middle of the thirties, had little relative importance compared to the increased potential production of the northern districts, estimated at over 3,000,000 tons.[5] Moreover the export

[1] 'Report of 1830,' pp. 268 and 269; 'Report of 1836,' p. xxxix.

[2] Dunn, 'The Coal Trade of the North of England,' p. 216.

[3] *Ibid.* p. 203; 'Report of 1873.'

[4] According to Dunn the export of coal in 1836 amounted to 623,000 tons, in 1842 to 1,411,000 tons.

[5] Cf. 'Remarks on the present State of the Coal Trade' 1843, quoted in Dunn, p. 232.

duty of 1842 necessarily limited the use of this safety valve, as English coal consequently was unable to compete in the French market with French and Belgian coal. The export, exclusive of "smalls," showed a decrease of 480,000 tons as against the preceding year.[1]

The tendency to an increase of production and consequent depression of prices—the result of the growth of the mines and the comparatively slow increase of demand—was not in itself sufficient to cause the dissolution of the cartel. Earlier cartels had been founded in precisely similar conditions, with the precisely similar aim of so regulating by joint agreement the growing productive power of the mines, which was in excess of demand, that prices should not be depressed by increased competition. These were the motives which led to the formation of the cartel of 1771, and with this aim the mines on the Tees joined the cartel on the Tyne and Wear in 1833 after severe competition. Might it not be possible again to lessen the effect on prices of the opening up of new mines by a joint limitation of the actual output? Might not the allocation of production in accordance with demand even now result in a level of prices which would secure the further existence of both favourably and unfavourably situated mines?

The cartel did, in fact, follow the only system which appeared to promise salvation. It limited output to an ever-increasing degree in comparison to potential production. In 1837 it put up for sale 80 per cent. of the original basis, in 1840 this percentage fell to 55·7, and in 1843 to 44. Thus the contingent furnished by particular mines became steadily smaller.[2] One mine, the basis of which had been fixed in proportion to its estimated power of production at 50,000 chaldrons, was permitted to sell only 22,000 chaldrons in 1844, although in 1838 it had been permitted to sell 40,000.

The members of the cartel might perhaps have borne

[1] Dunn, 'Coal Trade,' pp. 231-234.

[2] *Ibid.* p. 229; also 'Report of 1873,' Mr. Elliot's evidence.

patiently with this system of increasing limitation of output had the result aimed at—the keeping up of prices—offered them any equivalent for the great diminution of actual as compared to potential production. But now a second danger shook the existence of the cartel to its very foundation: the price limit within which north of England coal enjoyed a monopoly both in London and on the coast began to fall.

It is not easy to give figures for the growing competition which north-country coal had to encounter in the markets of the south after 1840. It is however a striking fact that in 1836 only 2300 tons of coal were carried to London by inland water-ways, while in 1840 the traffic had increased to 22,000 tons, and in 1844 to 72,000 tons. Similarly, in 1844 carriage by railway began to assume larger dimensions.[1] Nor was the growing competition with northern mines confined to London. As the increasing severity of the rivalry between canals and railways forced down freights, Midland coal began to arrive on the coast. Finally, the increasing output of South Wales meant increasing competition for north-country coal, and after 1840 Scotch coal was also put on the English market in increasing quantities.[2]

In this way the "competition price," that price limit at which it had been profitable to obtain supplies from other sources, fell considerably both in London and on the coast. This was first apparent in 1844. From Dunn's statement it seems that consigners were the first to feel the impossibility of keeping up the cartel price, and that they suffered for some time from the difference between cartel price and market price. In 1844 the inevitable happened. The cartel price, which had been fixed at 30s. 6d. for best coal, had to be reduced to 25s.[3]; in other words to a level, which,

[1] 'Report of 1871, E,' p. 45.

[2] Dunn, 'The Coal Trade of the North of England,' pp. 220, 227, 229-230.

[3] Dunn, 'State of the Coal Trade,' p. 203.

according to expert opinion in 1836, meant the loss of all profit on poorer qualities of coal.[1]

The position of the cartel now became more and more serious. On the one hand the strictest possible limitation of output; on the other hand a price which in comparison with the former standard was extraordinarily low, and which did not in any way compensate for diminished production. It is clear that the desire for an increased allotment grew continually stronger among those mineowners whose mines, even with low prices, could be worked at a profit, as long as there was a proportionate increase of output. Owners of less valuable pits were anxious to see a still further reduction of the allotment furnished by the more favoured mines. So a conflict, or rather a crisis, in the cartel was inevitable. Even so friendly an observer as Dunn recognised the impossibility of carrying on the organisation in its existing form. He wrote in 1844: " The evils of regulation heretofore have been the limited quantity allowed to each colliery under the abridged trade; but this has been felt more severely by the long worked and smaller collieries, where, in many instances, the quantity has been so limited, and the price so depressed, that nothing but a losing trade could result; and a strong feeling has prevailed, that their relief could only arise from a concession of the quantities disposed of by great and highly valued collieries for the general good. This feeling has been so urgently advocated that the present regulation agreement contains a clause for a general revision and settlement of the basis of every colliery in the trade; every individual thus satisfying himself with the hope that such general review will benefit him at the expense of others. This is the present understanding, but in the opinion of experienced persons, such period will never arrive, inasmuch as the investigation would be too endless, and would in all

[1] 'Report of 1836.' Even Mr. Wood, who opposed the high price fixed by the cartel, considered at that time that a price of 24s. 6d. was necessary, cf. q. 2480 ff.

probability create greater and more general dissatisfaction than that which prevails at present."

And "experienced persons" were right. There was no revision. Why should mines working at a profit limit their output still further for the benefit of those not so working whilst competition in the south and on the coast was becoming more severe, and whilst no limitation of the vend in the north could force prices up to their former level? On the contrary, it was now to the interest of the paying mines to meet the fall in prices caused by competition elsewhere by an increase in output, which would enable them still to work at a profit. But the owners of valuable mines, who had formerly loudly advocated the cartel as the "preserver" of the inferior mines, had now no further interest in taking steps to their own detriment for the general benefit. Their indifference was shown by the fact that no revision took place, in spite of the needs of the non-paying mines. The long strike of April 1844 accentuated the effects of the drop in prices. Thus the year 1844 saw the break-up of the coal cartel.

From this time north of England coal has been sold by open competition among the mineowners.[1] In 1845 one more effort was made to reorganise the shattered cartel as another and closer association.[2] A number of large mine-owners in Durham formed a scheme for buying up all the north-country mines and amalgamating them in one company. Circulars and prospectuses were printed, but the scheme failed in consequence of the opposition of some of the large coal magnates. A scheme proposed by the miners for a common regulation of production also failed.[3] The cartel presupposed that it was possible to monopolise the market. The conditions which had annihilated this

[1] On the question of the failure of a new coal cartel after 1845, cf. details by Dunn in the 'Mining Almanack,' London 1849, pp. 152-3.

[2] 'Report of 1873,' q. 7525-7528.

[3] Thorold Rogers, 'Industrial and Commercial History of England,' p. 617; also 'Report of 1873.'

assumption became increasingly prominent after 1844. Although the output of coal grew rapidly in the north in the fifties and sixties, it increased still more rapidly in other districts of Great Britain. The output of South Durham increased from about 11 million tons in 1856 to about 17 millions in 1872. But the output of S. Wales for the same time increased from 5½ to 10 millions, of Scotland from 9 to 15 millions, and of the Midlands from 4½ to 10½ millions. In Yorkshire, Lancashire, and the western counties output had also increased rapidly, and the production of the N.E. district therefore lost in importance relatively to the total production.[1]

The possibility of intercompetition between the separate districts had been greatly increased by the growing development of means of communication. The great economic advantage enjoyed by the northern districts had been due for centuries to the exceptional cheapness of sea carriage as compared with land carriage. The progress made by the canal and railway systems and by means of communication in general now began steadily to reduce the importance of sea transport. Inland districts were better able to supply the markets which had hitherto been dependent on sea transport. In 1850, 55,000 tons of coal had been carried to London by rail, 85,000 by canal; in 1868, 2,988,000 tons were carried by rail and canal jointly. In the years following transport by rail and canal grew rapidly in importance. Of 7,556,000 tons of coal consigned to London in 1872, 5,000,000 were carried by rail or canal. Moreover, the traffic statements of the railway companies interested showed that a large portion of the supply came from districts other than the North-East. The Midland Railway

[1] 'Report of 1873,' p. 324-325. Owing to the peculiar arrangement of the statistics, Cumberland has to be included in any figure which can be given for the total production of the northern coal district, though economically it does not belong to that district. On this basis the production of the northern district between 1856 and 1872 rose from 20 to 30 million tons, and the total production of England from 71 to 123 million tons.

carried 1,615,000 tons, the London and North-Western about 1,000,000, the Great Eastern 687,000, and the Great Western 581,000.[1] The means by which coal was supplied to London had therefore undergone an entire transformation since the palmy days of the cartel. We have seen that whilst the amount consigned to London in 1872 had increased to 7,500,000, the northern districts sent 2,200,000 tons by sea, and if we credit them with the amount carried by the Great Northern Railway only about 1,000,000 by rail. In the thirties supplies had only been obtained from other districts than the north-eastern in emergencies, but now these other sources contributed more than half the supply of the metropolis. The report of the Committee of 1873 drew attention to this revolution in market conditions in these words: "We do not believe that any combination either of employers or workmen can by artificial means succeed in permanently affecting the ordinary results of the relations of demand and supply by adjusting the quantity of coal produced to the demand, or can permanently affect the price resulting from the state of the market." [2] The severe competition between the numerous areas of production which ruled in the central market and which was bound to increase with any rise in price, rendered hopeless the union of a single district in a cartel for the raising of prices. On the other hand, the multiplicity of geographically separated producing districts made any combination between them difficult. Although England, as Sir George Elliot said,[3] could not in the seventies reckon on imports of coal from abroad and therefore mineowners, in spite of free trade, had a monopoly of the home market, no cartel was formed to exploit this monopoly.

It was impossible to foresee that with the dissolution of the Vend an organisation had broken up, which fifty years later would be characteristic of many industries in many

[1] 'Report of 1873,' p. 317. [2] *Ibid.* p. 10.
[3] Cf. *Ibid.* q. 7641 ff.

different countries. Its history was rather regarded as an attempt to prevent the competitive struggle proper to all departments of industry from running its "natural" course, and its final collapse as a fresh proof of the correctness of the classical economists' doctrine of competition.

PART III

THE MODERN ORGANISATION OF ENGLISH INDUSTRY ON A MONOPOLIST BASIS

CHAPTER VII

INTRODUCTORY. TRANSITION TO THE PRESENT TIME

DURING the eighteenth, and still more in the first half of the nineteenth century—that epoch of unexampled industrial development—the industries of England present a picture of increasing production, rapid increase in the number of single undertakings and, in each separate area of production, the keenest competition between the various manufacturers only giving way occasionally and under pressure of certain exceptional conditions to a monopolist organisation.

For several decades this state of affairs remained substantially unchanged. When the Parliamentary Committee of 1886 published its comprehensive report on the depression of trade and industry, experts were still complaining of ruinous competition as loudly as they had done in 1833. Lord Brassey, who was the best judge of the industrial life of the time, ascribed [1] the crises at the end of the seventies to "British manufacturers having gone far beyond their rivals abroad in the rashness with which factories have been multiplied." But among the voluminous official reports of the eighties there is no hint that any effort had been made anywhere by means of any combination to weaken that competition which was so much deplored.[2] It is true that in the iron industry a few preliminary schemes for a

[1] Lord Brassey, 'Papers and Addresses,' London 1894, pp. 215-216.

[2] Cf. 'Reports on Depression of Trade and Industry,' London 1886.

systematised reduction of competition were brought forward, though they were not mentioned before the Parliamentary Commission. They were local combinations, mostly for the purpose of reducing the output of pig iron.[1] Similar loosely organised unions can be detected in times of trade depression in the thirties.[2] But, as in that case, the agreements of the eighties exercised no decisive influence on sale conditions in the iron industry, nor had they the least permanent character. To compare them in any way with the cartels and syndicates of the present is to put them in a false light. They would hardly have found a mention in English political economy of that day if it had not been thought possible to see in them, as Thorold Rogers does, smaller editions of certain trusts which shot up in the United States at the end of the eighties.[3]

Though Rogers believed he saw in 1889 that "the beneficial operation of competition was at an end," and looked forward to the systematic formation of cartels and trusts in England in the near future, his prophecy was not fulfilled for ten years. On the contrary, the problem in England seemed rather to be why cartels and trusts should develop extremely slowly or not at all, while in Germany, France, America, and other great industrial countries such monopolist associations should spread so rapidly. Thus Prof. Liefmann writes[4] "when the cartel problem was very prominent with us, England, usually the first in economic developments, had hardly heard of it," founding his opinion on the results of personal study at the end of the nineties. It did not escape this careful observer that for some years past several monopolist undertakings had existed in Great Britain, specially in textile industries. There were not

[1] H. W. Macrosty, 'The Trust Movement in British Industry,' London 1907, p. 57 ff.

[2] Cf. *e.g.* 'The Mining Journal,' Dec. 17, 1836, p. 212; also Jan. 14, 1837, p. 11.

[3] Thorold Rogers, 'Industrial and Commercial History of England,' London 1892, p. 377.

[4] R. Liefmann, 'Schutzzoll und Kartelle,' Jena 1903, p. 7.

many, if those undertakings and combinations are subtracted which have often been inaccurately described as cartels and trusts,[1] but there were enough to disprove the assertion that no monopolist industrial organisations existed in the home of free trade.

The number of lasting monopolist combinations existing in Great Britain at the end of the last century and the beginning of the present were far fewer than in America and Germany, their structure, their organisation and their spheres of action were entirely different, and their growth was less rapid than in other countries. But whatever the causes of these differences, which must be looked into presently, may have been, these monopolist undertakings cleared the way for new developments of industrial organisation. No present writer on competition could ignore the possibility of organising industry on a monopolist basis, as W. B. Hodgson ignored it in his work on the subject in 1870.[2] But the criticism applied to this form of organisation in England differed very little from the views of monopolies held by classical economists. Even at the end of the nineties Prof. Edgeworth[3] put forward the theory that the self-interest of mankind by its very nature necessitated competition: "Competition is an almost ineradicable growth of self-interested human nature. 'Expellas furca, tamen usque recurret.' Combinations resisting the tendency of this force are liable to disruption." Thorold Rogers[4] expressed himself (1892) with greater caution. He believed in a further development of the syndicate and

[1] Liefmann, 'Schutzzoll und Kartelle,' p. 64, where reference is made to mistakes of this kind in Macrosty's book, also to Huber and Menzel. Likewise to the 'Deutschen Kartellenquête,' Berlin 1904, Heft 5, pp. 377-80, which contains a list of English monopolist associations, founded for the greater part on a misconception of the essential elements of these undertakings.

[2] W. B. Hodgson, 'Competition: Lectures on Economic Science,' London 1870.

[3] 'Palgrave's Dictionary,' vol. i. p. 379 A.

[4] Th. Rogers, 'Industrial and Commercial History of England,' p. 378.

trust system, whose beginnings he had observed. But, while not venturing to maintain that the position of the consumer was assured by the natural self-interest of the producer, whose whole attention was directed to competition, he nevertheless held fast by the law of equalisation of profit held since Adam Smith's time, which he looked upon as a palliative against any abuses caused by the monopolist element in combinations. "The most profitable process hitherto known and employed is for strong men, or a combination of strong men, to ruin weak ones by low or unremunerative prices, and having secured a monopoly, to commence a legal pillage of the public. But though the expedient may enrich individuals, it is essentially transitory. Sooner or later competition reappears and extraordinary profits are arrested."

It is not surprising that in the country where the doctrine of free competition had been accepted unconditionally for over a century, notwithstanding the change in the conditions on which that doctrine was based, there was nevertheless no sudden alteration of economic doctrine. This is the less surprising, as the change in Great Britain was taking place but slowly. It happened as with other economic theories. The classical economists' doctrine, that competition was equally to the interest of the consumer and of the producer, had been regarded as an invariable truth, not because it was in any way correct, but because for a long time it was borne out by existing facts. In agriculture similarly the doctrine of the superior value of cultivation on a large scale was maintained just so long as cultivation on a large scale was the dominant form of agricultural industry. And economists who regarded the development of small cultivation, notwithstanding its rapid growth, with incredulity and suspicion, were equally slow to appreciate at its true value the rise of monopolist associations.

But when it was seen, towards the end of the last century and the beginning of the present one, how firmly industrial organisation on a monopolist basis was taking root in both Germany and America, how international monopolist companies were springing up, and how the monopolist movement was showing itself in England, then Englishmen began to realise that their former conception of competition failed to apply universally. Industry was being steadily reorganised in the largest industrial countries on a monopolist system, and this reorganisation produced entirely new economic phenomena. The theory of competition was becoming an exposition of things as they would be rather than of things as they are. " Free competition and free trade are now things of the past. We live in an age of ever-extending monopoly," as Professor Brentano wrote in April 1904.[1] That competition among wholesale manufacturers which had been looked upon hitherto, and particularly in England, as the inevitable result of an immutable law of economics, now became merely a possible condition of industrial organisation and out of date at that. The development of flourishing monopolies is now an accomplished fact.[2] But even at the time when no monopolist organisation existed in English industry, objection ought to have been taken to this explanation if there had been any desire to prove as an actual fact what was after all only an opinion. The very principles underlying that explanation were questionable. For an industry can owe its monopolist position as regards a foreign country to other causes than a tariff or an advantage in freights. International agreements may come into play, and, finally, competition can force down prices far below that limit " at which imports from abroad into a free trade country seem possible," a fact early emphasised by Prof. Liefmann.[3] Later on we shall be able to give several instances to prove

[1] L. Brentano, 'Die beabsichtigte Neuorganisation der deutschen Volkswirtschaft,' 'Süddeutsche Monatsheft,' 1904, p. 255.

[2] This fact has been amply recognised even before the war in discussions on Free Trade and Cartels, cf. Brentano, p. 260, and Pierce, 'The Tariff and the Trusts,' New York 1907, p. 56.

[3] Liefmann, 'Schutzzoll und Kartelle, p. 8.

the actual realisation of this possibility in England. For the moment we turn our attention to a further " explanation " of the slight development of cartels and trusts in England, which, although of an entirely different kind from the foregoing, has in common with it a want of positive proof—I mean the opinion that the objection of English manufacturers to cartels and trusts is psychological. The chief exponent of this theory is Prof. Liefmann,[1] who maintains that " the chief reason for the absence of cartels in many branches of English industry lies in the fact that the doctrines of extreme individualism still retain a firm hold over English manufacturers. The idea that ' free ' competition is the ' natural ' condition of economic life, that it best secures the advantage of all, is still extremely common and extremely powerful among them." His opinion, shared by Prof. Jenks,[2] is certainly plausible, if we take into consideration the conservatism (somewhat strange at the present day) of English people in economic matters. In England the lack of cartels and trusts has often been held up as a sin of omission on the part of manufacturers. But no positive proof has ever been adduced that the lack of such organisation in the eighties and nineties was due to any such psychological aversion. The influence of the doctrine of free competition on the English manufacturer was taken as given, and his indifference to monopolist organisation seemed to follow from it. But concrete confirmation of this inference is all the more desirable as several facts are entirely against it, and tend to weaken the hypothesis connecting the slow development of cartels and trusts with the psychology of the manufacturer. The history of the early coal cartels is most important evidence that monopolist associations existed even at a time when the doctrines of classical political economy had far more weight with English people than they have now. And as Prof. Liefmann supports his conclusions as to the influence of

[1] *Ibid.* pp. 8-9, and in ' Kartelle und Trusts,' Stuttgart 1920, p. 152.

[2] Cf. Jenks in ' Industrial Commission,' vol. xviii. p. 9.

individualism by the case of present-day competition in the English coal mining, we are forced to enquire why that individualism did not show itself when the mineowners created in the Newcastle Vend the most powerful coal cartel which has ever yet existed, and maintained it for seventy years. The monopolist organisation of copper production at the end of the eighteenth century is another important instance of the possibility of forming a cartel in former times, and Babbage in the thirties describes a bookseller's [1] cartel, the aim of which was " to put down all competition," and which exhibited a striking similarity to the " Börsenverein der deutschen Buchhändler," as we can prove, though exact details are wanting.[2] Further, we notice in the eighties and nineties, when neither cartel nor trust existed, repeated attempts by large firms to initiate a monopolist organisation of their particular branch of industry. There were, for instance, at the beginning of the eighties, attempts at forming a syndicate in pig iron, though they were not long successful. In 1894 a coal syndicate was formed in the north of England with the object of fixing a minimum price and of regulating conditions of output, but this also only lasted a few months.[3] At the end of the eighties a syndicate was projected but never realised in the paper trade, the only monopolist branch of which at present is the wall-paper industry. Among other unsuccessful early monopolist organisations is the well-known Birmingham Alliance, which, created originally in 1891 in the interest of the bedstead industry, transferred its activity subsequently to other trades. It was an effort to regulate the prices of the various trade products in conjunction with an organised association of workpeople. But these associations could not permanently withstand the pressure of outsiders and of

[1] ' Economy of Manufactures,' London 1833, ed. 3, p. 312.

[2] Cf. for details Levy, in Schmoller's ' Jahrbücher,' 1908, pp. 1538-1540.

[3] Cf. for details Levy, in Schmoller's ' Jahrbücher,' 1907, pp. 1689-1690.

foreign competition, and at the present time free competition obtains in these trades also.

Attempted cartels and trusts, which failed either because they never passed beyond the stage of a project, or because they had not sufficient vital power to carry them on for any length of time, can be seen in other branches of industry in the same years. It was clearly not through any lack of will on the part of manufacturers that the powerful and effective cartels and trusts of Germany and the United States did not exist in England. That their efforts to carry out their desires were unavailing was the result of competition, either that of the foreigner or that which arose at home.

It must therefore be recognised that the undoubted anti-monopolist conscience of the English nation and its belief in economic individualism has always been subject to limitation when the individual Englishman thought of himself as a producer and not as a consumer. The cartels and projected cartels of the past clearly show that English manufacturers have tried to form monopolist organisations wherever they saw a prospect of making any profit. English shipping firms inaugurated between 1870-80 the now well-known " shipping rings," and English business houses gave the first impetus to the nitrate cartels of Chili early in the nineties. Facts such as these show that the English man of business is a much greater lover of cartels than he would be if his adhesion to the principle of individualism were as firm as is generally supposed. Let us turn lastly to the testimony of Prof. Clapham,[1] the author of the best extant work on English textile industries. " It is true that in all branches of the trade the promoters of a combination have to deal with special obstacles, not the least of which is the strong local feeling and pronounced individualism of the manufacturer ; but these things have been overcome before, and may be overcome again, when there is a gain to be made or a loss to be avoided." Thus, as the subjective

[1] Clapham, 'Woollen and Worsted Industries,' London 1907, p. 154.

conditions of monopoly have obviously existed in spite of the doctrine of individualism, we can only conclude that the external essentials of monopolist control were not as fully developed in England as in other countries up to the outbreak of the war. What these " defective " elements are can be shown only by more intimate knowledge of the conditions of production and sale in those branches of industry in Great Britain which are still governed by competition, and especially in coal-mining.

The war and post-war periods have produced a very considerable development of trusts and cartels. The great growth in the number of associations since 1914 must not, however, be regarded as an entirely new feature of British industry, but rather as an acceleration of a gradual progressive tendency independent of the special influences of the war. The increase of monopolistic and quasi-monopolist organisations in the great English industries since 1914 was so important that the Ministry of Reconstruction issued a comprehensive report on the subject in 1919. The Committee included well-known economists like J. A. Hobson and Sidney Webb. Its report, to which is appended a special memorandum by Mr. Percy Ashley, begins: " We find that there is at the present time in every important branch of industry in the United Kingdom an increasing tendency to the formation of Trade Associations and Combinations having for their purpose the restriction of competition and the control of prices. Many of the organisations which have been brought to our notice have been created in the last few years, and by far the greater part of them appear to have come into existence since the end of the century." [1] It nevertheless appears probable that, even if the new combinations were fewer in number than those in existence before the war, the relative increase in only five years was much greater than in the period from the end of the nineties to 1914. The report gives a list of

[1] 'Ministry of Reconstruction, Report of Committee on Trusts,' Cd. 9236, new edition, London 1924.

ninety-three combinations—cartels, syndicates or loose associations. It is significant that a few years later so well-informed a paper as the 'Statist' allowed an expert to contribute a series of thirty-four articles on the 'Trust Movement in British Industry' (including bank amalgamations and shipping rings). These show the growing tendency to trustification, though some of the new combines were not successful and did not last.

These articles, which came to an end on July 5, 1924, throw a flood of light upon the new formation of monopoly organisations up to date, and have been issued in volume form by the author, Mr. Patrick Fitzgerald, under the title 'Industrial Combination in England.'[1] This notable work confirms in the most conclusive way the increase and importance of the contemporary formation of English trusts and cartels and the growing movement towards concentration. An important event in this connection is the formation of the Chemical Trust in 1926.

How the wartime conditions conduced to an acceleration of the movement towards cartels in England is authoritatively set out in a memorandum appended to the Report on Trusts. The official and semi-official organisation of English trade and industry brought about by war conditions laid the foundations of association, especially in purely business questions such as rationing, import and export licences, shipping space, war regulations in factories, etc., which were much better settled in combination than in isolation. The process of combination was also greatly helped by the action of the Government in summoning conferences of the chief representatives of all branches of industry. It is noted that one effect of the Excess Profits Tax was to encourage the buying up of unprofitable businesses by highly profitable concerns, for such purchases were in effect paid for by moneys which would have otherwise gone in Excess Profits Duty to the Revenue. A factor of great technical importance was the more extensive use from 1914 onwards

[1] Pitman, London 1927, pp. 1-7, *passim*.

of machinery and standardisation in English industry. The immediate effect of this on the position of the very large concerns was, by still further enlarging these concerns, to pave the way to concentration.[1] An important consideration, not mentioned in the Report, is the fact that the movement towards cartels and concentration in the last decade has been found easiest where it has been a question of quite new branches of industry, in which from the outset a few large concerns dominate production, or where new inventions and improved machinery have involved larger units of management. Here the conditions for forming cartels and trusts are evidently quite different from those which obtained in industries which, like the English textiles, have developed in a century and a half from the small domestic handworker into the factory and mill system, but had at the outset to face a long-drawn competitive struggle with small producers. In the latter case it is possible for small concerns to survive for a considerable time; in the former the modern system of production organised on a gigantic scale accompanies the birth of a new branch or method of industry. The modern chemical industry, for example, has never known small masters in the same way as the textile or boot trades. The Committee on Commercial and Industrial Policy after the War has rightly pointed out that Germany enjoyed superior business management, although she became a great industrial power later than England, because she had not the handicap of a traditional organisation and was able to employ the cartel system.[2] It is thus possible to understand how the rise of new industries in England during and since the war and the operation of the Safeguarding of Industries Act, 1921, have favoured the creation of large concerns and made concentration much easier in their case than in that of small, separate and rival concerns developed by a long historical process. We must, however, note that

[1] 'Report on Trusts,' p. 20, *passim*.

[2] See 'Final Report,' London 1918, Cd. 9035, pp. 21-22.

many combinations formed in England since 1914 have not been able to hold out, and have succumbed during the stress of the great period of depression.[1] In these cases the competitive character of English industry has asserted itself anew.

[1] See 'Statist,' Sept. 30, 1923, 'The Trust Movement in British Industry': xx. 'The Effect of Depression.'

CHAPTER VIII

THE SPHERE OF COMPETITION

A CONSIDERABLE number of cartels and trusts in all parts of the world are essentially dependent on the existence of mineral deposits which are easily convertible into a monopoly. In the first place, certain minerals, being found only in a single country or in one or two countries, are from the outset a monopoly to the rest of the world. In this connection may be mentioned the powerful monopolies of the potash deposits in Germany, nitrate in Chili, marble in Italy, petroleum, copper and borax in America, nickel in Canada, zinc in Germany, Belgium and America, and diamonds in the Transvaal. Secondly, certain areas of production, such as the coal and iron ore districts of America and Germany, hold monopolies, if not in the world's market, at least in a given national area, generally as a result of the freight charges which a foreign competitor would have to face.

The naturally narrow limits of such mineral wealth and the marked tendency of mining from the very beginning to accumulate fixed capital have created relatively early and with comparative ease close monopolist combinations or a semi-monopolist predominance of particular interests in all such areas of production.

Great Britain, on the other hand, has no monopoly over other countries in any mineral whatever. Her mineral productions are now reduced to very few products. In 1923 they reached a total of £279·4 millions, of which coal alone accounted for £259·7 millions. Iron ore came next with £3½ millions. The other minerals are divided among products of which Great Britain furnishes only a small part of her own needs. A certain small if not important exception consists of stone, earths, and salt (this last £1·45 million).[1] None of her chief mineral products is present in sufficient quantity to obtain anything like monopoly in the world's market. But from the point of view of its own national market it is a striking fact that precisely those very important raw materials and other products which are worked abroad as the closest monopolies, are subject in Great Britain to very marked competition. One most prominent instance is that of the coal trade.

Here we have to deal with a branch of English production which, although it has more and more lost during the last thirty-five years its former monopoly of the trade of the world, has, on the other hand, never been effected by foreign competition in the home market.[2] In the eighties and nineties, even if an English coal trust had put up coal prices considerably, it would have had no cause to fear imports from abroad. Jeans writes[3] in 1894: "There would appear to be no insuperable difficulty in the way of founding and carrying on a combination to keep up the price of fuel at home, so far as foreign competition is concerned, and this is more than can be said of most other industries." Prof. Ashley in 1903[4] was of opinion that if "very high" prices were to rule in the English market for a few months German and French coal might perhaps be attracted to the country. But as a practical matter the importation of

[1] 'Statesman's Year Book,' 1925, pp. 45-55.

[2] For the statistics on which this statement is based cf. D. A. Thomas (later Lord Rhondda), 'The Growth and Direction of the Foreign Trade in Coal,' in 'Journal of Royal Statistical Society,' London 1903, p. 491. For later statistics see the detailed summary in the 'Report of the Royal Commission on the Coal Industry,' London 1926, i. 4-9, Cmd. 2600.

[3] J. S. Jeans, 'Trusts, Pools, and Corners,' London 1894, p. 67.

[4] W. J. Ashley, 'The Adjustment of Wages,' London 1903, p. 49.

oversea coal has never (except during the coal dispute of 1926) been discussed in England. And it is not probable that foreign coal would be imported in the case of merely "very high" prices. It might be imported if prices were extraordinarily high in the English market, and at the same time very low in Germany, Belgium, or even America. But even in 1900—the year of the great rise in the price of coal—when, with the additional impetus of the Boer war, prices were unusually high, German and American competition was not felt, though prices in Germany and America had not risen to anything like as high a level as in England. The increasing competition of these two countries was only to be detected by the fact that they competed more successfully than before with English coal in the export trade to non-English parts of the world. In some areas where English coal had previously enjoyed a monopoly, foreign coal even drove it from the field. Thus in 1900, for the first time, American coal appeared on the shores of the Mediterranean, while German coal competed with English on the north-west coast of France.[1] But England itself during the coal famine had no recourse to imported coal.

In 1901 there was a marked fall in English coal prices; in Germany and America they remained unchanged.[2] It was perfectly plain that, in this condition of the international market, a coal cartel in England could have hindered the fall in home prices, which only affected the home market, and in September 1901 certain important firms urged the creation of a cartel with great eagerness. Even opponents of the cartel system could not maintain that such a cartel by causing prices to rise would attract competition from abroad to England, so they had to be content with pointing out that in the long run a rise would increase the competition of the foreigner in certain export

[1] D. A. Thomas, 'Growth and Direction of Foreign Trade in Coal,' p. 491.

[2] Cf. Uhde, 'Die Produktionsbedingungen des Steinkohlenbergbaues,' Jena 1907; and D. A. Thomas, 'Growth and Direction of Foreign Trade in Coal,' p. 491.

markets.[1] But the failure of the cartel and trust schemes of that time was certainly not due to any fear of provoking importation from abroad.

It was due to a very different cause. The same facts which had worked the ruin of the old Vend in spite of its seventy years of existence are at work to-day, and prevent the creation of a monopolist organisation in the English coal industry. As we have already seen, these facts were the multiplicity of the sources of production and their mutual competition, owing to increased means of communication since the latter half of the nineteenth century. Coal is produced in all parts of the country. There is no such localised concentration of production as in Germany (Rhenish-Westphalia and Silesia) and in America (East Pennsylvania anthracite and soft coal districts). Experience has shown repeatedly and clearly that the cartel system has little prospect of success where coal is so universal. The Durham Coal Association of 1894 lasted but a short time after its increased prices had quickened the competition of Yorkshire coal on the London gas-coal market. A similar fate befell a Lancashire and Cheshire Coal Association in 1894.[2]

In Wales the conditions were more favourable, and from 1870 up to the present time projected cartels have found here a suitable field for operation.[3] But, excellent as Welsh steam coal may be, it has to compete when prices are high with coal from the north of England,[4] so that in this case also any organisation to be effective must be able to control both districts.[5]

[1] 'Economist,' 1901, p. 1433.

[2] Macrosty, 'The Trust Movement in British Industry,' pp. 88-92.

[3] 'Report on Coal,' 1873, q. 7522 and 7529.

[4] Macrosty, 'The Trust Movement in British Industry,' p. 86; Ashley, 'The Adjustment of Wages,' p. 26.

[5] This has again been noticeable recently, at the beginning of 1907. When at that date coal prices rose quickly the 'Economist' said (Feb. 2, 1907, p. 188): "There is no influence of any combine in the matter, though there has been formless gossip about a hypothetical ring in South Wales to capture the London trade. We should imagine that

It must not be forgotten that the above-mentioned districts do not all produce the same quality of coal, and in so far they do not always compete with one another, some districts in this way having a preference in the market. But if any one district were to attempt to put up prices to any marked extent consumers could obtain coal supplies from other districts, though possibly of different quality.[1] Thus we find in the official report of 1873 mention of "the variety of coals produced, which though primarily used for particular purposes, will at certain prices be used for others."[2] The only exception in this respect is the anthracite district in the extreme west of South Wales.[3] No other region of Great Britain produces similar coal.

With this single exception, unimportant as compared with the total amount of coal produced, we are brought to the conclusion that monopolist combinations in separate districts could only have an extremely limited sphere of action. An effective monopolist organisation could only be formed if all the coal districts were combined in a systematic cartel or trust.

But the difficulties are great, as the excitement caused by Sir George Elliot's trust scheme, published in the 'Times' of Sept. 20, 1893, clearly showed. The scheme, which was never realised, was opposed by the trade on the following grounds: that it would be impossible to take into consideration the special conditions of production and sale in particular districts; that the number of mines to be combined was too large—they were estimated at 3400 pits; and that as most of the mines belonged to private com-

London consumers could manage to get along quite well without Welsh coal at all, seeing that they derive most of their supplies from the North and the Midlands." So that Prof. Liefmann's opinion ('Schutzzoll und Kartelle,' p. 11), that the Welsh coal mines could form a cartel independently of those in the Newcastle district, is incorrect.

[1] A certain rise of prices is possible in individual cases. Cf. Ashley, 'Adjustment of Wages,' p. 49, note 1.

[2] 'Report on Coal,' 1873, p. 10.

[3] Macrosty, 'The Trust Movement in British Industry,' p. 86.

panies, the difficulty of buying them out would be all the greater.[1] The first objection was probably the most weighty. And in a lesser degree there were in each separate district a variety of separate interests to be considered, which entirely did away with the idea of a joint cartel, for the continued independence of individual firms would make any combined agreement on questions of price and production impossible.

In 1926 the question of the economic organisation in English coal-mining—and especially the question of the hitherto unrealised coal cartel or even of a coal trust—was raised anew in all its bearings owing to a coal dispute of unexampled magnitude. In May 1926 a great strike, which had been threatening for a year before, broke out, after a Commission of Enquiry—the Royal Commission on the Coal Industry, 1925—had been appointed, and had gone thoroughly into the whole questions of production, sale, organisation and social conditions in English coal-mining. The Report of this Commission, issued in March 1926, confirmed the impression already current among those who had not exact figures to go upon as to the constitution of the industry. The chapter entitled 'Structure of the Industry' begins with the words: "The principal characteristic of the industry, in comparison with other productive and distributive industries, is its diversity." [2] It then sets out the differences, geological as to quality of coal, geographical as to freight, social as to wage regulation and labour conditions of the various districts, leading up to the conclusion, "all these diversities are special to the mining industry." Attention is called to the great number of undertakings and their lack of uniformity. "There are now in Great Britain about 1400 colliery undertakings owning about 2500 mines." In another passage: "It is a fact of some significance that the Westphalian coalfield,

[1] Jeans, 'Trusts, Pools, and Corners,' p. 62. For the present time see 'Report on the Coal Industry,' 1926, pp. 239-241 and *passim*.

[2] 'Report,' p. 44.

the principal European competitor of our industry, is organised differently from our own. The output of that field in normal years is in the neighbourhood of a hundred million tons, but the number of separate undertakings responsible for this large output is only seventy." [1]

"In the reconstructed coalfield of the Pas de Calais, again, the units of production are of the same order of magnitude as in Westphalia. In 1925 an output of 20 million tons was produced there by only 16 undertakings." This alone serves to show the difference of the English system, with its multiplicity of undertakings. The Report gave a number of particular instances of this fact which had not heretofore been generally known. But it must not be overlooked that even in the case of English coal-mining amalgamations have taken place. In 1908 Mr. David Thomas, later Lord Rhondda, founded the Cambrian Trust which then produced about four million tons yearly. We have to-day an example of concentration in the Doncaster Collieries Association,[2] which controls an output of some five to six millions per annum. But such instances are of little importance if we keep in view the number of small undertakings and their conditions of working. The fact that some pits turn out coal at 12s. per ton and others at 30s. shows clearly the difference due primarily to the distinction between large scale and small scale production. The experts of the Commission found a mine in the Rhondda Valley employing only two labourers. Another, with a capital of £350, employed twenty-four.[3] The coal strike threw a flashlight upon the out-of-date character of these whole conditions, which made any uniform regulation of social questions in English coal-mining impossible owing to the structural confusion of the industry in England. The second recommendation of the

[1] 'Report,' p. 57. The English output for 1924 was about 244 million tons.

[2] See 'Iron and Coal Trade Review,' July 3, 1908, p. 64.

[3] See the section 'Obsolescence of the Mines,' pp. 45 ff.

Commission deals with amalgamations : "The amalgamation of many of the present small units of production is both desirable and practicable." [1] But it must be borne in mind that a movement towards concentration, as we now understand it, is a process lasting many decades, paving the way for amalgamations by excluding other concerns which are crushed out of existence by those forming the amalgamation. Modern English coal-mining did not in the earlier decades attempt any such concentration, though the range of prices would have made such a step feasible. Although protected against the Continent by low costs of production it has not since the collapse of the Newcastle Vend attempted to supersede competition by means of common action. To effect this now at a stroke is a matter of immense difficulty,[2] and the consequence is that from many quarters now comes a demand for nationalisation, as a means of removing the disadvantages due to differences of conditions through equalisation by the State, the taxpayer coming to the help of the weak producers.

Very different are the obstacles to cartels or trusts in the second most important branch of British mineral products. The iron ore mining industry has made no progress in England in the last decades. Since the outbreak of the war it has tended to decline. Its output was 16 million tons in 1913, only 10·8 in 1923, 11·2 in 1924, 10·1 in 1925. But even to-day, when American and Franco-German iron districts have long disputed her pre-eminence, Great Britain still occupies the third place in world production.[3]

In the United States the Steel Trust has dominated the

[1] p. 233.

[2] Since the dispute of 1926 intelligently managed undertakings have energetically supported the movement for amalgamation. Thus in 1926 the Amalgamated Anthracite Collieries Co. and the United Anthracite Collieries Co. united into one company by exchange of shares. The new Company has a capital of nine millions sterling, with Sir Alfred Mond as President. See 'Berliner Börsenkurier,' November 19, 1926.

[3] For the figures see 'Statistical Abstract of U.S.A.', 1924, p. 696; 'Economist,' Sept. 4, 1926; 'Statesman's Year Book' for 1925, p. 56.

production of iron ore since the beginning of the century. Formed in 1901 it has developed its position by special arrangements with the railway magnate Hill in 1907. The formation of American trusts was and still is favoured to a certain extent by the very localised character of the iron deposits. Of a total production of 54·2 million tons in 1924 no fewer than 45 millions came from the district of Lake Superior.[1]

In Germany, before 1918, Minette iron, now the most valuable iron ore, had been monopolised by the manufacturers of finished products. In Siegerland there is the Iron Syndicate in iron mining proper, while but a small portion of the large iron production of Lorraine-Luxemburg reaches the market directly, most of it being further manufactured by the large iron concerns themselves—a fact which makes any special monopoly organisation such as a cartel or a syndicate for the most part superfluous.[2] This is at least true so far as sales to outside smelters in the Minette and Saar regions is concerned, as the big sellers, who are comparatively few in number, can command a complete view of the whole market and check mischievous underbidding without any special system of regulating prices. It is only in the case of the relatively small sales to outsiders in Rhenish Westphalia that Spanish competition detracts from the power of the large mines to influence prices by their monopoly.[3]

By the Versailles Peace Treaty the advantages of the combination of the possession of iron mines with the manufacture of steel passed in part to France with the annexation of certain iron-producing areas which were formerly German. But for our present purpose this has made no change, these territorial alterations causing no break-up of the great undertakings. In America, as well as in Continental

[1] 'Statistical Abstract of U.S.A.', 1924, p. 696.

[2] Heymann, 'Die gemischten Werke im deutschen Grosseisengewerbe,' Stuttgart 1904, p. 261.

[3] G. Goldstein, 'Die Entwicklung der deutschen Roheisenindustrie seit 1879.' 'Proceedings of the Verein zur Beförderung des Gewerbefleisses,' 1909, pp. 477-8.

Europe, both the production and manufacture of iron are concentrated in certain localities, and therefore adapted to cartels and amalgamations.[1]

In England things are very different. As late as 1903 Jeans was able to write "that the majority of the works engaged in pig-iron making in this country are pig-iron makers only, having to buy all their raw materials."[2] But in Great Britain, too, the tendency for related branches of business to combine has been making headway,[3] and many iron and steel works have their own mines. There is, however, no question of any development on monopolist lines, such as some writers have thought this tendency denoted.[4] There is nothing in the Cleveland district or elsewhere corresponding to the monopolist concentration of France, Germany or America. Even if this were the case it would still be impossible to speak of a monopolisation of the iron ore supply in England. The official figures for the consumption of iron ore in 1923 were 16,300,000 tons, of which no less than 5,800,000 tons were imported.[5] As the quality of the imported ore, which comes chiefly from Spain, is much higher than that of English ore, we may assume that 50 per cent. of the present English pig-iron output is manufactured from foreign ore. If the English were to employ more extensively in the future the Thomas process,[6] which they have neglected hitherto, home ores, to which it is well suited, would certainly be more largely used.[7] Even then

[1] For the special movement towards concentration in iron ore, coal, and steel in France after the war to 1925 see the Report of J. R. Cahill, Councillor to the British Embassy, 'Report on the Economic and Industrial Conditions in France,' London 1925, pp. 215 ff.

[2] Jeans in 'British Industries,' London 1903, p. 14.

[3] Jeans, 'The Iron Trade of Great Britain,' London 1906, p. 175.

[4] Von Schulze-Gaevernitz, 'Englischer Freihandel und Britischer Imperialismus,' Leipzig 1906, p. 271.

[5] 'Statesman's Year Book,' 1925, p. 56.

[6] According to 'Iron and Steel,' 1908, p. 9, Great Britain produced in 1907, by the Thomas process only, about 1,900,000 tons of steel out of a total of 6,522,000 tons.

[7] Jeans, 'Iron Trade of Great Britain,' p. 15.

the low rate of freight to England for Spanish and Swedish ore,[1] and the relatively small cost of inland transport in England itself, would be against any movement in the direction of monopoly. Even in Rhenish-Westphalia there is competition between the Lorraine and Spanish ores, though the foreign ores have to pay much higher rates of freight, and this would necessarily be still more largely felt in England; consequently, one important reason for forming monopolist organisations in the iron industry of other countries—the exploitation of the protective effect of freights—does not exist in England. Again, in the case of the quarrying of stones and earths (specially sandstone, slate, limestone, chalk, clay) monopolisation is out of the question owing to home competition. The supply of these minerals is so abundant and distributed through such an extremely large number of competing districts (as in the case of coal) that any monopolist movement is impossible. The trade also in many of the branches of production is extremely small and the plant comparatively undeveloped, so that in these cases even local monopolist associations would give an immediate stimulus to fresh competition.[2]

A special report on Building Material Trades, presented to the Committee on Trusts, states that the raw materials, so far as they are of mineral origin, are uncontrolled.[3]

Thus in England competition is still the ruling principle in the three most important mineral products. As we shall see later on, the same thing cannot be said of the fourth, salt, but its importance as compared to the sum of English minerals and of their three chief groups is insignificant.

We can therefore affirm generally: firstly, that England has no raw material in minerals possessing that monopoly

[1] For the comparison with Germany see Goldstein, 'Verhandlungen des Vereins zur Beförderung des Gewerbefleisses,' 1908, p. 430, note 2.

[2] Cf. for the diffusion of production all over the country, 'Mines and Quarries,' part iii. 1908, pp. 159-162, 238 *et seq*. The statements on pp. 242-243 of the small amount of trade done by the slate quarries are typical.

[3] 'Report on Trusts,' 1924, p. 35.

in the world's market which favours the development of cartels or trusts; and, secondly, that it is precisely in the most important of the existing raw mineral products that the conditions are most unfavourable for monopoly. Monopolist combinations are consequently for practical purposes excluded from the sphere in which their success in other countries has been most marked.

Turning now to the finishing trades, in which, from their very nature, monopoly resting on natural scarcity is out of the question, what are the elements of successful monopolisation which are "deficient" in England? It is obvious that the protective effects of freights, which in England bear very lightly on heavy raw materials, can only influence the manufacture of high-priced goods in rare cases. The higher priced the goods, the more clearly must the English manufacturer recognise the fact that freight rates give him no advantage over the foreigner in the home market, which consists of an island with but a small inland area. The absence of protective duties in all those manufacturing industries which are or may be influenced by foreign competition considerably increases this openness to attack, and Free Trade is therefore a sufficient explanation of the non-existence of cartels and trusts in a large section of English industries. To-day, however, some reservations must be made.

Certain branches of the iron trade are an excellent example. Before the war Jeans writes with reference to the absence of monopolist associations in the production of pig-iron:[1] "The main reason for this fact is that while in protectionist countries prices may be regulated by such combinations within tolerably wide limits, here prices must be largely determined by the behaviour of the foreigner. An arrangement made to-day to sell at a certain regulated price may be completely upset to-morrow by the action of an outside country. Although the output of iron and steel throughout the world is now so enormous, the iron market

[1] Jeans, 'British Industries,' p. 35.

is so sensitive that an offer of 25,000 or 50,000 tons of pig-iron or steel in markets like Glasgow or Middlesbro' at 5s. or 10s. below current prices would completely demoralise the market and almost create a panic."

Before 1914 the English iron market was subject to the constant danger and pressure of possible foreign importation. Even when the price of pig-iron in England fell below the level of American or German prices there was little inducement to adjust the level by means of a cartel for a short period. To-day the English iron and steel industry is in a similar position as regards imports and exports. In 1925 the imports of iron and steel and their products amounted to 2·7 million tons, the exports to 3·7 millions.[1] According to the 'Economist'[2] the English iron industry is "now exposed to the full blast of the storm of world competition," and this holds good for every branch of the industry. Since the war the costs of production in all these branches have very greatly increased. The 'Economist' speaks of a fifty per cent. increase in costs, while the output to meet home and foreign demand shows a notable decline.[3] The estimated capacity of steel production is 12½ million tons. In face of the possibility of so great an over-production the desirability of an amalgamation of the various branches of the iron industry seems obvious. Yet the iron and steel industry of to-day is still far removed from the measure of concentration obtaining on the Continent. When in the summer of 1926 the question of joining the iron agreement between Germany, France, Belgium and Luxemburg became acute, it soon appeared that the English iron industry felt little inclina-

[1] 'Economist,' Feb. 13, 1926, p. 52; see also Fitzgerald, p. 43.

[2] 'Economist,' *ut supra*, p. 54.

[3] The 'Economist' for Feb. 13, 1926, gives the following figures of output. Tons (000 omitted):

	Pig-iron.	Partly manufactured.
1913 - - -	10,250	7,660
1921 - - -	2,611	3,652
1924 - - -	7,320	8,220
1925 - - -	6,238	7,397

tion to enter the combination. Various reasons may be assigned, but many journals pointed out at the time that, owing to the imperfect movement towards concentration, the English iron industry was in no condition to enter an international cartel. About the same time Sir Walter Peter Rylands, as President of the Iron and Steel Institute, expressed the opinion that protection was necessary to bring about a practicable cartel organisation—an idea which he further developed in one of the leading commercial papers.[1] However doubtful this policy may appear—especially when we consider the cartels and trusts which we have yet to describe as existing in spite of free trade—it is clear that the English iron and steel market still remains in the domain of competitive production. None the less, there have long been associations in the trade which, without regulating the output after the fashion of a cartel, have sought and still seek to influence prices. It is not without importance here to look back upon the conditions as they were twenty years ago. It is precisely because the possibility of cartelising the English steel industry has been denied in many quarters that we must pay attention to the struggles towards organisation at the beginning of the century as exemplified in the manufacture of ship and boiler plates. Here, also, we have competition between several districts, Scotland, the north of England, and the north of Ireland, each more or less equally favoured by position. But within each district only a small number of firms made ship and boiler plates, and the desire to monopolise the local market soon brought makers together.[2] Local monopolist associations like the Scotch Steelmakers' Association, founded as early as 1886 by the union of the

[1] See 'Manchester Guardian Commercial,' July 8, 1926; also Levy, 'England und die Konzentrationsbewegung in der deutschen Industrie. Wirtschaftliche Nachrichten für Rhein und Ruhr,' Aug. 18, 1926.

[2] According to Jeans, 'Iron Trade Report,' p. 62, in 1906 ten works made ships' plates, producing a yearly average between 1888 and 1903 of about $1\frac{1}{2}$ million tons, of which the Consett Company, in Durham, alone produced 300,000 tons.

four leading firms, arose. The Association practically abolished local competition, in the hope of thereby becoming better armed against freebooters from rival districts. The other districts followed suit about 1900;[1] and the union of the comparatively few masters in each district prepared the way for a wider organisation, when, at the end of 1903, the period of "dumping" ceased.

The monopolist organisation, which thus arose and exists to this day, devotes its main energies to the geographical division of the market. The two main rivals, the Scotch Steelmakers' Association and the north of England makers, have since 1904 entered into agreements which secure each party the undisputed right to certain areas, and thereby make it possible to maintain prices within those areas. Scotland withdrew from north of England markets, and received in return Belfast.[2] The effect of this arrangement was not long hidden. An Irish firm had remained outside the "combine" and undercut their prices in Belfast, with the result that they were forced to sell much cheaper than on the Clyde and in the north of England district where the understanding could be maintained. The combine accordingly commenced to "dump" in Ireland, and the Clyde shipbuilders complained that this policy gave an advantage of £2000 on every 7000 tons ship to their Irish rivals.[3] In 1908 the Midland steelmakers also came in. The Midland consumers struggled, we are told, in vain against the prices of the local association. They sent their orders to the Clyde makers, and the following extract from the 'Iron and Coal Trades' Review' for September 1908 shows the result.[4] "The English makers drew the attention of the Scotch makers to the position, and the latter, out of loyalty to their compact, have raised their quotations for plates in

[1] Macrosty, 'Trust Movement,' p. 66 *seq.*

[2] 'Economist,' 1906, p. 1133.

[3] 'Economist,' 1906, pp. 1407, 1662, 1675. Similar complaints in the 'Engineer,' March 16, 1909, p. 7.

[4] 'Review,' Sept. 18, 1908, p. 1177 a.

the English districts concerned by 2s. 6d. a ton. This will force the English consumers back to their old supply. The new quotation is actually 2s. 6d. a ton over what is named for local deliveries in Scotland, and is about 10s. a ton above what is asked on exports for foreign markets. It is fully five years since this understanding originated, and year by year it has gradually extended its borders until now it is the most important of the kind in the country."

Differentiation between home and foreign markets is not here, as in the case of several English combines, a mere unfounded rumour nor the exceptional concomitant of one or two export contracts. On the contrary, trade papers regularly quote both prices. The 'Iron and Coal Trades' Review' for January 1909, for instance, gives the following:[1]

SCOTCH HOME PRICES.

	1st Jan.	10th March.	8th June.	16th Sept.
Boiler plates, -	£7 7 6	£7 2 6	£6 17 6	£7 2 6
Ship plates, -	6 12 6	6 7 6	6 2 6	6 10 6

SCOTCH EXPORT PRICES.

	1st Jan.	1st April.	1st July.	1st Sept.
Boiler plates, -	£6 18 9	£6 18 9	£6 15 0	£6 17 6
Ship plates, -	6 0 0	5 15 0	5 12 6	5 15 6

It seems at first strange that export prices of this kind are possible in the home of free trade without encouraging reimportation. But the geographical distribution of the exports must be remembered. Of the 200,000 tons of plates exported from England in 1908 the great majority went to India, Japan, Norway, Australia, Canada, and similar countries [2] whose distance involves high freights for such heavy articles. In this case, therefore, home prices could be maintained above export prices by the amount of return freights, whereas, in the case of raw iron exports, which go mostly to Germany, Holland, France, and Italy, even a monopolist combine would find their maintenance a difficult matter. The most important condition of success

[1] p. 11. [2] 'Trade and Navigation Accounts,' pp. 146, 148.

was, of course, the control of home prices by the suppression of competition. The question became a very burning one at the end of the steel boom in the winter of 1907, and as soon as the first signs of falling demand were felt, works were closed under a general agreement, and compensation paid to their owners by the remaining firms.[1]

Similar proceedings may be noted yet earlier in the case of the National Galvanised Steel Makers' Association and the South Wales Siemens Steel Bar Association. But it was, and still is, characteristic of these Associations that they covered only a limited area of the iron and steel industry of England, and were induced to adopt a common economic policy by special circumstances, such as local concentration, questions of quality, or peculiar temporary conditions (high prices abroad), orders for execution within a limited period, etc. These combinations are not comparable with the closely bound German cartels and syndicates or the United States Steel Corporation, lacking as they do the character of a unit embracing the whole national industry. They increased enormously during the war, but there was never any organisation of a national monopoly. The 'Report on Trusts,' 1919, sums up the whole list of these combinations—five in the pig-iron industry, three in preparing raw steel, seven in rolling mills, besides combines in cast steel, wrought iron, bar iron, and numerous branches of the iron industry. But the 'Report' points out that most of these associations did not concern themselves with the regulation of output.[2] Meanwhile, with the disappearance of the special circumstances—*i.e.* since about 1921—a large number of such combines in the iron industry have disappeared. "The power of many of these combines," says the 'Statist,' "broke down under pressure of the crisis, though they greatly increased during the post-war stimulus."[3] Thus the Cleveland Ironmasters' Association, which had been a member of the English Association

[1] 'Economist,' 1907, p. 1503. [2] p. 2, and Fitzgerald, p. 41 *et seq.*
[3] June 30, 1923.

since 1916, swept away all restrictions upon free competition in July 1922. The combines in the bar iron industry, the North-East Coast Steel Makers' Association, the West Coast Iron Committee, and South Wales Siemens Steel Association, which had long worked in unison to keep down competition, broke away from their associates and gave competition free play. Other combinations are important, such as the Cut Nails' Association. The output of hobnails in England seems to be the monopoly of two undertakings, one of which is an affiliated Norwegian business (the Mustad combine). But all these partial combinations must be regarded from a different angle from national cartels or trusts.

Their function lies rather in tying local competition up to certain members so as to make the most of local opportunities as to price and tides of fortune, than in a comprehensive influence over the output of the whole industry and therewith the price level. It is an understanding, and not a cartel. A monopolistic organisation in the English iron industry is more likely to grow out of the concentrating movement of the great industries of to-day than out of these small organisations. In the last decade large firms have crystallised in a fashion which may have great significance as a stage on the way to monopoly. We must distinguish between such groups: the Tees group consists of four large concerns—Dorman, Long & Co.; Bolckow, Vaughan & Co.; Cargo Fleet, associated with the Furness Co.; and Pease and Partners. Follow the three leading firms in South Wales: Baldwins; Guest, Keen & Nettlefold; and Ebbw Vale. Then comes the United Steel Co., a company formed during the war, which branches out into Sheffield, Cumberland, Lincolnshire. Add to these three groups the most important Scottish manufacturer, David Colville, and we have the basis of a British iron trust. Yet the 'Economist' declares that the financial conditions of these concerns are "so different that they constitute a very powerful hindrance to any practical large scale movement towards concentration in the British iron industry." [1] We must regard the whole sphere of this industry as competitive rather than monopolistic. Fitzgerald is of the same opinion: "We come to the conclusion that, in spite of the increase of combines and associations, competition still reigns supreme in the iron and steel industry." [2]

In attempting to mark out that sphere of English industry in which free trade is still a defence against monopolist prices, we must consider all those industries (i) where the importation either of the same goods or of substitutes is easy; and (ii) where English prices are normally the same as import prices (freight included). In all such cases a monopolist rise in prices created by a limitation of competition would simply encourage the foreign competitor. The silk,[3] the boot and shoe trades, and the motor-car industries fulfil these conditions. In these industries we find a great number of employers of about equal importance competing with one another.[4] The paper industry—except the wall-paper trade—has no cartels or trusts worth mention. Free trade is no doubt largely the cause of this, as a protective policy gave its first impetus to the prosperity of the paper trust in America. A Paper Makers' Association, which regulates certain trade usages, existed before the war, but according to contemporary evidence it had no influence upon prices. As we shall see later, there is now in the paper trade a marked development towards large scale business and concentration. But the 'Report on Trusts,' 1919, makes no mention of a tendency to monopoly in the trade. Strong foreign competition is undoubtedly the cause of this. The English Paper Trade is one of those industries which pressed earnestly and still presses for protection from the foreigner.[5]

[1] 'Economist,' Jan. 9, 1926. [2] p. 53.

[3] For foreign competition cf. (with the necessary reservation) 'The Report of the Tariff Commission,' vol. ii., London 1905, pp. 3088-3092 ff.

[4] 'Economist,' March 20, 1926, p. 577; and June 19, 1926, p. 1189.

[5] For further details see 'The Free Trader,' Jan. 1926, pp. 27-29.

Often enough English attempts at monopoly have broken down owing to foreign competition. A well-known early example is the collapse of the Birmingham Bedstead Makers' Alliance in 1900. It had doubled the price of bedsteads since 1891, but the final result was that " foreign competition was stimulated " and the cartel fell to pieces.[1] Twelve years passed before it was set up again. As the internal conditions for cartel-making were present it was naturally led by the war and the subsequent diminution of foreign competition to make a strong combine. Under the name of the Bedstead Makers' Federation it represents about eighty per cent. of the trade. Its main concern is the fixing of minimum prices.[2]

The significance of free trade as a means of defence against the monopolist price policy of a national organisation of manufacturers may be deduced from the well-known fact that within the last half-century England has imported in yearly increasing quantity many classes of goods in which she formerly had the predominance over other countries, at least in the home market. Free trade has of late years contributed essentially to the non-existence of monopolist associations in all such branches of industry. In former days they might quite possibly have been organised on monopolist lines, so far as foreign competition was concerned.

This fixes, however, only one of the limits of competition in English industry. Where for any cause, in spite of free trade and the slight protective effect of freights (as in so-called sheltered industries), there is immunity from foreign competition, the formation of a monopolist organisation becomes independent of these factors ; on the other hand, high freights or even protective duties do not in themselves necessarily entail the creation of a cartel or trust. It remains to determine the sphere of competition within the bounds of home trade, *i.e.* to distinguish the essential factors

[1] Jeans, ' British Industries,' p. 202.

[2] ' Report on Trusts,' p. 39 ; and ' Statist,' March 7, 1923.

which prevent the substitution of monopolist combination for competition, if home trade is regarded as a self-contained entity.

The industrial competition on which the classic economists based their observations is still dominant in a considerable proportion of English industries at the present time. The ' Report on Trusts ' states : " There are many industries, trades, and services, great as well as small, in which combination has made hardly any headway, and competition is still the determining factor in the fixing of price." [1] The shipbuilding industry is quoted as a case in point, and reference is made to another English report which states that " most of the shipbuilding and marine engineering firms in this country are independent and there is no community of financial interest between them as an industry. Competition is always keen, and shipowners have no difficulty in getting numerous tenders at all times when they offer specifications." But for some time British shipbuilding has lost its power of dominating the world market and dictating prices. In 1925 it saw several orders for motor vessels go to German and Dutch competitors, showing clearly the strong international competition to which English shipbuilding is now subject.[2] During dull times competition by every means becomes very acute, and firms lacking orders for their own specialities plunge into other markets, and contracts are accepted at prices below costs of production. " Other industries and trades are to be found in which the rival manufacturers or traders are hardly on speaking terms, much less at that stage of mutual confidence which permits concerted regulation of the trade."

In the English textile industry competition and monopoly exist side by side. On the one hand we have a number of large firms whose position has been built up by ten years'

[1] 'Report on Trusts,' p. 20.

[2] Cf. 'Shipbuilding Depression,' by Capt. F. C. Brown; in the 'Manchester Guardian Commercial,' Jan. 28, 1926, p. 73.

movement towards concentration, which practically represent special branches of the industry to which we return later. On the other, the textile industry exhibits a very great diversity of conditions among works and undertakings, rendering impossible any domination of the market by the formation of trusts and cartels.

This is pre-eminently the case in the textile industry in its simplest stages, both in cotton spinning and wool spinning and weaving. The joint action of manufacturers and trades unions in 1904, which shortened hours of labour and therefore limited production, has not approved itself as a means of moderating competition and over-production, although Mr. Macrosty [1] enumerates it in his 'Trust Movement' as being the first step to further organisations. On the contrary, that organised limitation of production, with its consequent increase of profits, has made competition keener than ever. The value of exported grey yarn rose from 11·25d. in the years 1900-1903 to 13·55d. in the four following years,[2] while the number of joint-stock undertakings, which had only increased by twenty-four between 1900 and 1903, had risen to ninety between 1904 and 1907.[3] "Certainly the great trade boom of 1905 and succeeding years was ushered in by a prolonged spell of organised short time in 1904, but trade booms are rather uncommon in Lancashire just now. It seems pretty clear that the great reduction in the output of yarns and cloth helped to dislocate the relations of supply and demand, and by bringing almost unparalleled profits stimulated an immense excess of the means of production." For this reason, according to the 'Manchester Guardian,' manufacturers both in Oldham and Bolton were in 1909 against any "organised" limitation of hours of labour.[4]

[1] Macrosty, 'The Trust Movement in British Industry,' p. 123.

[2] 'Statistical Abstract,' London 1908, p. 255. Prices for each year are taken from this source.

[3] Cf. 'Statist,' Feb. 23, 1908, p. 381.

[4] Cf. 'Manchester Guardian,' March 2, 1909, p. 5.

During the war and the general scarcity of cotton wool and cotton goods in England, proposals by the manufacturers against over-production naturally did not come into question, but in view of the depression in English textiles since 1921 such proposals have come again to the fore. Early in the summer of 1925 the Masters' Federation of Cotton Spinners sought to persuade their members to agree to all-round short time. But it was clearly very difficult to get these proposals accepted.[1] The situation in the summer of 1926 was unaltered. An article in the 'Economist' shows how little resulted from these endeavours for common action: "The majority of firms look upon restriction of output as in itself desirable, but as things are the average production is no more than half the capacity of the plant. The Masters' Federation has revived suggestions for fixing minimum prices. A definite plan for this purpose was carried by a large majority. But it was recognised that the plan would not be practicable until conditions in the industry were fairly settled."[2] The lack of unity among the cotton spinners[3] is clearly the reason why a fixation of prices would create the danger of new competition, and this would only intensify the depression. This danger is naturally no greater to-day than in the case already described. In the same way multiplicity of firms is characteristic of the woollen industry. Professor Clapham states[4] that it is still common to find mills occupied by more than one manufacturer and firms starting with small capital. The small trader rents a few rooms or perhaps a whole floor in a wool mill; while looms belonging to two different

[1] 'Economist,' Feb. 13, 1926, p. 66.

[2] 'Economist,' July 17, 1926, p. 101.

[3] The heavy pressure of bad trade brought about a new attempt to common regulation of prices in August 1926. The American Yarn Association Ltd. was founded, and fixed minimum prices for its yarns. No fewer than 200 firms attended the meeting to form this Association, which shows how much the spinning business is divided up. Cf. 'Economist,' August 21, 1926.

[4] Clapham, 'Woollen and Worsted Industries,' pp. 129-130.

firms and driven by machinery which belong to neither are often found in one and the same factory. This system of providing factory space, machinery and requisite power to firms with small capital (the Tenement Factory or Machine Renting system) is naturally extremely favourable to the growth of smaller concerns. It has been a matter of much complaint of late that this organisation is being exploited by speculators in order to persuade the hands to make themselves independent without starting on a sound basis.[1] In like manner, the commission system, which exists in every department of the wool trade, but specially in spinning and weaving, encourages the rise and continuance of the small capitalist as a manufacturer by the side of the large concerns.[2]

It is the more remarkable that these conditions should be predominant in the textile industry, as it is precisely within the limits of the same industry in the last ten years that the English trust movement has largely developed. Whilst in spinning and weaving, on the whole, competitive conditions of trade are still to be seen,[3] we find in several finishing branches of the trade, as well as in some of its special grade products, a marked concentration. This fact shows the impossibility of accepting without qualification the statement often made,[4] that, as the manufacture of

[1] Cf. George Brodnitz, 'Betriebskonzentration und Kleinbetrieb in der Englischen Industrie,' Conrad's 'Jahrbücher,' 1908, pp. 188-9.

[2] Clapham, 'Woollen and Worsted Industries,' pp. 130-131.

[3] Exceptions are to be found. In 1918 the Amalgamated Cotton Mills Trust united the leading spinners in all branches. Founded with a share capital of £1 million, it increased by further purchases to £7·25 millions in 1921. We have here at the same time a vertical combination, the Trust owning dye and bleaching works and other trades as well as spinning and weaving. But there is no question of monopoly. On July 31, 1921, there were about 56 million spindles in Great Britain. Of these the Trust with its 61 concerns had only 1,587,552. 'Statist,' May 6, 1922.

[4] Cf. Brentano, 'Die beabsichtigte Neuorganisation der deutschen Volkswirtschaft,' p. 260: "On the other hand the more the manufacture of highly finished articles develops, the more easily new works are formed and the number of competitors increases."

high-class goods increases, the chances of a coalition will diminish because the number of concerns will then be more numerous than in the earlier stages. It entirely depends on how far the technical development of each grade has advanced. Under certain circumstances it is just the high grades in which the particular impetus to concentrate has been given. There is, for instance, all the world over, less concentration in the production of pig-iron than in the manufacture of steel rails.

Many facts could be adduced to illustrate the special difficulties of forming monopolies in finishing trades. Monopolist associations find their progress hindered wherever there is a great differentiation in the quality of the products of the finishing industry. This is particularly noticeable in England. For many branches of English industry have, in view of the competition of countries which can supply in bulk articles of inferior value at lower prices, directed their attention more and more in the last decade to the production of specially highly finished goods. In this way distinctive qualities and brands arise which give individual manufacturers so strong a position against other competitors that they reject all proposals for coalition. This appears to be the case in the woollen yarn industry. Imports affect yarns "which are either not spun in Bradford or whose manufacture does not pay there."[1] The quality of English woollen yarns is admitted to be the finest known, but many very different kinds are made; in consequence, no monopolist organisation can be formed, as Prof. Clapham expressly points out.[2] With reference to this particular case he writes: "For as a rule only the producers of articles that come into fairly direct competition with one another are easily moved to set bounds to the force of that competition by means of joint action."

Important as it is to recognise this condition of things, the fact must nevertheless not be lost sight of, that some-

[1] Chapman, 'Work and Wages,' London 1904, p. 190.

[2] Clapham, 'Woollen and Worsted Industries,' p. 154.

times where firms owing to the manufacture of special brands hold an exceptionally advantageous position, the chances in favour of a monopolist organisation seem particularly great, as such firms would have very little fresh competition to fear if they were to raise prices by joint agreement. As we shall see further on, many monopolist associations, in the woollen industry in particular, owe their success to this fact. But we must remember that the monopolist position arising from the possession of special makes is then always held and jointly exploited by a not very considerable number of firms. In general, therefore, the question seems to be whether a concentration of manufacturers of highly finished goods has taken place or not, and whether new undertakings will increase competition with ease, or slowly and with difficulty.

In the case of many highly finished manufactures (and fine grades) we find England confirming the view that it is comparatively easy to create new competing undertakings if demand increases. As in other countries, the size necessary for a profitable business in such branches is relatively small compared to the total production of the country, and therefore there is less need of fixed capital than in the case of raw material or half-manufactured goods. We find accordingly that (i) the number of existing undertakings is comparatively large; and (ii) it increases rapidly when demand grows and profits rise—two conditions which make it extremely difficult to shut out competition.

Pre-war examples are numerous enough. The Bedstead-makers' Alliance had seen new factories grow from 40 in 1891 to 56 in 1899, and its own importance diminish correspondingly.[1] In the worsted yarn industry large joint-stock companies first appear at the beginning of this century, but the old-fashioned "family business" still preponderates.[2]

To-day, after many years of depression and over-produc-

[1] Macrosty, 'Trust Movement in British Industry,' p. 81.

[2] Clapham, 'Woollen and Worsted Industries,' p. 153; Hooper, 'British Industries,' p. 95.

tion in all branches of English industry, the factor of new competitors is naturally less of an obstacle to the formation of a cartel. But the increase of production after 1914, and continued after 1918, has caused such an increase of competitors that new difficulties of a serious character are opposed to such an agreement, especially at a time when every firm is striving to underbid others for orders.

As compared with other countries, specially with the United States and Germany, the size of undertakings in many branches of English industry is relatively small, because the need for vertical combination is less. In a country where protective duties and monopolies of raw goods hinder the manufacturer of finished goods from obtaining supplies of materials, and where, at the same time, it is impossible for the finishing manufacturer to make the consumer pay directly for the monopolist higher price of material, an intimate connection with raw production and half manufacture is unavoidable. The most important of the few raw products of England are not under a monopoly, and an artificial rise in the price of raw materials owing to protective duties is out of the question. Accordingly, the process of combination has been a much longer one in England than in countries where the industrial element saw in it a means of protection against an abuse of power on the part of producers of raw materials and half-manufactured goods.

This has been clearly brought out in the Report of 1918 on 'Industrial and Commercial Policy after the War.' In Germany the large steel manufactories are always combined undertakings, whereas Jeans in 1906 represents the combination of different branches of business only as being "increasingly recognised."[1] The extraordinary multiplicity of coal mines already alluded to, the free competition governing the coal trade, and the necessity of importing pure ore, deficient in phosphorus, from Spain or Sweden,

[1] Cf. Jeans, 'The Iron Trade of Great Britain,' p. 175; 'Financial Times,' July 7, 1909, p. 4.

make any idea of vertical combination in the English iron industry almost unthinkable. It is significant of the relative unimportance of vertical combination in any English industry that the 'Report on Trusts' touches briefly upon it, mentioning only one example, the soap industry of Lever Brothers, which has established overseas the production of oil-bearing plants and seeds.[1]

As vertical combination makes ever-increasing demands on the capital of the united undertaking, the relatively small amount of influence exercised by such combinations in English industry means that it is easier to start competing works in England than in the United States or in Germany. Further, whilst the vertical combination in the latter countries has often led to a complete monopolisation of raw materials, this development, which would entirely exclude competition in finishing manufactures, is non-existent in England. It is quite conceivable that more English paper manufacturers might think it advisable to follow the example given by a few of their number, and to acquire forests and wood-pulp mills abroad. If the scheme were really able to make such undertakings more profitable, it would force subsequent new mills to keep up the pace, and by considerably increasing both the amount of capital necessary and the risk run, would probably make it more difficult than before for any such mills to be founded. Yet they might, though with difficulty, spring up. In the United States and in Germany, however, matters are different. Monopolies of raw materials in all kinds of industries make it impossible to start new works in any finishing manufacture. Witness the American Paper Trust, which owes its power to the fact that, aided by high duties on wood and pulp, it has monopolised the native forests and consequently lamed fresh competition.[2] Witness again the

[1] p. 20.

[2] Cf. Levy, 'Einfluss der Zollpolitik auf die wirtschaftliche Entwicklung der Vereinigten Staaten von America,' Conrad's 'Jahrbücher,' 1906, p. 646. Liefmann refers to earlier monopolies of raw materials, p. 25.

steel trade in America and Germany, in which the creation of new undertakings on a large scale is hindered by the monopolisation of the deposits of ore.[1] Similar cases often occur in countries where extensive monopolies of raw materials exist side by side with finishing manufactures; but they are not to be found in England where there are only isolated monopolies of raw materials, and even these, as we shall see later on, have only a comparatively limited sphere of operation, the great mass of raw material required by English manufacturers being imported duty free and at low freight rates. It might be thought within the bounds of possibility to create a trust in English finishing manufactures by the aid of a foreign raw material monopoly, and one such attempt has been made by the American Borax Trust which owns a few refineries in England. But generally speaking it has not been found possible by monopolising raw materials to promote monopolies in remote stages of finishing manufactures otherwise exposed to competition.

There are therefore a number of circumstances which serve to explain the continued existence of competition in many English finishing trades. Two of these circumstances —the existence of a large number of undertakings and the comparative ease with which this number may be increased —are very marked in one English industry in particular in which the conditions of competition stand in sharp contrast to those in Germany and America. This is the tin-plate industry.

Inasmuch as foreign competition is in fact unknown and need not be theoretically excluded for purposes of argument only, tin-plating offers an excellent illustration of how the home trade itself may necessitate the continuance of competition. The English or, more particularly, the Welsh makers have a dominant position in the world's market. The tin-plate industry of the United States was in the

[1] Heymann, 'Gemischte Werke im deutschen Grosseisengewerbe'; Levy, 'Stahlindustrie,' *passim*.

nineties the spoilt child of the American steel trade, the youngest but the most difficult to rear, and is the standing example of a protected "infant industry."[1] During the war it made enormous strides owing to the tremendous demand for canning. The manufacture of tin-plate in the United States rose from 1410 million pounds in 1910 to 3168 million in 1923 and 2975 million in 1924.[2] An export of tin plates might have developed, but in proportion to the home production it played no great part. In 1924 the exports amounted to 360 million pounds (as against only 109 millions on the average of the last four years of peace),[3] about one-eighth of the home product. The British export in 1924 and 1925 exceeded 500,000 tons.[4] But the officially published 'Survey of Overseas Markets,' 1925,[5] shows that the tin-plate exports of England, in spite of increasing American and German competition, dominate the foreign markets for this commodity, except in the United States, which was formerly a great market for Welsh tin plates. Nevertheless, the tin-plate industry in England, strongly established as it was before the war, has not been able to establish a monopoly with the function of regulating prices. This is all the more striking as ever since 1862 the tin-plate industry in Germany has possessed a syndicate in the Weissblechverkaufskontor, and the American industry, which is of much more recent growth, having existed only since 1892, became subject in 1898 to a trust, the American Tin-Plate Company, since 1901 a member of the Steel Corporation.

What is the explanation of this peculiar position? As regards comparisons between Germany and England, it is at once noticeable that in Germany five works suffice for the

[1] Cf. Levy, 'Entwicklungsgeschichte einer amerikanischen Industrie' in Conrad's 'Jahrbücher,' 1905, vol. xxix. 145.

[2] 'Statistical Abstract,' 1924, p. 698.

[3] *Ibid.* 512.

[4] 'Economist,' Feb. 13, 1926, p. 60.

[5] London 1925, p. 732. See the references there quoted, especially to Italy and Brazil.

relatively small production of tin plates, and the creation of a cartel is, therefore, naturally a simple matter. They have practically no German competitors. Tin-plating, in spite of the protective duty, is not a very paying industry,[1] for the cost of the necessary skilled labour is high, and as owing to cartels and duties it is so difficult to obtain a supply of raw material that only a " mixed " works is in a position to make tin-plate making profitable,[2] existing works have kept their monopolist position undisturbed. The larger production of England admits of a correspondingly greater number of concerns. This is due to two reasons: first, in tin-plating trained manual labour still plays the chief part, machinery being of less importance, and, therefore, the size of a profitable business is relatively small; secondly, in Wales, tin-plate works pure and simple, which buy tin-plate bars, are no worse off than larger " mixed " works, as there are no duties to send up rates, and on the contrary half-finished goods can often be bought from abroad at " dumping " prices.[3] This enables the smaller capitalists to exist beside those who combine steel and rolling works with tin-plating. Many considerable difficulties must be met with in projecting cartels among so great a number of undertakings.[4] When the American Trust was founded in 1897 the manufacture of tin plates within the Union amounted only to 250,000 tons, and only about thirty-eight works had to be bought up in order to

[1] Cf. 'Kontradiktorische Verhandlungen,' Heft 9, p. 153, *passim*. The opinions of different manufacturers, who remarked on the fact that there is no trained race of workers in the German tin-plate industry, seem quite credible. The importance of such a race of workers specially in this branch of industry, is recognised in England also. Cf., for instance, 'Tariff Commission Report,' vol. i. 1904, § 889.

[2] *Ibid.*, particularly page 120, also pp. 118, 119. From the accounts given there by Messrs. Capito & Klein it is easy to see what difficulties lie in the way of the supply of raw material.

[3] Cf., for instance, 'Tariff Commission Report,' vol. i. §§ 1155 and 1145, where the introduction of a duty on semi-finished goods is opposed by manufacturers in the interest of the tin-plate industry.

[4] 'Report, British Iron Trade Association,' 1907, p. xviii.

control 90 per cent. of the production, many of which had been rash speculations and were very nearly bankrupt.[1] In Wales, on the contrary, there are practically no unprofitable works. All have an excellent type of workman at their command and a firm hold on traditional markets. As an expert explained to the Tariff Commission—"We cannot make a monopoly in the tin-plate trade, because it is divided up into such small units." [2] The war brought about the formation of a Tin-plate Trade Association, but according to the 'Report on Trusts' it was of little importance. A more important fact is that in October 1922 the manufacturers combined to form a plan for stabilising prices, which as the "stabilisation tin-plate agreement" remained in force till May 1925. The minimum prices were then cut. The Association thereupon broke up, and prices were left open to competition.[3] The prices of tin plates immediately fell, proving the influence of the combine in keeping up prices. But the episode shows clearly that the ground is not yet ready for effective monopoly organisation in the Welsh tin-plate industry.

The main factors which make the suppression of competition among English manufacturers at the present time impossible or in the long run inadvisable have now been considered, and the general outline of the sphere of competitive industry in England should be clear. But in the last thirty years the limits of unrestricted competition have been increasingly narrowed by a number of circumstances which have given a growing impetus to monopoly in certain trades. These circumstances we must now investigate.

[1] Levy, 'Stahlindustrie,' p. 180 ff. [2] *Ibid.* p. 986.
[3] 'Economist,' May 9, 1925 p. 945; Fitzgerald, p. 44.

CHAPTER IX

EXISTING MONOPOLIST ORGANISATIONS IN ENGLISH INDUSTRY

(*a*) THE MOVEMENT TOWARDS CONCENTRATION

PERHAPS the most far-reaching innovation in competitive industry during the nineteenth century has been the appearance of what is called the concentration of industrial units. The course of development has been by no means uniform, as a review of any reasonable number of English industries shows. With rising demand the number of separate makers may be permanently increased, as in cotton spinning, even though as time goes on the average size of each separate unit is very much larger than it was. On the other hand, we also find the peculiar position, sometimes by no means new, that an *increasing* demand is satisfied by a continually *decreasing* number of firms, the greater productive power of the single unit reducing from decade to decade the aggregate number of firms.

Nowadays this concentration, which John Stuart Mill noticed in the case of gas and railway companies, is not confined in England to staple industries. We meet it also in other cases; in shipping, in banking, in both wholesale and retail trade, in hotelkeeping, in newspapers, and in urban traffic schemes, etc.

We are not now concerned with the historical origins of this general tendency, nor need we investigate in detail its causes. It interests us only from the point of view of industrial competition. We regard it merely as a special variety of industrial development, one of many directions which manufacturing on a large scale may take. Every factor which can exercise any considerable influence on the origin and development of such an industry—changes in facilities for communication, increased competition, new inventions and discoveries, and so on—can equally be the basis of a concentration of industrial units. The primary result of enormous industrial undertakings is the increased efficiency of each unit. If, however, the circumstances of the case are such that the demand for the commodity in question can be satisfied by fewer concerns of greater productive power, we then arrive at the special case of a concentration of industrial units. The productive power of an economically profitable undertaking grows so much faster than the aggregate of goods actually produced in the industry, that production is gradually concentrated in the hands of an increasingly small number of concerns. And just as a multiplicity of undertakings makes it difficult to suppress competition, concentration, if combined with a reduction of the competing undertakings,[1] makes it proportionally easy.

Nowadays concentration often appears at the very beginning of a new industry, when the productive power of an economically profitable unit is such that a few units alone suffice to meet the entire demand. But more usually it is the result of a lengthy process, in which the technically more efficient overcome, after severe competition, the less productive, and acquire their markets. The history of the English paper trade is an interesting example. Statistics of the licences granted show that in 1801 there were 413 paper factories; in 1811, 527; ten years later, as many as 564. Between 1803 and 1831 the amount of paper taxed in the year rose from about £31,000,000 worth to twice that amount.[2] In other words, the increase in the number of paper mills was accompanied by a corresponding increase

[1] The case of an undertaking containing many separate branches of trade concentrated in itself is different.

[2] Porter, 'Progress of the Nation,' pp. 367-9.

n production. The next period shows a different picture. Between 1841 and 1845 there were still on the average 497 mills, but the number then sank steadily. In 1904 there were only 279.[1]

The production of paper rose from 43,350 tons in 1841 to 773,550 tons in 1903, but the number of mills fell from nearly 500 to 282. Continual improvements in machinery, the inaccessibility of certain older works to markets, and the increasingly strong competition of the more efficient mills were, according to Spicer,[2] the causes of this concentration.[3]

A particularly characteristic example of the concentrating movement, illustrating not only the tendency of the English paper industry but the strength of the movement generally, is provided by the most recent development of one of the great undertakings in this branch of industry, the Inveresk Paper Company. In the autumn of 1926 it raised its capital from £650,000 to £1,200,000, the chairman explaining this as due to the great expansion of the Company through the purchase and absorption of other firms. He mentioned at the general meeting twelve businesses which the Company had either bought up or controlled by acquiring a majority of their shares. To this the Company presently added the endeavour to graft on to its organisation factories of raw and partly-manufactured material, a vertical combination. "It is our declared intention," said the chairman, "to bring a group of leading papermakers into good relations, and to secure their position by an assured supply of raw materials to be produced by ourselves." [4]

To this class of undertaking belongs also the International Pulp and Chemical Company, which originated in the purchase of the majority of the shares of the German Koholyt Company, with which the Inveresk Co. was associated in the manufacture of cellulose and various chemical products. The Company then sought to connect

[1] A. Dykes Spicer, 'Paper Industry,' 1907, p. 248. [2] *Ibid.*, p. 248.

[3] *Ibid.* pp. 4-5.

[4] See Report of General Meeting of Inveresk Paper Co., 'Economist,' Oct. 23, 1926.

itself with the publishing business in order to secure an exclusive market for its own paper. It bought up the 'Illustrated London News, 'Sphere,' 'Tatler,' 'Graphic,' 'Bystander' and other journals, and formed a special company—Illustrated Newspapers, Limited. We have here a typical example of the way in which a vertical may develop from a horizontal combination, following a course comparable to that upon which Lord Northcliffe had embarked in 1907 in the newspaper business. Lord Northcliffe pointed out that an increase of only one farthing a pound in the price of paper cost the Amalgamated Press £70,000 a year. He caused his undertaking to acquire possession of forests and cellulose and paper factories in Newfoundland, a policy which it had no cause to regret, especially during the war.[1]

In the production of pig-iron the tendency to concentrate appeared much later. From 1796 to 1880 the number of furnaces in existence rose steadily from 124 to 926, and there was a corresponding increase in production from about 125,000 tons to about 7,700,000 tons.[2] But after 1880, though production increased, the number of furnaces fell—to 908 in 1884, 790 in 1890, and 514 in 1907.[2] It is interesting to compare the decrease in the number of working furnaces with the output:[3]

Year.	Furnaces working.	Production of pig-iron in tons.
1865	629	6,365,000
1880	567	7,749,000
1885	434	7,415,000
1890	414	7,904,000
1900	403	8,959,000
1905	345	9,608,000
1913	338	10,260,000
1923	203	7,441,000

[1] See 'Times Financial and Commercial Supplement,' Dec. 20, 1907, and 'Paper Maker,' Jan. 1, 1909, p. 67.

[2] A. Meade, 'The Coal and Iron Industries of the United Kingdom,' London 1882, pp. 829 ff.; 'Iron and Coal Trade Review,' Jan. 8, 1886, p. 51, Jan. 2, 1891, p. 7; 'Mines and Quarries,' 1908, p. 205.

[3] 'Mines and Quarries,' 1907, p. 210; and 'Statesman's Year Book,' 1925, p. 56.

It is obvious that this development has not been so regular as it would have been but for the intervention of the war. It is none the less noteworthy that in 1923 an output of pig-iron, nearly similar to that of 1880, was accounted for by about one-third of the number of furnaces in blast.

The special cause of the tendency to concentration, in this instance, lay in the changes in the construction of furnaces. They have been so often described in the case both of Great Britain and of other countries that it is unnecessary to re-state them now, and, in any case, we are interested in the fact of concentration only. Many firms or concerns owned more than one furnace, and therefore the figures given above are no exact measure of the decrease in competition with which we are concerned.

But statistics of particular districts show that a considerable concentration of interests accompanied the concentration of ironworks. I will quote some of them. In the most productive pig-iron district of Yorkshire, eighteen firms owning 92 furnaces, produced 1,747,000 tons in 1885; in 1907 there were only thirteen concerns, producing 2,537,000 tons. Of the 92 furnaces in 1885 Bolckow, Vaughan & Co. owned 21; in 1907 they owned 25 out of a total of 77. During the same years the number of furnaces in Durham fell from 60 to 39, while output increased from 730,000 tons to 1,144,000 tons. Of the 39 furnaces Bell Brothers, in Middlesbrough, owned 12, the remaining 27 were divided between seven other firms, and since 1885 the total number of firms has decreased by five.[1]

Since 1914 the building up of concerns in the English iron industry has made great progress. Finishing manufactures—including shipbuilding and the tin-plate industry—have developed into vertical combines which have naturally been preceded by a corresponding horizontal combination of coal-pits and furnaces. The Workington Iron and Steel Co. is an example, founded in 1908 by a fusion

[1] 'Mines and Minerals,' London 1886 (C. 4771), pp. 152 ff.; 'Mines and Quarries,' London 1908, pp. 206 ff.

of various undertakings, the most important of which were the Cumberland Works of Cammel, Laird & Co., and comprising 22 out of the 36 Cumberland furnaces. In 1918 it passed over to the United States Steel Co., which absorbed a large number of small firms and a few larger ones like Steel, Peech & Tozer. Exact figures are wanting, but we may take it from the 'Economist' that in 1923-4 (when the crisis was less pronounced than at present) they yielded £3·6 million net profit as against £2 million in 1913-4, though the steel production of England has only slightly increased—a striking demonstration of the movement towards concentration.[1]

The cases so far quoted illustrate movements towards concentration arising from a permanent enlargement in the normal size of an undertaking. Where this increases more rapidly than the total output requires it leads to an absolute decrease in the number of works, and in most cases also of undertakings. It must be left to a history of industrial concentration to describe the specific technical improvements which led in each case to an increase in producing power, the economic circumstances which made it profitable to adopt them, and attendant features of the movement :—the extinction of inefficients through bankruptcy, their purchase and closing down, amalgamations, and so on.[2] We are only concerned with the contrast between the development of concentration in recent times and the present day, and the absolute increase in the number of works in the days when industry on a large scale commenced at the beginning of the nineteenth century—a

[1] "The Plight in the Iron and Steel Industry," 'Economist,' Jan. 9, 1926, p. 49.

[2] The 'Statist,' May 6, 1922, gives an interesting example of amalgamations after 1918. During the subsequent boom in the cotton industry the shortness of stock made it necessary to provide larger and more numerous stores. Their purchase by good firms was a departure from the old practice of floating a new company with capital subscribed by the public. But reaction from this tendency to combine soon followed with the trade collapse of 1920-21.

contrast which existing statistics unfortunately only make possible in a few though not the least important branches of industry.

Nowadays combination among works which produce the same commodity gives rise to a further concentration—the so-called " horizontal " combination. Technical changes in the process of manufacture or in productive power are in such cases either absent or at least not decisive. Combination more often results from purely economic causes. Separate undertakings hitherto working in competition combine to obtain higher profits by uniting all existing works in one concern. Where this kind of combination arises there is very probably a simultaneous concentration of plant; and it is also conceivable that technical improvements are made in the works of the united undertaking. But while concentrations like that in pig-iron could be regarded as exclusively due to increased productive power, horizontal combinations are the result of systematic efforts on the part of manufacturers to organise more completely the production and sales of all works concerned, concentration of plant being only one means among many.

Mr. Macrosty has collected a great deal of information concerning horizontal combinations and the resultant concentration of undertakings in British industry before the war in his exhaustive book. He shows how the organisation of many works into a single combine has developed in the most diverse spheres of industry, in fact practically everywhere. That leaders of industry well understand the advantages of such combination and make it the centre of their efforts in organisation may be seen, apart from Mr. Macrosty's instances, from a remarkable speech made in 1908 by Sir Christopher (now Lord) Furness. As director of one of the largest firms in England for the manufacture of ships' engines, Richardsons, Westgarth & Co., Limited, he suggested on the 29th of December, 1908, a fusion of that undertaking with various other similar concerns. To him this might well have appeared as a mere repetition of a proposal which had led to the foundation in 1900 of the firm of which he was then a director—a combination of Th. Richardsons Limited, Sir C. Furness, Westgarth & Co., and William Allan & Co., representing a paid-up capital of £790,000 sterling.[1] The new amalgamation was intended to embrace a number of undertakings which had together supplied no less than 1206 ships with engines having 2,150,000 horse-power in 1902-1908.

There remains to be mentioned the form of concentration known as the "vertical" combination. As we have seen, this is much less common in England than in Germany or America. Owing to the absence of the tariff duties, of high freights, and monopolies in raw materials which increase the cost of supplies of raw materials and half-manufactured goods abroad, the necessity of vertical combination is less imperative for the English manufacturer, and in any case in finished articles vertical combination as a means of monopoly is practically unnecessary in England. It is used merely to suppress ordinary middlemen's profits and to increase the profits on the last stage of production by combining different intermediate stages. As a rule therefore it follows a concentration of plant or a horizontal combination. This is especially the case in the high-grade finished goods, in which it only becomes profitable to take over the production of raw material or half-manufactured articles when a very large concern is formed, or many undertakings are amalgamated. In lower grades, however, an ordinary modern firm can usually profit from vertical combination, and we find it, for instance, in recent developments of the English steel trade, as a result of the increasing expansion of separate concerns.

The tendency of English industries to combine in vertical combinations has considerably increased during and since the war. We have already referred to various cases (iron, steel, shipbuilding, paper, and soap), and can add to these in discussing particular monopolist organisations in England

[1] 'Stock Exchange Official Intelligence,' 1908, p. 139.

at the present day. On the other hand, account must be taken of difficulties, already discussed, which are specifically English, and will perhaps only be lessened by a change of trade policy, viz. a transition to high tariffs. The organic importance of this tendency to combination—vertical, horizontal, or both together—was emphasised by Lord Furness in a noteworthy speech to the shareholders of his Company in 1908, as something new. But to-day it is a generally accepted view in England, though it has not spread so far as on the Continent or in America.

It is very significant that a movement parallel to the concentration of great industries is to be found developing on similar lines in other spheres of economic life in England—notably in banking and transport. The horizontal combination of banks, beginning early in the eighties, culminated in the predominance of five great concerns comparable with the German D banks (Disconto, Deutsche, Darmstädter, Dresdner, to which must now be added the Berliner Handelsgesellschaft). The English "Big Five"—Midland, Lloyds, Barclays, National Provincial, and Westminster—have, it is true, in no way sought or attained a monopoly of banking. So also, as already mentioned, the railways early developed a tendency to exclude competition, like railways all the world over. Fitzgerald states [1] that between 1840 and 1870 the number of separate railway companies fell from 1100 to 130. Immediately before the war fourteen large groups dominated railway business, and these again were knit together by alliances and "tacit understandings." The war, with its compulsory unification of railway transport, brought about a change whose influence persisted after the war. To-day the whole British railway system may be said to be in the hands of four companies, but by the Railway Act of 1921 they are prevented from fixing rates in a monopolistic or arbitrary fashion.

The whole movement towards concentration in these cases—as well as that of the Shipping Conferences in sea-

[1] p. 16.

transport—is subject only in part to the influences which we have described and have yet, in the case of the great industries, to analyse. Their development is mentioned here only as supplementary to the general movement towards concentration.

As to the possibilities of combination and its great importance the 'Report on Trusts'[1] says: "Great possibilities of industrial and commercial improvement lie beyond the confines of free competition, and are only to be realised by combination in one or other of its several forms; by informal consultation and co-operation, by formal association, or by actual amalgamation. These may be tabulated as follows:

"Buying (materials, plant, stores, etc.).
- Assured and steady supply of material.
- Unification of buying departments and staffs.
- Bulk instead of detail purchase.
- Greater opportunity for comparison and selection.
- Cheaper credit and better discounts.
- Standardisation of materials.

"Making.
- Standardisation of product.
- Specialisation in product.
- Improvements in plant.
- Use of by-products.
- Equalised distribution of work.
- Quality.

"Selling.
- Transport economics.
- Unification of selling departments and staffs.
- Extension of export trade.
- Collective advertising.
- Lower costs of distribution, fewer middlemen.

"Knowledge.
- Interchange of data and experience.
- Standardisation and interchange of costings.
- Collection and dissemination of trade statistics.
- Promotion of scientific and technical research.

[1] p. 16.

"The above are the possibilities of combination, not the necessary accompaniments or the invariable achievements. It should be stated at once that no association among the many hundred existing in the United Kingdom at the present time, and few of the numerous mammoth amalgamations, have come as yet anywhere near realising them in full."

In spite of this sceptical tone of the official report, its enumeration of the possibilities of combination is of the greatest significance. It shows both the way and the tendency to follow it on the part of English industry. Special circumstances in capacity and situation make development slower than on the Continent or in America, but the progress is durable and admitted. There is here a sharp distinction between the time before and since 1914. The deep depression of trade has made it essential to lower costs of production and to seek for more economical methods of management. But a further special characteristic of the English movement towards amalgamation has yet to be mentioned.

Experience of German or American "vertical" combinations would lead one to expect that such combinations would greatly influence the movement towards concentration in England. But this is not so. As we have seen, the economic urgency of "vertical" combination in the land of free trade, low freights, and no monopolies in raw materials is less, and therefore the "mixed" works do not necessarily force the remaining undertakings to follow their example. In Germany and America the large firm which has grown to be a "mixed" undertaking can usually manufacture the final product at such a much lower cost that only similar combination can save the rest from its competition. This consideration and the fear of not being able to combine later when all raw material is completely monopolised generally leads to the rapid "vertical" combination of more and more firms. As all are not in a position to meet the large capital demands of "vertical" combination, where a distinction between "simple" and "mixed" undertakings arises, it tends ultimately to concentrate production in the hands of the latter. But in England few traces of this connection between "vertical" combination and concentration are as yet to be seen. The "simple" rolling works have only slowly yielded to the greater strength of the "mixed" works. The British shipbuilding and armament firms are still an arena of free competition, though many firms have for a long time formed "vertical" combinations, comprising shipping, coal and iron ore industries. Such are Palmer's Shipbuilding and Iron Co., Armstrong, Whitworth & Co., Vickers, Sons & Maxim, John Brown & Co. It is very possible that in the future there will be in Great Britain in single or combined industries "vertical" combinations which will form a horizontal concentration with large "mixed" works absorbing the whole pure industry and all its product. It is sufficient at present to indicate this tendency provisionally. There will be no change so long as the "pure" industry is favoured by the conditions to which we have already referred. It is not "vertical" combination that causes the concentration of plant and undertakings,[1] but, *vice versa*, concentration of plant or horizontal combination that leads to vertical combination. In other words, vertical combination is one of the economic advantages which may possibly be obtained by these two forms of industrial organisation.[2]

This conclusion is of great moment for its bearing on the importance to the growth of monopoly in England of the movement towards concentration which we have described above. As we have already seen, the significance of concentration in the history of cartels or trusts lies primarily in the fact that a decrease in the number of rival firms

[1] The American wire industry is a clear example of this. Cf. Levy, 'Die Stahlindustrie,' p. 241 and pp. 243-5.

[2] It is typical that the Fine Cotton Spinners' Association, founded in 1898, acquired in 1900 a colliery.

makes it easier to suppress competition. Secondly, the difficulty of founding a new undertaking increases in the exact proportion in which that undertaking—to be an effective competitor—requires a large amount of capital and a wide sphere of activity, and the more certain it must be, as will be explained later, of finding a profitable market for the great increase of commodities which it adds to the total output of the trade. "Vertical" combination has hitherto had but little influence in England (unlike other countries) on the concentration of undertakings concerned in a given branch of production. It can therefore be neglected for the moment in considering the conditions necessary for the creation of monopoly. Concentration of plant and "horizontal" combinations, on the other hand, have proved to be very important antecedents to industrial monopolies in modern England. Both by diminishing the number of competing firms and by adding to the difficulties of new competitors they increase the general possibility of monopoly in an industry. But it by no means follows that they will in every case lead to the rise of a monopolist combination. To enumerate, as Mr. Macrosty does, numerous cases of concentration of works which have nothing in common with monopolist control of the market, in a book on the "Trust Movement" is to ignore the fact that concentration and monopoly are two different things. Waring and Gillow's, to take one of his examples, and one that represents the result of several amalgamations,[1] may be the largest firm of furniture manufacturers in England; but it has in no way a monopoly in furnishing and decorating, and in view of the great number of similar firms in existence no likelihood of forming one. The inclusion of such firms in an enumeration of English trusts merely because they are notably large undertakings is as confusing as the identification formerly so common of all the various kinds of combinations of interest, *e.g.* ordinary English associations, with syndicates and cartels. It would be as reasonable to

[1] Macrosty, 'Trust Movement,' p. 325.

see the advance of the trust movement in every large hotel company or in every large stores.

What is true is that every concentration of producers has a natural tendency to assist monopoly. But monopoly or trust or cartel implies the preliminary exclusion of competition as such, either completely or to a considerable degree. Even highly concentrated undertakings need immunity no less from foreign than from domestic competition if they are to create a monopoly. In the pig-iron industry, for instance, works and businesses have been concentrated on all sides, but up to the present foreign competition has prevented any monopolist combination from gaining a footing. Similarly the effectiveness or otherwise of domestic competition depends on the degree of concentration attained in each particular instance. Two cases must be distinguished. Concentration may be adopted as a means to permanently greater production in each factory or undertaking, which may finally result in the acquisition of a monopoly or something very like it by the undertaking which proves to have the greatest efficiency. Lord Furness's plan of 1908 would not only have created an undertaking of greater efficiency than the aggregate of all the individual undertakings it amalgamated. It would also have created an undertaking exercising a monopolist control over the production of ships' machinery on the North East coast. The horizontal combinations made by each individual undertaking in its own particular branch of trade would have ended in a final " efficiency " combination, formed to reduce the cost of production, but at the same time a " monopolistic combination." In this case the movement towards concentration would have run its full natural course before ultimately culminating in monopoly. But long before this stage is reached manufacturers may seize upon concentration as a possible means of creating monopoly. Concentration of works or horizontal combination reduces them to a relatively small number, say twenty or thirty, and in given circumstances a monopolist organisation is then possible without any increase of economic efficiency either immediate or prospective worth mentioning. In the first case, concentration aiming at increased efficiency leads directly to the monopoly of the survivor; in the second, it merely results in the possible systematic suppression of home competition by reducing the number of competitors and facilitating their combination. In either case the movement towards concentration—if concentration of works and horizontal combinations aiming solely at increased efficiency are included under that term—must have reached an advanced stage.

If on the other hand the number of existing works or undertakings is very high, as in the paper trade, even a good deal of concentration would find it difficult to suppress competition. And further, if concentration would reduce the actual number of factories but, given increased prices and profits, the rise of new factories is relatively easy as in tin-plating, the individual manufacturers must see from the beginning that the absolute suppression of mutual competition in order to reach high monopoly prices may, under certain circumstances, involve greater risks to their future than its continuance.

Concentration, therefore, only leads to the rise of cartels and trusts under given conditions, one very important factor in which is foreign competition. Where freedom from such competition coincides with certain possibilities of development by industrial concentration and horizontal combination, the ground is prepared for monopoly.

We must now examine the actual history of monopolist combinations in the light of these two main conditions, freedom from foreign competition and completeness of domestic combination.

(*b*) THE CHIEF EXISTING ENGLISH CARTELS AND TRUSTS

If we review English industries from the standpoint of their relative freedom from foreign competition, we shall find that they fall into three groups. The first group consists of industries sheltered only *conditionally* from the foreigner;—industries helped by no special advantage in production over other countries, but enjoying the natural protection of freights; industries only subject to foreign competition on rare occasions when protected syndicates are compelled to dump; or, finally, industries in which foreign competition only takes the form of imports of inferior qualities or of substitutes. Wherever such circumstances or a combination of them arise, competition between manufacturers usually keeps prices under the limit which would pay the foreign exporter, though it would allow a monopolist organisation to take advantage in its prices of the freedom from foreign competition existing within that limit. The second group comprises industries holding an unconditional monopoly against the foreigner, and in which a monopolist organisation in fixing its prices and regulating its production, will have regard to consumption, to the rise of other home competition, to the possibility of re-imports, and so on, but not to foreign competition; in other words, industries in which either imports are impossible for technical reasons, or in which decisive advantages in the quality of goods, or extremely low cost of production, secure a monopolist position to the home trade. The third group consists of those in which security from foreign competition is assured, as it always may be, by international agreements.

We will commence with the consideration of various monopolist combinations in the first group, starting with one closely connected with the production of raw materials.

THE PORTLAND CEMENT TRUST

All the evidence we have so far considered shows how comparatively rare it is nowadays for an English industrial monopoly to be protected from foreign competition by freights. But there are certain trades in which the relatively high cost of transit, where distances are considerable, favours the English manufacturer. The case of minerals would naturally suggest itself, but we have already seen that these are not very numerous in England. There can be no question of protection in the case of iron, for the superior quality of Spanish and Swedish iron more than covers the extra costs of freights, while cheapness of production alone is enough to secure coal and salt from foreign competition in the home market. But in the cement industry, which is entirely dependent on the supply of clay and chalk, freights are of some importance.

The industry is concentrated in the Thames and Medway valley, near to the chalk pits of Kent and Essex, which produce three-quarters of the entire output.[1] It is therefore favourably situated with regard to supplies of raw material, and owing to the two rivers, the proximity of the sea and of a great consuming centre (London) can find an outlet for a considerable part of its produce at a very small expenditure on freights. The coincidence of all these factors gives cement makers better facilities for production and sale in this district than perhaps anywhere else in the world.[2] The English makers, with their usual conservatism, for many years neglected possible improvements in quality, and accordingly suffered increasingly severely in some foreign markets from German competition. After 1900, however, English processes began to improve, and at the present time experts consider that English cement is fully comparable to that of other countries, both in quality and in cheapness of production.[3]

When there is a good demand for cement in the world's markets, and consequently no dumping from Germany, Belgium, or France, the Thames-Medway district is effectively sheltered from foreign competition by its low rates of freight. For a long time strong competition between the rival manufacturers prevented this advantage being fully utilised. But in the late nineties there appeared to be

[1] 'Mines and Quarries,' pp. 157, 158.

[2] F. H. Lewis, 'The Cement Industry,' New York 1900, p. 201.

[3] Lewis, p. 200; and Fitzgerald, p. 105.

considerable likelihood that this competition would be suppressed. Thirty-one firms, one of which had a productive power of 160,000 tons or 10 per cent. of the entire output of 1899, controlled 89 per cent. of the total production,[1] the concentration being no doubt due to the bad market conditions of the nineties. Improvements in machinery since 1872 and the almost complete displacement of manual labour made considerable capital necessary for the foundations of new concerns and thereby impeded their rise; [2] and finally the universal boom in the cement trade since 1897 removed any fear of dumping.[3] The prospects of the Portland cement trust, founded in July 1900 under the name of the Associated Portland Cement Manufacturers, were accordingly exceptionally bright, although the frequency of chalk and clay deposits put any scheme of forming a monopoly of supplies out of the question. The trust included 27 of the above 31 firms, and had cartel agreements with the remaining four.[4]

At its foundation, however, the trust controlled only 45 per cent. of the total English output. Exposed as it was to severe competition it soon strove to include further concerns, and in 1912 it united 33 additional firms under the title British Portland Cement Association, in which the original Trust had a 70 per cent. share. It then controlled 75 per cent. of the production. In 1918 it developed further into the Cement Makers' Federation, uniting the Cement Makers' Alliance, the Ireland Cement Manufacturers' Alliance and the Tyne and Tees Alliance. To this new combination naturally belonged the trust, so that the Federation in which the trust had no overwhelming majority of votes controlled about 90 per cent. of the whole British Portland cement output. Foreign competition

[1] Macrosty, 'Trust Movement,' pp. 108-9.

[2] D. B. Butler, 'Portland Cement,' London 1905, pp. 4 and 9.

[3] In America the cost of starting a cement works was estimated at a million to a million and a half dollars. See 'Mineral Resources,' Washington 1906, p. 923.

[4] Macrosty, p. 108.

always imposes limits upon the activity of combination in this industry. The import of cheap "natural cement" exercises a moderating influence. Unknown till 1895, it rapidly increased after 1897 and latterly amounted to between £150,000 and £300,000 annually. It was in no way caused by the trust's operations on prices; it commenced at the moment when cement commanded a price it had not reached since 1892. England both exports and imports an increasing amount of cement, the explanation being that the imports are of an inferior quality. Natural cement can, in point of quality, in no way compete with Portland cement, but owing to the high price of the latter it is used for cheap buildings as a substitute. Statistics of the value per cwt. of the exports compared with that of the imports also show how much less valuable the imported cement was and still is. Those who required Portland cement at any price found no substitute in natural cement, cheap though it was, and the trust was therefore in so far not damaged by it. The cement industry shows how diminished competition from abroad since 1914 has favoured combination. It is true that for some years there has been a more lively importation, in 1920, 38,438 tons, in 1921, 105,711, in 1922, 133,106, reaching the level of pre-war imports. At the same time the export fell off from 617,000 tons in 1920 to 400,000 in 1923, owing to the gradual increase of the old Continental export area.[1] The openly avowed aim of the Federation was, according to the 'Statist,' "the fixation of minimum prices for cement sold by members of the trust in the country and the regulation of conditions of sale." A Committee for fixing export prices was set up for a time. In view of the very strong position of the trust in the country it is not surprising that some of its most influential members were anxious to avoid the reproach of monopoly. Thus the Chairman of the Associated Portland Cement Makers, at the annual meeting of March 29, 1926, said, "We have to do with a business in which there can be

[1] 'Survey of Oversea Markets,' 1925, pp. 40, 142, 216, etc.

no monopoly. We must reckon with increasing competition, home and foreign, especially where there is a depreciated currency." As in many cases of English monopolistic organisation, the increasing possibility of foreign importation sets a limit to price policy. But that the policy is by no means impracticable is plain from the efforts of the Federation, and is clearly stated in the 'Report on Trusts' without particular names being mentioned.[1]

THE STEEL WORKS ASSOCIATIONS

We have already seen that, looked at as a whole, the English iron and steel industry is much more subject to competition than to monopoly. Despite the existence of numerous combines in nearly all its branches, of far-reaching associations, horizontal and vertical, and of enlargement of technical units, it cannot be compared with the American Steel Trust or the great German iron cartels of the last decade. The uneconomic character of the English iron market is perhaps a symptom of the lack of unity in the organisation of the industry. England is still as much an importer as an exporter of iron. In 1925 she exported 3·7 million tons of iron and steel and their products, and imported 2·7 million tons, a greater import than in 1913, while the export diminished by about 1 million. The material exported is as a rule different from that imported. The 'Economist'[2] says: "During 1925 most of the English iron and steel prices have exceeded those of Continental manufacturers. In many cases the difference has been about £2 per ton, and British firms have found it profitable to buy partly manufactured goods instead of making them in their own works. The tinplate works of Wales and the great factories have been able to improve their competitive position in world markets by buying Continental bars and ship plates at dumping prices."[3]

In these circumstances it is clear that the activity of

[1] p. 36. See also Fitzgerald, p. 105. [2] Feb. 13, 1926, p. 52.
[3] *Ibid.* p. 54.

monopolies in the English iron industry is limited, and so far as the standardising of prices is concerned narrowly limited, though we have adduced particular instances in illustration of its earlier development and of its position and policy of price-regulation before the war.

Nevertheless, in the last ten years combinations have been formed in the English iron and steel industry which in their own (sometimes local) spheres have established a close monopoly, and have exercised all the functions of a monopoly. Such a combine is the National Light Castings Association in the iron foundry business which supplies gutter pipes, rain pipes, iron rails, stoves and other materials used in the building trade. Founded in 1911 the combine openly declared its aim to be the prevention of undercutting prices. It enjoyed a certain protection from foreign competition as the advantage in freights to English manufacturers is considerable. It began at once to aim at a partitioning of output and a fixing of the quota of production of individual members. Those who wish to dispose of more than their quota pay a sum to the pool, out of which other members who have not produced their full quota receive a supplementary payment. Minimum prices were laid down for retail sales. Certain discounts were given to those who bought only from members of the combine, which forbids its members to sell direct to consumers. Within a year of its formation the combine included 95 per cent. of all branches of the industry. A similar and equally strong combine is the Cast Iron Pipe Association, which, according to an official report of 1924, includes practically all the producers in this trade.[1] In the finishing industries of the iron industry, such as the Bolt and Nut Associations and the Cut Nails Association, similar combines are to be found.

One of the most important of the English steel works combines is the Steel Rails Cartel. As this sprang out of an international agreement we defer our account of it. On

[1] 'Statist;' July 7, 1923; 'Report on Trusts,' p. 39.

the whole the iron and steel industry remains above all in an area in which monopolist organisation has established itself only slowly, and in particular cases after a long period of moderate combination in some branches and with occasional breakdowns. The heavy depression of the last few years, which still endures in spite of the hopes formed at the beginning of 1926, is not conducive to the development of monopoly in the English iron and steel industry. The manufacturers come together as soon as possible when special circumstances make a rise of prices feasible, but not when overproduction and difficulty of marketing their output at home and abroad are prevalent.[1]

THE INDUSTRIAL SPIRIT CARTEL AND THE WHISKY TRUST

Here again the impetus necessary to create a cartel was given by the decline of foreign competition after 1903. In 1902-3 not less than 1,212,000 proof gallons of methylated spirit were imported into England: in the following years, mainly owing to changes in production and markets in Germany, imports fell to 334,000 gallons in 1904 and to only 4300 gallons in 1907-8. At the same time the home production rose from 5,388,000 gallons in 1903-4 to 6,455,000 gallons in 1907-8.[2] Increasing immunity from foreign competition, due to the constantly rising price of foreign spirit, soon led to a combination of the few competing firms. For many years concentration had been at work. The Distillers' Company, for instance, which was mainly concerned with whisky distilling, was due to a fusion of seven Scotch firms in Edinburgh as far back as 1877. And it was now, therefore, only necessary to bring eight large distilleries into line to control the entire manufacture of industrial spirit in the United Kingdom.

In November 1907 seven of the eight existing firms founded the Industrial Spirit Supply Company,[3] with a

[1] See Fitzgerald, pp. 41-53, for further details.

[2] 'Manchester Guardian,' March 5, 1909, p. 12.

[3] These facts were taken from the severely technical account in a trade paper, Ridley's 'Wine and Spirit Trade Circular,' Nov. 8, 1907, pp. 828-9.

capital of no more than £1000, the shares being taken up by the constituent firms. The eighth remaining firm entered into an agreement with the new company. The loose compacts already existing were replaced by the definite regulation of output and sales. The company managed the entire industrial spirit sales of all the firms in the cartel, as no spirit could be bought for methylation except through it. It regulated the production of each firm according to an allotted quota proportional to the number of shares it held, and fixed the common prices. It further distributed orders among the individual firms after duly considering freights, a practice which was expected when the cartel was founded to produce considerable economy. A difficulty arose from the fact that a number of distilleries themselves manufactured methylated spirits, while others sold their spirit to finishers through agents who required to be paid; but the resulting advantage of the "mixed" distillery was met by a provision in the articles of association that it must pay to the funds of the cartel an amount per gallon produced equal to the agent's commission.

The founding of this cartel—described in the 'Report on Trusts' as the Industrial Spirit Supply Association—immediately resulted [1] in agreements among buyers as to a minimum price for methylated spirit. The circle was thus completed, and definite monopolist organisation from raw material to finished product achieved. After the approved fashion the cartel at its foundation foreshadowed steady, moderate prices; but within two years its success gave rise to loud complaints of its operations. It was accused of not lowering its tariff as it should have, in view of the provisions of the Finance Act of 1906, which reduced the duty on industrial spirit, and of having, on the contrary, raised the price of methylated spirit from 1s. 8d. to 2s. 2d. since the passing of the Act. The London distilleries put the blame on the high price of raw materials, especially maize,

[1] 'Manchester Guardian,' *cit. supra.*

but the 'Manchester Guardian's' correspondent estimated that the manufacturers, in spite of that, succeeded in obtaining "a highly satisfactory difference between price and cost," due solely to the strong position of the cartel.

A monopolist organisation which has a powerful and active influence is the whisky trade, which is closely related to that of industrial spirit. Whisky enjoys in British home and overseas markets, as well as in foreign markets, a position of monopoly highly favourable to large firms owing to special brands and its use as a national drink.

The concentration of whisky distilling has been slow but steady. The "Distillers' Company Ld.," of which we heard in connection with the Industrial Spirit Syndicate, and which has now matured into a trust, started as early as 1877 with the amalgamation of six Scotch firms. In 1902 and 1903 the company bought up three more distilleries, and acquired half the shares in the most important Irish distillery.[1] In 1907 it purchased the Vauxhall Distillery Company, representing a share capital of £376,000, thereby increasing its possessions to seventeen distilleries in England, Scotland, and Ireland.[2] In Scotland, the chief distillery district, it had only two competitors, with whom it before long came to an understanding as to common prices.[3] As a result the Scotch combine, as it was called for short, proceeded in the autumn of 1907 to raise the price, an action which called forth some interesting remarks from the correspondent of the trade paper.[4] "The advance of twopence per gallon in the price of new whisky reported last month was sensational enough in its way, but not content with that it is now rumoured that the distillers meditate a further advance of a penny a gallon. One thing certain is that the distillers can advance prices by another penny just as easily as they advanced it by two-

[1] Macrosty, 'Trust Movement,' p. 241.

[2] 'Times Commercial and Financial Supplement,' Oct. 4, 1907, p. 4.

[3] 'Kartellrundschau,' 1907, p. 670.

[4] Ridley's 'Wine and Spirit Circular,' p. 818.

pence last month. Users will have to pay it, and get it back from their customers as best they may."

In contrast to many other monopolist organisations which were weakened by the crisis the whisky trade showed a great development in 1925, when the Distillers' Company combined the three great distilleries of England and Scotland—Dewar, Buchanan, and Walker. At the same time two powerful firms of gin distillers—Boord & Co. and Sir Robert Burnett & Co.—were taken over with a number of works engaged in producing industrial spirit. The "policy of expansion," as it was called, resulted in an augmentation of capital and reserves of the Distillers' Co. from £6·8 millions in May 1925 to £13·6 in May 1926. The importance of this step may be measured by the fact that the capital of the outside large firms did not exceed £800,000. The device of reckoning the shares acquired by the combine as investments concealed the magnitude of the effective capital of the single undertaking, and made it appear less than it really was. But the Distillers' Co. was able to strengthen its position in the trust, for a trust it is in fact. In 1926 the 'Economist' states that the policy of expansion had worked unexpectedly well. The chairman of the Company, Mr. William H. Ross, in his report for 1925-6 says that the Company is in a very strong position to deal with all contingencies of economic necessity. Time will show what influence upon prices this now powerful organisation will exercise.[1]

THE WALL-PAPER TRUST

Although, as we have seen, the paper trade had never offered a hopeful field for monopolist combination on account both of foreign competition[2] and of the still considerable number of competing works, in 1900 a fusion of

[1] For further details, see the balance sheets, etc., 'Economist,' July 17, 1926, pp. 127-8; Nov. 20, pp. 868-9; July 10, 1926, p. 4.

[2] A warning note is uttered in the 'Survey of Overseas Markets,' 1925, p. 159, as to the increasing competition of Finland with England in the paper market.

31 wall-paper factories, under the name of the Wall-paper Manufacturers Ltd., was effected. According to Mr. Macrosty,[1] the trust had working agreements with three other firms, and controlled about 98 per cent. of the production of wall-paper and other decorative materials. In 1908 only seven manufacturers, according to Mr. Philips' statement, appeared as outsiders to the trust. Nine other firms were bought up by the trust in 1915.[2] This branch of the highly finished paper industry was therefore distinguished from the rest of the trade by close concentration of undertakings, and consequently suited for the formation of a trust. It was also the least threatened with foreign competition. Experts have told me that most English wall-paper makers, owing to the high quality of their goods and the peculiar dimensions current in England, have nothing to fear from the foreigner, except that the cheaper and inferior foreign papers might take the place of the English if the price of the latter became very high. This also explains the fact that while England imports and exports wall-papers in about the same quantity, the value of the exports is considerably greater.

The powerful position of the Wall Paper Trust has not diminished since the war. The memorandum by Mr. Percy Ashley appended to the ' Report on Trusts ' refers specially to this and the Portland Cement Association as examples of industries which by powerful combination have established a quasi-monopoly. " The output of wall-papers not controlled by the combination is insignificant." [3] In 1921, according to the ' Statist,' it was " strong enough to check a sharp fall of prices," [4] although it ended the year with a loss. But the following years show an increase of net profit above the pre-war average. This cartel is undoubtedly one of the most successful in English industry.

[1] ' Trust Movement,' pp. 309-11.

[2] Cf. ' Paper Trade Directory,' London 1908, pp. 127-129.

[3] ' Report,' pp. 39-40.

[4] October 27, 1923.

THE ELECTRICAL INDUSTRY AND CABLE CARTEL

On the whole the electrical industry shows far fewer signs of trust or cartel building in England than in Germany or America. It belongs, generally speaking, to the sphere of free competition. It is especially subject to foreign competition. Imports of electrical fittings and apparatus (excluding machines and wires) have risen from £242,000 in 1897 to over £1,000,000 in the years 1905, 1906, and 1907. In 1913 it rose to £1·6 millions, in 1924 to £3·3 millions, but it must be noted that prices in the latter year were so much higher than before the war that the quantity imported was probably not materially increased.[1] On the other side are high figures for export (£10 millions in 1924), but in this case also we are concerned with one of those English industries which both imports and exports, the articles concerned not being identical in quality. In many branches, and sometimes the most important, foreign products are often superior to those of the English electrical industry. The predominance of foreign countries is due firstly to the greater reputed utility of German, Belgian, or American goods (a fact often neglected or underestimated by complaining British producers, but supported by adequate expert testimony),[2] and secondly, to the economic advantages of foreign countries which enable them to produce and place on the market various electrical goods at a cheaper rate than the English makers.[3] The causes of the backward state of the electrical industry in England are various. Some find the main cause that checked its development in the over-favourable purchase terms granted by the legislation of the early eighties to local authorities.[4]

[1] 'Statesman's Year Book,' 1925, p. 61.

[2] Cf. evidence in Chapman, 'Work and Wages,' p. 136.

[3] 'Report of the Tariff Commission,' vol. iv.; 'The Engineering Industries,' London 1909, under 'Electrical Industry, Foreign Competition'; and W. Koch, 'Die Konzentrationsbewegung in der deutschen Electroindustrie,' München 1907, p. 19.

[4] For details cf. A. G. White, 'The Electrical Industry,' London 1904, pp. 19 and 23 ff.

Others attribute it chiefly to the want of technical education.[1] Prof. Chapman recalls [2] the fact that production in England is not connected with so important a demand as in America and Germany, and that therefore less use has necessarily been made of division of labour and of technical improvements. A later important opinion will be found in the ' Report on Commercial and Industrial Policy after the War,' which bases its observations upon the authoritative judgments of all branches of industries. It states [3] that the total electro-technic output of all kinds amounted before the war to £22½ millions in England, compared with an estimate of £60 millions for Germany. And yet the value of such imports in England was five times larger than in Germany. The backward state of the English electric industry is said in this Report to be due to defective legislation, to the traditional predominance of steamships in England (while the young German industry has adopted new types), to German protective tariffs, etc. But it signalises also the policy of amalgamation and combination adopted by the German electric industry as conducing to these consequences: "In opposition to this policy the tendency to concentration has made little advance in England: numberless small firms exist which compete with one another, and the result is high costs of production and general economic waste."

These general characteristics accentuate the exceptional position of the one branch of the English electrical industry which exhibits at the present time the conditions necessary for creating a monopolist organisation. The cable industry —under which term we include, for simplicity's sake, the production of current conductors, power cables, telephone and telegraph cables, electric wires, and so on—is, unlike all other branches of electricity, still far superior to

[1] Chapman, p. 137. ' Engineering Industries Report,' §§ 423-4.

[2] ' Work and Wages,' p. 136; and ' Report,' *ut supra*, 477-8; 65, 475, 949, etc.

[3] pp. 14, 41.

its foreign rivals.[1] The 'Report on Commercial and Industrial Policy after the War' stresses the fact that the superior quality of electrical machines and apparatus in Great Britain is in a "far from favourable position, save for the notable exception of the cable industry." [2] It has also a considerable export trade.

For this foreign market England has chiefly to thank its colonies. They require a very superior quality. And other countries, whose production is largely restricted to cheaper and comparatively inferior wire, have not been able to satisfy the demand. Moreover, in England itself consulting engineers prefer English wires,[3] which have, therefore, in practice the advantage of a monopoly in the English market.

The exploitation of this advantage by a monopolist organisation is further simplified by the fact that in this case, again in contradistinction to the general condition of the electric industry, only a few large firms have to be considered. Their size, originally considerable, has much increased in the last twenty-five years. The well-known Callender's Cable and Construction Company had before the war a turnover of £1,000,000, as compared with only £100,000 to £150,000 about 1900. "A small firm," their representative recently stated, "cannot do electric cable work. To begin you must have £500,000." [4] Moreover, cables can be standardised, which further adds to the ease of a union of competitors.

The Cable Makers' Association started as early as 1898. It was made clear that further competition would lead to depreciation of quality, and this was to be avoided by fixing a minimum price. The 'Report on Trusts' states that the Cable Makers' Association, one of the powerful

[1] Koch, p. 19. [2] 'Report,' p. 14.

[3] So I was informed by the director of a large firm; cf. also 'Tariff Commission Report on Engineering Industries,' § 486 and the 'Electrical Contractor,' Oct. 1908, p. 102.

[4] 'Report,' §§ 484-5.

cartels which have survived the war and its after-time, is avowedly organised for, *inter alia*, the control of prices, while the British Electrical and Allied Manufacturers' Association is believed to exercise considerable influence in this respect through its associates and subsidiaries. The price policy of the Cable Association before the war was not uncontested. It is clear that imports were then coming in though of inferior quality and merely substitutes. In 1905 the original standardisation had to be abandoned, and members were allowed to manufacture inferior qualities, to be quoted for sale as Non-Association Cables.[1]

SALT TRUST AND SALT SYNDICATE

Of the chief mineral raw products of England, three only —coal, stone and earth, and salt—occupy monopolist positions in the home market through low cost of production and favourable market conditions. We have seen the reasons which prevent an organised attempt to profit by this position in the case of the first two, but English salt works have been for years ruled by monopolist associations. As salt, unlike coal, was practically concentrated in one county, Cheshire, it was relatively easy to form understandings, and this culminated in 1888 in the formation of the Salt Union, a trust of sixty-four firms embracing about 90 per cent. of the production. The number of firms included in the trust was comparatively large, but it must be remembered that they were by no means all of equal weight, so that the number of really important competitors joining the combine was far smaller than these figures would at first suggest. The prospectus of the Union, which enumerates[2] among the property of the undertaking such things as steamers, boats, locomotives, railway lines and trucks, quays, and landing-stages, shows how far separate firms had developed industrial combination in the matter of transit. The immediate result of the formation of the

[1] Cf. 'Electrical Review,' 1905, p. 1050; 'Report on Trusts,' p. 39.

[2] Macrosty, 'Trust Movement,' p. 182.

Salt Union was an enormous rise in the price of salt. If we compare the prices shown by the value of the exports we find they are as follows :[1]

	Export Price per ton. s.		Export Price per ton. s.
1878-1887 -	12·65	1890 - -	17·98
1888 - -	10·81	1891 - -	17·77
1889 - -	16·15		

Allowance must be made for the great increase during these years in the price of coal, which represents 80 per cent. of the cost of production. But while the pit price of coal in Cheshire only rose from 6s. in 1881 to 8s. 6d. in 1890, the works price of salt rose in the same period from 6s. 1d. to 10s. 3d.[2] The combine could not, it is true, permanently maintain the high prices, and in the nineties they fell again considerably. But up till now they have not again reached the low level of the eighties, though the export price sank temporarily to only just above 13s. in 1898.

Higher prices and annually improving profits, however, led to an increased number of outsiders. When the Union was formed the Directors anticipated an output of 2,000,000 tons, the total production being then (1887) 2,206,000 tons.[3] In 1907 the total output of the United Kingdom was 1,984,656 tons, to which the Salt Union contributed only 909,000![4] But as a very considerable portion of the country's output of salt was still concentrated in the Union, no insuperable difficulties existed to agreements between them and the outsiders. Such agreements began at the end of the nineties, and became more definite after 1900, when the Union and the outsiders actually agreed upon a division of production between them.[5] In 1905, however,

[1] 'Statistical Abstract,' 1891, pp. 140-1.

[2] 'Wholesale and Retail Prices,' London 1903, pp. 3, 189.

[3] Macrosty, p. 182.

[4] 'Mines and Quarries,' p. 235, and 'Statist.'

[5] Macrosty, pp. 185-6.

these still fairly loose compacts came to an end, and an immediate fall in price followed, export prices sinking from 16·36s. in 1904 to 14·22s. in 1906. But the prophecy of the Union chairman in 1905 that "outside makers would see that it would be more profitable to work half or two-thirds of their pans at a profit than work the whole at a loss," was soon fulfilled. In the autumn of 1906 both interests combined to form the North-Western Salt Company, a syndicate which now regulates the sales both of the Union and the outside makers. According to the statement of its first chairman, Mr. G. H. Cox, at the annual meeting of the Salt Union on March 27, 1907,[1] all the salt-makers and wholesale dealers, with a few exceptions, joined the undertaking. As in the case of Spirit Supply Company the share capital is small (£10,000 in £1 shares). Each member has an allotted quota of production, a "basis of tonnage," and the actual output of each firm is dependent on the total output fixed, a system which vividly recalls the Newcastle Vend. Each firm is represented by one director in the syndicate, the Salt Union on account of its importance having two.

The effect of the syndicate was soon seen. As early as the second half of Sept. 1906 a trade paper announced[2] that "a meeting of the [N. Western Salt] Company was held at which the prices of salt were reviewed, and wherever the absence of contracts made it impossible they were increased by small amounts ranging from 3d. to 6d. per ton." Export prices rose from 14·22s. in 1906 to 15·52s. in 1907, an increase partly justified by the higher prices of coal, but never approached before the days of the syndicate; and the profits of the Salt Union increased from £87,000 in 1906 to £127,075 in 1907, the output of salt being practically the same. This was the largest net profit since 1896.[3] It is undoubtedly the case that monopolist organisations

[1] Information given by Sir A. Mond.

[2] 'Oil and Colourman's Journal,' Sept. 15, 1906, p. 767; Sept. 22, 1906, p. 855.

[3] Cf. 'Statist.'

in the English salt industry have sensibly affected home prices. When the syndicate arose in 1907 it was stated at the general meeting of the Salt Union on March 27 that "a thoroughly sound and practical working scheme for regulating the tonnages and prices of the salt trade as a whole had been found." In 1909 the Union reported [1] that "the North-Western Company which regulated prices had worked effectively." It had "carefully considered the circumstances attending the trade at home and abroad, and had from time to time arranged prices accordingly, so that they might rest assured that no markets had been lost by an attempt to exact *too* high prices. On the contrary, especially low ones had been agreed to in several instances, where there was a prospect of opening out fresh channels of trade or retaining old ones in the face of competition." The report clearly shows how absolute the power of the syndicate over prices is, and recognises its expression in the different treatment of different markets according to the interests of the company. That English salt-makers dumped even before this date can certainly be proved; and at times complaints against them were as rife on the other side of the Atlantic as among English manufacturers at the dumping of American trusts.[2]

The Salt Trust and Salt Syndicate are among the combines which have effectively survived the war. The report for 1925 shows a net profit of £396,000 against £227,000 in 1913. The chairman of the Salt Union stated at the general meeting of March 23, 1926, that it was all the more agreeable to show a satisfactory result at a time when most great industries were in a sorry plight. A dividend of 12½ per cent. was declared. But the Salt Trust has plenty to do to meet the production and handling of output in view of the heavy over-production. The chairman observed that "the active firms in the salt trade must say to themselves that there is no room for them so long as the old-

[1] 'Chemical Trades' Journal,' March 27, 1909, p. 314.

[2] 'Industrial Commission,' 1902, vol. xiii. p. 260.

established works can only produce profitably to half their capacity." This shows clearly that the trust is ready to wreck new outsiders if possible. But in view of the present over-production it seems hardly likely that new outsiders of importance will enter the business. On the other hand the import of salt is small. The 'Salt Union Report' for 1925 gives the imports for that year as about 64,000 tons, while the English output was over 2,000,000 tons (figures for 1923 from 'Statesman's Year Book,' 1926, p. 50). England is still, as before, a great exporter of salt, especially to the Far East. The trust has, as heretofore, the possibility of an effective influence on prices.[1]

THE FINE COTTON SPINNERS' AND DOUBLERS' TRUST

The English textile industry is, so far as the greater part of its products is concerned, very firmly entrenched against foreign competition. Certain branches like silk weaving may be exceptions, in certain cheaper qualities competition from abroad may have much increased of late, but such facts cannot in any way overshadow the economic superiority of this very important branch of English manufactures. The Reports of Mr. Chamberlain's Tariff Reform Commission, it is true, bring these discouraging signs so much into the limelight that one is almost induced to regard them as more than mere exceptions. To quote but a few of the Commissioners' opinions from their Report on the woollen industries,[2] we find it, for instance, stated that " Great Britain has lost one branch of trade after another, until there is now practically no foreign market in which the firms who have given evidence before the Commission feel themselves secure.... The export trade of British woollen manufacturers is being step by step reduced to one in special articles and fancy goods, or of raw materials and half-manufactured articles.... The profits of the home trade have diminished by increased competition amongst

[1] 'Economist,' March 27, 1926, pp. 641-2, and March 20, 1926, p. 564.

[2] 'Tariff Commission Report,' vol. ii. London 1905, §§ 1446 and 1448.

themselves and by foreign importations. The home trade, therefore, has tended to become more insecure during recent years. This state of insecurity makes it more and more difficult to get new capital into the trade, to build new mills, or to maintain in the proper state of efficiency those that already exist." The unsophisticated reader of such statements, innocent of the fact that they must be intended to prove that English textiles need protection at any price, might actually believe textiles to be "going." But he will gain quite a different impression if he studies the export statistics of textiles rather than the *ex parte* statements of certain selected firms, which could by no stretch of imagination be regarded as representative of the textile trade. The average annual exports in round millions sterling were : [1]

EXPORTS.

	1893-1902.	1903-1907.	1913.
Cotton yarns and goods, -	67·7	91·2	126·4
Woollen yarns and goods, -	23·5	28·1	35·7
Other goods, - - - -	11·7	13·4	16·0
Total, - - -	102·9	132·7	178·1

IMPORTS.

	1893-1903.	1903-1907.	1913.
Cotton yarns and goods, -	5·0	9·2	9·2
Woollen yarns and goods -	13·3	13·2	10·0
Other goods, - - - -	19·2	19·3	9·8
Total, - - -	37·5	41·7	29·0

These figures show, in the first place, that English textile exports have of late years considerably increased, and have risen much more in the aggregate than imports, and secondly, that it is just in the most important export branch of textiles (accounting for more than two-thirds of the whole textile exports) that importation is almost negligible. Since the war the usual comparisons with former times are difficult and misleading. The higher prices vitiate a comparison of values, the statistics of imports and exports of

[1] 'Statistical Abstract.' Cf. 'Statesman's Year Book,' 1925, p. 61.

cotton yarn have undergone technical changes, and since 1924 the figures for the Irish Free State are excluded from the statistics of the United Kingdom. Bearing these facts in mind we may quote the following comparison, specially calculated by the 'Economist':

EXPORT OF YARNS FROM THE U.K.

	Lbs.	Value.
1913, - -	210,099,000	£15,006,291
1925, - -	189,532,000	30,500,647

These figures afford no ground for the earlier pessimism. The fact that the value of the exports of cotton yarn and goods rose from £126·4 millions in 1913 to £199 millions in 1924, in spite of the much higher prices, is not an unfavourable symptom for an industry which has so much to bear from the world-wide economic crisis of the post-war period.[1] English textiles, as a whole, are therefore not exactly "overtaken" or "endangered" or "driven from the field" by foreign competition. But the real importance of the statistics can only be seen when we remember the kind of exports in question. English textile manufacturers have been wise enough to turn lately more and more to the making of high-quality goods, in which they are unsurpassed in any other country; and this has enabled them to compete even behind the high tariff walls of America and the Continent while preserving their English market in such goods unchallenged.

Experts and scientific writers have so frequently discussed the facts of this phenomenon and admitted their correctness[2] that it is here only necessary to draw atten-

[1] Cf. 'Economist,' Feb. 13, 1926, p. 66; and 'Statesman's Year Book,' 1926, p. 56.

[2] S. J. Chapman, 'Work and Wages,' London 1904, pp. 67, 169, 190, and 194; *idem* 'The Cotton Industry,' London 1905; J. H. Clapham, 'The Woollen and Worsted Industries,' London 1907, p. 303 and *passim*; L. Helm in 'British Industries,' pp. 89 and 143; A. L. Bowley, 'National Progress in Wealth and Trade,' London 1904, p. 47; 'Economist,' Feb. 16, 1907, under "Woollen Trades"; Von Schulze-Gaevernitz, 'Englischer Freihandel und britischer Imperialismus,' pp. 273 and 292 ff; Hasbach, 'Zur Characteristik der englischen Industrie,' 3. Aufsätze; Schmoller's 'Jahrbücher,' 1902 and 1903 *passim*.

tion to it. Especially noteworthy for more recent times is the conclusion arrived at in the 'Report of Commercial Policy after the War' on the basis of the enquiries made by a special committee on the cotton trade. It says[1] the Textile Trades Committee declares "that all the opinions collected by us seem to indicate that the strength of the British cotton trade, both in yarns and in piece goods, is practically uninjured in competitive world markets though important changes have taken place in the character of the business.... The finer makes of men's woollen stuffs are pre-eminent in home and colonial markets." War and post-war conditions have greatly increased the output of cotton yarns and cotton goods in the English spheres of competition, while the development of the Indian and Japanese cotton industry and the increased American tariff have militated seriously against the English textile output, as shown in detail in the 'Survey of Overseas Markets,' 1925.[2] The Committee on Industry and Trade, 1925, states clearly the relations between the English textile industry and world markets in the following words:[3]

"The new local manufactures are, generally speaking, concerned at the outset with the simpler and coarser classes of goods, and the immediate result is not only to restrict international commerce, but to drive it more and more on to the finer qualities of manufacture.... It follows that, while the total volume of international trade open to competition may be diminished, there is a probability that an increased share of what remains will be captured by the exporting country most capable of adapting its production to special qualities of goods. We find to-day that the reputation of our country for good qualities surpasses that of its competitors in most markets."

The fact that the English textile industry possesses, owing to the high quality of its goods, a world-wide superi-

[1] p. 16.

[2] pp. 452-3, 287-9, 417-9. See also Levy, 'Der Weltmarkt 1913 und heute,' Leipzig 1926.

[3] p. 11.

ority in most of its products is one of the main foundations of the monopolist associations now existing in the trade. Given the possibility of excluding home competition an association can always be formed. As we have already seen, this possibility does not always exist, because in the lower grades of both the cotton and the woollen and worsted industries the number of separate undertakings is so great, and the creation of new undertakings so easy, that the systematic restriction of competition and the raising of prices by a monopoly is out of the question. But the conditions in high-quality textiles are quite different.[1]

One of the most successful combinations in the textile industry is the Fine Cotton Spinners' and Doublers' Association. Founded in 1898 by the amalgamation of thirty-one firms, it soon after acquired further undertakings and practically controlled the whole English production. The association's prospectus itself claimed that the business had a kind of " monopoly value," and emphasised the fact that the old-established reputation of the amalgamated firms for expensive yarns "placed an obstacle in the way of new competitors." As to foreign competition, " the spinning and doubling of the finest counts require large experience and excessive care, and it can be only successfully carried on where the workpeople are skilful and highly trained. It is doubtless for this reason, coupled with the climatic advantages of Great Britain, that this branch of the cotton trade has not suffered appreciably from foreign competition." [2] Owing to the comparatively small number of competing firms and the difficulties facing new competitors, this advantage can be fully used. The fact that though dozens of new mills started spinning during the great boom of 1907, they in no way competed with the fine yarns of the

[1] When not otherwise stated, the facts as to associations in the textile trade are drawn from the very valuable material given in Macrosty's ' Trust Movement,' p. 117 ff.

[2] ' Prospectus of the Association,' May 6, 1898, p. 3. The ' Statist,' May 6, 1922, shows that this is still the case : " These rings of the textile industry are as good as free from open competition."

association shows that the expectations of the prospectus were not unjustified.[1]

In 1911 the trust made a novel experiment, hitherto unknown in the textile industry, when it bought for £750,000 an interest in two cotton plantations near the mouth of the Mississippi in order to make itself independent of the fluctuations in price of raw cotton. It was not, indeed, until 1920 that this became profitable, as the plantations of the trust were repeatedly damaged by floods.[2] The Fine Cotton Spinners and Doublers are on the whole an example of a flourishing concern. This is the more remarkable because conditions in the English cotton industry in recent years have been by no means easy and satisfactory owing to the condition of the world market for their products, *i.e.* reduced purchasing power, particularly for the more expensive products, and the violent fluctuations in the raw cotton market. In 1913 the trust declared a dividend of 8 per cent; in 1923, 12½ per cent.; in 1924, 14 per cent.; 1925, 15 per cent.; and 1926, 12 per cent. The concentration of factories played a large part in these results, as shown by the report of the chairman, Mr. Herbert W. Lee, who on May 21, 1923, declared himself sceptical about the possibility of keeping together the spinners of coarse yarns, but at the same time added: "We on our side are fortunate to have with us large concerns, of which our own is the largest, and this enables us to moderate our costs of production and to deal with our customers in such a way that we have no unjustifiable losses to bear."[3]

THE SEWING COTTON TRUST AND SEWING COTTON SYNDICATE

The Fine Cotton Spinners' Association arose out of the competition of a comparatively small number of firms of equal strength. In the derivative sewing thread trade concentration developed in quite a different manner. A

[1] 'Economist,' August 1, 1908, pp. 204-5. [2] 'Statist,' May 6, 1922.
[3] 'Economist,' May 22, 1926, p. 987, and May 29, p. 1055-7.

single undertaking, J. & P. Coats, had grown from small beginnings in 1826 to a limited liability company, with £5,750,000 capital in 1890. In 1895 and 1896 four other firms of similarly extensive character were amalgamated with J. & P. Coats, with whom they had for many years been allied through a sales association. In 1897 most of the twenty smaller firms standing outside this immense undertaking united in forming the English Sewing Cotton Company, which, after the inclusion of further firms in 1899, had a share capital of £3,000,000. The relations of these two great rivals were smoothed by the fact that Coats held some of the new company's shares. At the same time an American thread trust, "The American Thread Company," was formed, both Coats and the English Sewing Cotton Company holding commanding interests. The English thread trust, which now owned important factories in Spain, Canada, Russia, and other countries, besides America, thus acquired an international character.

Conflicts as regards sales between the rival large firms were, it is true, not entirely obviated by the holding of shares in common. But the decision of the Sewing Cotton Company, whose position was far less assured than that of Coats, to sell their products in association with the latter through the Central Thread Agency, brought greater unity. As in the salt trade the syndicate with its common sales led to a close connection between the trust (Coats) and the outside makers, here concentrated in a single undertaking (The Sewing Cotton Company). The strength of the combine in foreign markets is due to the special nature of the articles it sells. "Our strength," declared the Report of the Sewing Cotton Company in 1908,[1] "lies largely in the fact that the names and brands of our various goods are asked for by consumers in so many parts of the world." This is even more true of Coats. "In spite of foreign tariffs, and of foreign competition, we hold our own".[2]

[1] 'Report' of July 23, 1908, p. 4.

[2] 'Textile World Record,' Oct. 1907, p. 87.

Undoubtedly it exercises a great influence on prices, and knows that it can fix them at its will without being hindered by any consideration except the elasticity of the demand, as the above report shows. "As far as possible, we have avoided a policy of high selling prices that would tend to lessen consumption or dissatisfying our customers." Whatever the customers may have thought of the prices, their monopolist nature is shown by the fact that they resulted not from the workings of competition, but from systematic regulation by the chief makers.

The 'Report on Trusts' has recently stated that the two firms, Coats and Sewing Cotton, "are believed to control together the whole sewing thread industry of the United Kingdom, with the exception of a certain amount of specialised trade, and are also in a powerful position abroad.' The Sewing Cotton Company was able to pay a dividend of 20 per cent. in the bad textile years from 1922 to 1926.[1]

BLEACHING AND DYEING TRUSTS

In the bleaching industry the trust, the Bleachers' Association, now twenty-five years old, depends for its chief protection against external competition on its monopoly of the water supply.

As the association's prospectus puts it, "the great and ever-increasing difficulty of obtaining a sufficient water supply makes the position of established bleaching works very strong, whilst the laws against the pollution of water tell against the erection of new works." Advantage had already been taken of this peculiar monopoly possessed by the works round Manchester to make agreements as to prices long before the formation of a closer organisation in 1900 in the Bleachers' Association, a union of fifty-three firms. Similar circumstances led to the formation of the Bradford Dyers' Association in 1898, which also resulted from the organisation of an existing local monopoly. The

[1] 'Report on Trusts,' p. 40; and 'Economist,' July 17, 1926, p. 110

conditions which favoured this development are clearly set out in the prospectus.[1]

They were (1) freights, which secured undertakings near Bradford from external English competition; (2) the necessity of close local connection between dyers and their customers, a factor which enhanced the value of this advantage in freights; (3) the special qualities and abundance of the water supply; and (4) the existence of a limited class of workmen for high-grade work. On these grounds the Dyers' Association considered their position "almost unassailable." As 90 per cent. of the production was in the hands of twenty-two firms, the formation of a combine was easy. In 1903 thirteen more firms joined, and the monopolist organisation became complete. In this case, therefore, a much more complete concentration took place than in bleaching.

But the Bradford Dyers are not the only holding concern left in the field of English bleaching. The 'Report on Trusts' states[2] that the dyeing branches of the cotton and woollen industries are dominated by a small number of powerful consolidations, of which the chief is the Bradford Dyers' Association. There are also the British Cotton and Wool Dyers' Association (forty-six firms), and three smaller concerns in the velvet, cord and worsted dyeing industries; and a cartel of firms not comprised in the great trust, the Lancashire Cotton Piece Dyers' Price Association.

The Dyers' strong position and their intentions as regards prices were to a certain extent revealed in the 1898 prospectus, which, though like that of the sewing thread combine attempting to reassure consumers, bore emphatic testimony to the possibility of regulating prices without competition. "Whilst it is apparent that the inclusion of about 90 per cent. of the entire trade within this Association amounts to what is practically a monopoly, the directors recognise that the interests of the Company are largely identical with those of the manufacturers and

[1] Prospectus of Dec. 14, 1898. [2] pp. 39-40.

merchants of the district, and though there are no doubt cases in which some readjustment and regulation of rates are clearly reasonable ... it is no part of the present scheme to inaugurate an era of inflated prices." Similar language was used by the chairman of the company in 1904:[1] "We have ever refrained from the adoption of those forcible methods which are a temptation to the executives of large organisations. We have never taken unto ourselves the rôle of monopolists." But the buyers do not seem to have declared themselves entirely content with the prices actually charged. On the contrary there were so many disputes that the Bradford Chamber of Commerce managed to get a central agency between the combine and its customers established. This agency, the Bradford Piece Dyeing Board, was composed of merchants and of members of the association, and aimed at forming price agreements running for considerable periods of time, and harmonising the interests of both parties.

Mr. Clapham, who justly calls the Bradford Dyers "the most successful of British industrial combines," quotes a number of facts showing their commanding position in regulating production and markets, and he rightly explains the creation of the above agency as due to the imperative necessity for merchants to cultivate "friendly relations" with this powerful organisation.[2]

An interesting account of the association's attempts to differentiate prices is quoted by Mr. Macrosty[3] from the 'Yorkshire Post.' Contracts were made with merchants under which they were bound to send all the goods which they required to have dyed to the combine. The merchant might make exceptions, but he had to enumerate (i) the classes of goods to be excepted, (ii) the outside firm in whose favour the exception was made, (iii) the amount of goods to be left them, and (iv) the reasons for so doing.

[1] 'Report of the Association,' Feb. 26, 1904.

[2] Clapham, 'Woollen and Worsted Industries,' pp. 151-4.

[3] 'Trust Movement,' p. 160.

If he agreed to these conditions, the combine could see at once the strength of its position in each branch of the trade, and adapt its different scales of prices accordingly. But after a while dealers began to regret such contracts, and this ingenious system of attacking outsiders came to an end.

The Bradford Dyers are among the prospering textile concerns. In 1923 and 1924 they distributed a dividend of 25 per cent.; in 1925 "only" $13\frac{1}{8}$.[1]

The cotton and wool dyers' combine, the Cotton and Wool Dyers' Association, formed in 1900 by the amalgamation of forty-six firms, is less powerful. As the association dyes all kinds of yarn, not woven materials, and does not, like the Bradford Dyers' Association, make special articles of particular reputation, the original position of the separate firms was not so secure as at Bradford; whilst any manufacturer using yarns could make himself independent of the combine by erecting his own dyeing works, especially if he only made plain cloth and simple blue or black stuffs.[2] This branch of dyeing is moreover scattered over several districts—the combine has works in Lancashire, Yorkshire, and Glasgow—which makes it more difficult to make arrangements with new outsiders than in a locally concentrated industry like that of Bradford. It is, therefore, not unnatural that the cotton and wool dyers have been much less successful financially and in fixing prices than the Bradford dyers.

THE CALICO PRINTERS' TRUST

The bleachers' and dyers' associations threw but little light on the tendency to industrial concentration. The associated firms represent of course but a small number of undertakings, though they amount to some dozens in all, but it cannot be shown whether the immense size of the

[1] 'Economist,' Feb. 20, 1926, p. 357.

[2] Clapham, pp. 151-2. Fitzgerald, p. 21, treats the price policy of this trust with strange indifference.

united undertaking in fact impedes the rise of many new competitors. The difficulty of founding new firms is due far more to the peculiar circumstances of the water supply, the demand for known patterns, and the need of a special race of workpeople. It was facts such as these which secured to the not very numerous existing works a monopolist position, and considerations of what was the most efficient unit of size for a bleaching company or dye works.

With calico printing matters are different. Forty-six manufacturing firms were included in the Calico Printers' Association when it was founded in 1899; and this would at first sight lead to the conclusion that there had been no very strong concentration, none at least at all comparable to that in the steel and iron trades. But we can prove[1] (what is not always possible) that these forty-six firms were of very varying competitive power. In all they owned 830 printing machines and produced about 85 per cent. of the calico printed in England. Seven of them owned 350 machines between them and represented 36 per cent. of the total production. Gartside's alone owned 74.[2] As early as the end of the nineties many undertakings no longer paid, and by June 1905 no less than 20 factories were closed. The number of undertakings of serious moment in 1899 was therefore much smaller than might be supposed from the list of firms included in the association. It further appears, if we investigate the dates at which the associated undertakings were founded—and this is typical of the movement to concentration—that 37 of them were founded before 1860, 5 between 1860 and 1880, and 4 after 1880. To all appearances the most recently founded were smaller concerns, for they only employed 6 or in one case 13 machines. Possibly they supplied some particular demand. These figures only include firms still existing after 1898, and even so are not complete, but they clearly show how slowly in recent years the number of firms in the calico trade has increased.

[1] 'Prospectus,' Dec. 8, 1899, p. 3. [2] Facts given in the Prospectus.

Concentration and the survival of a very small number of the most efficient undertakings facilitated the combination of the majority of existing works. On the other hand, the Calico Association is now an " efficiency " combination with which no single firm, even if of suitable size for economic working, could easily vie. The expense of acquiring new inventions and discoveries, or of securing the best designers and prickers is excessively great for a single firm; whilst the combine, by supplying the needs of a number of works at one and the same time, is in a position to satisfy these important requirements in calico printing at the very lowest cost.

The financial report of the Calico Printers justifies the conclusion that it had established a strong position in the course of the year, in spite of the violent crises through which at the outset the organisation passed. In 1907 and 1908 it passed its dividend, and again in 1914 and 1915, while in 1917 and 1918 it paid only 5 per cent. But in 1920, 1924 and 1925 it paid 12½, 10 and 15 per cent. Another similar large concern, which is not of course to be considered a pure trust, is the United Turkey Red Company, which with the Calico Printers' Association is jointly interested in and controls the British Alizarine Company, the only maker in the United Kingdom of alizarine dyes. This combination is related with the chemical trust founded in 1926, to be described later, and has become of special importance.

The calico trade, being one of the main textile exports, is quite secure from foreign competition. It fixes the world's price and, especially in specifically English qualities, holds a monopoly in the home market.

COURTAULDS, THE ARTIFICIAL SILK TRUST

The manufacture of artificial silk in England has had a rapid boom in the last decade, and especially in the last few years. The following are the figures[1] of output of artificial silk in thousands of lbs.:

	1922.	1924.	1925.
World production, - -	79,738	141,164	197,000
United States, - -	23,500	38,750	50,000
Great Britain, - -	15,340	23,947	30,000
Germany, - - -	12,584	23,672	26,000
France, - - - -	6,292	12,333	23,000
Italy, - - - -	6,292	18,480	28,000

It will be seen that England holds the first place among European producers and that there is a strong increase of competition from all sides. In spite of its high output the English artificial silk industry was not able fully to meet the home demand in recent years. In 1925 though 30 million pounds were produced 7 million pounds were imported, chiefly from Italy. The importation of foreign artificial silk, though the English trade was flourishing and the quality of its wares superior,[2] moved the English manufacturers to seek protection, which was accorded for five years under the Finance Act of 1925. A large increase of English artificial silk factories is expected to follow.[3]

It is not surprising that in a new industry of this character, which needs a large capital to start, rests partly upon the acquisition of valuable patents, and has not been built up in the presence of long-standing small undertakings which have first to be amalgamated, monopolistic organisation can be effected without much opposition. It is represented to-day by the firm of Courtaulds, which has its headquarters in Coventry, founded in 1904 and reorganised in 1912. Very soon after its formation the Company sought to broaden its basis of production abroad. In 1910 it set up a factory in the United States, then in Russia and Germany. In 1916 it bought up the patents and undertakings of its only English competitor, the British Glanzstoff Manufacturing Co. In 1922 the 'Statist' reports[4] that "the Company has full control of the artificial silk industry of

[1] 'Manchester Guardian Commercial' of April 15, 1926; Summer number on 'Artificial Silk,' p. 19.

[2] *loc cit. supra.* [3] Cf. the 'Free Trader,' March 1926, p. 81. [4] May 13, 1922.

the country." Their financial experience was phenomenal. The net profit from 1913 to 1922 was about £14 million. 1925 witnessed a record point of over £4 million net profit and 25 per cent. dividend.[1] The strong foreign competition which existed is now reduced partly through the duty imposed in 1925, partly through agreement with the international society of manufacturers in which Courtaulds have their share. The 'Manchester Guardian Commercial' published in 1926 the following diagram, which shows the distribution of the international producers and their relation to other great branches of industry:

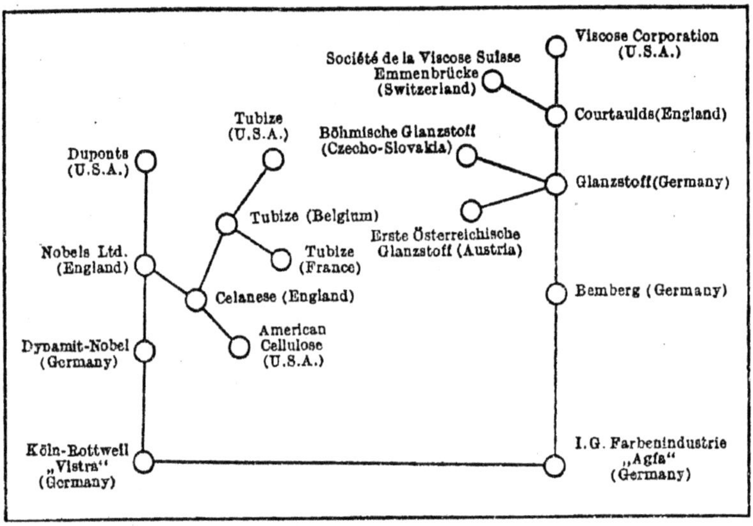

Nothing can be said as to the price policy of the trust until it is seen what influence the effect of the new duties will have. There can be no doubt that the trust is in a position to exercise a strong influence upon the prices of all manufacturers of artificial silk. But until an international cartel is formed limits are set to its power, and these must be respected. In 1925 the trust lowered English prices considerably, as they were out of harmony with foreign prices. It is perhaps due to this fact that since the trust returned to higher prices the import—as estimated by the

[1] 'Economist,' Feb. 27, 1926, p. 401.

'Economist'—of special artificial silk yarn increased from 110,116 lbs. in January to 197,171 lbs. in June 1926. Nevertheless the trust was obliged to follow quickly the lowering of prices in America and other producing countries.[1] An outsider whose importance must not be underrated, the British Enka Artificial Silk Company, set up against the trust in the autumn of 1926. It is a branch of a Dutch silk factory, and has opened a large factory in Liverpool. It has an output capacity of 20,000 lbs. of artificial silk daily, and must be regarded as a formidable competitor to Courtaulds.[2]

THE CHEMICAL INDUSTRY TRUST

The foundation of the great Chemical Trust in the autumn of 1926 is without doubt the most important event in the development of the concentration and trust movement in England during the last few years. The 'Manchester Guardian'[3] announced the occurrence in a leading article entitled "A British Trust at last!"

The four great concerns which were amalgamated are Brunner Mond & Co., United Alkali Co., Nobel Industries Ltd., and British Dyestuffs Corporation. These have between them a capital (ordinary and preference shares and debentures, etc.) of no less than £42,549,930, an unprecedented figure. The first two firms can look back upon a long process of trust formation, the Nobel Co. was greatly extended during the war,[4] and the Dyestuffs Corporation is entirely the product of war and post-war experience.

The United Alkali Co., which manufactures soda by the Le Blanc process, was formed in 1890 out of 48 firms which claimed to control almost the whole output by this process. Since then it has had to cope with two new difficulties, (i) the growth of foreign competition based on the manu-

[1] 'Economist,' July 17, 1926. [2] 'Economist,' Oct. 30, 1926, p. 722.

[3] Oct. 28, 1926.

[4] Schuster und Wehberg, 'Der Wirtschaftskrieg, Teil I.: England,' Jena 1917, p. 132.

facture of soda by the ammonia process, (ii) the increase of similar competition at home, where its chief opponent was the Brunner Mond Co., which had been founded by an original chemical genius of the name of Mond, father of the present Sir Alfred Mond, M.P. After 1900 steps were taken to bring about an international agreement, including the British producers.[1] Specially important was the understanding between Brunner Mond and the Solvay Works which dominated the German soda cartel.

During the war it appeared how dependent England had been upon Germany for chemical products, and especially dyestuffs. The embarrassment of the war, as well as the desire to be self-sufficing if possible in future, brought about the formation on August 25, 1914, of the Chemical Supplies Committee and the founding of British Dyes Ltd. on March 5, 1915. From this developed later the Dyestuffs Corporation Ltd. It is not now necessary to recapitulate the foundation, organisation and the criticisms of the productions of this undertaking.[2] It need only be mentioned that the technical and administrative difficulties of the British Dye trust have not been got over till recently, that in 1925 the most important members seceded from this semi-official undertaking on the ground that there was no satisfactory solution of the difficulties in which the direction was placed by its inadequate economic resources. Nevertheless the wish was fostered, both by the war and by the subsequent union of those interested in the chemical industry in Germany, to form a combination of chemical interests in England. Important amalgamations were formed, such as Castner-Kellner with Brunner Mond, and the Port Ellesmere Works with the large Levinstein firm which had occupied a leading position in the Dye Trust. In 1916 the Association of British Chemical Manufacturers was founded to repress unnecessary competi-

[1] Cf. Grossmann, 'Bedeutung der chemischen Technik,' Halle 1907, pp. 34-5; also Gothein, 'Deutscher Aussenhandel,' 1901, p. 711.

[2] For a precise account see Schuster und Wehberg, p. 125 ff.

tion and over-production. This combination was eclipsed by the formation of the single chemical trust in 1926, which took the name Imperial Chemical Industries Ltd., and has naturally a much stronger influence upon the procedure and market of the industry than any combine. Just as in the union of those interested in the German dye industry, so in this chemical trust it was necessary to take up the industries in which its different members were interested either for the purchase or sale of chemical materials. The firm of Mond was interested in anthracite coal pits, Nobel in artificial silk (British Celanese), and so on. The bringing together of these companies led to the formation of a powerful international association. But the trust, which is predominant especially in the output of heavy chemicals, is not without outsiders. The British Alizarine Co., already mentioned in connection with calico printing, and the well-known firm of Holliday have not joined the combine.

The power of the trust is so great that it seems not unreasonable for the consumers and their representatives to feel anxious about its effects. So far as prices are concerned, it must be remembered that the output of fine chemicals enjoys a protective tariff which was renewed in August 1925 for ten years for no fewer than 5000 so-called "key" chemicals.[1] The English dye trusts strongly protested. The 'Economist'[2] states: "Everywhere in Lancashire it is held that the chief cause of the decline of our export trade in cotton piece goods is to be found in the high prices which have to be paid for dyes. These make it impossible for our manufacturers to compete with foreign countries. At the annual meeting of the Blackburn Chamber of Commerce the chairman dwelt specially upon the fact "that for nearly a year the Dyestuffs Corporation had charged their customers 10d. a lb. for synthetic indigo, while our competitors paid only 8d.... Many materials which formerly were dyed and worked up in

[1] 'Economist,' Oct. 30, 1926, p. 716 [2] Feb. 13, 1926, p. 205.

England are now dyed in Belgium." So also the 'Shipbuilding Enquiry,' the report of an investigation by masters and men of the reasons for the decline of English shipbuilding in recent years in comparison with foreign rivals, comes to the conclusion that among other causes the increased price of enamel paint, due to the existence of monopoly, must be included.[1] Many criticisms were voiced by trade papers when the chemical trust was founded. The 'Manchester Guardian Commercial' claims[2] that "if the dye-makers demand protection the textile industry must in its own interests demand that some system be devised under which dyes can be bought in England at competitive and not at protectionist prices."

THE MINERAL OIL COMPANIES

The production and refining of mineral oil is still largely in the hands of the U.S.A. The output in thousands of barrels (each containing 42 gallons) is :[3]

	1911-15.	1924.
U.S.A., - - -	247,739	713,940
Mexico, - - -	22,791	139,497
Russia, - - -	66,521	45,312
Dutch East Indies, -	11,507	20,473
Persia, - - -	2,794	32,373
Rumania, - - -	12,499	16,625

The total world output has risen during the period mentioned from about 380 million barrels to one milliard barrels. In the United States outsiders have increased their production from 136 to 298 million barrels (estimated figure for 1925 over 300 million barrels). England has practically no share in the production of crude petroleum, but the petroleum question presents, nevertheless, an

[1] Levy, 'England und die Konzentrationsbewegung in der deutschen Industrie. Wirtschaftliche Nachrichten für Rhein und Ruhr,' Aug. 18, 1926.

[2] Oct. 28, 1926.

[3] 'Statistical Abstract of U.S.A. for 1925,' Washington 1926, p. 733.

extremely interesting problem of British economic organisation owing to the fact that England has gained an increasing control over the non-American oilfields, and is continually seeking to extend this control—a process in which great centrally organised undertakings play a decisive part. In spite of the fact, then, that the petroleum problem is not a purely industrial one, it must be treated here.

The following companies now control the oil business of Great Britain on behalf of its units scattered all over the world: Anglo-American, Shell Transport and Trading, Royal Dutch Shell, Anglo-Persian, National Benzol, Agwi Marketing, and Union Petroleum Products. Of these the first two are the most important. The Anglo-American was started in 1911 as a branch of the Standard Oil Trust. Its chief rival, the Shell, has had an understanding with the Royal Dutch since 1907. Both companies own oilfields all over the world, and great fleets of oil-tankers (about 1,300,000 gross tonnage in 1923). They sell about 10 per cent. of their output in England itself.

Next comes the purely English concern, the Anglo-Persian, in which the British Government is financially interested. It arose by fusion with the Burma Oil Company, and concerned itself chiefly with the exploitation of the Persian oil fields. But its active policy of expansion begins with its efforts to enter into the tanker and transport side of the business which the Dutch group had controlled up to 1922, thus absorbing some of the commerce and agency business of the Persian oil trade. After 1917 the Anglo-Persian acquired tank steamers, oil depots in the chief ports of the world, built its own large refineries, especially in Wales, acquired an interest in the Dutch Shell, united with itself five Scottish shale oil companies—Scottish Oils Limited—and bought up the former German concern, the British Petroleum Co., and other businesses.[1]

The tanker fleet of the Company is now about 650,000 tons.[2]

[1] 'Statist,' Dec. 22, 1923.

[2] 'Statist,' Dec. 22, 1923. Cf. also Liefmann, p. 257.

In the last ten years the Company's balance sheet has been exceedingly favourable, net profits rising from £2·2 millions in 1923, to £3·5 millions in 1924, and £4·39 millions in 1925. The import of crude oil into England has increased from a small amount in 1920 to 2170 million gallons in 1922, owing to the erection of refineries in the country. Naturally this progress of the Anglo-Persian awoke the fears of consumers as to their price policy. An expert contributor to a trade paper in 1920 believed the American oil trusts were kept in check by the European outsiders like the Shell and the Anglo-Persian, but that a union of these three groups would be a danger. Broadly speaking, oil prices in Great Britain tend to conform to American prices, but this tendency is operative only " in the long run." Thus we are told: " The fluctuations of American oil prices in 1925 had very little effect on European prices. In England the prices have been kept by the great companies at the level to which they were reduced in Sept. 1924." The influence of the oil concerns on price movements is still remarkable.[1]

BRITISH AND INTERNATIONAL RAIL SYNDICATE

The prospects of industrial monopoly in England have recently been improved by a circumstance which points to a great development of cartels and trusts in the future. Industries hitherto exposed to foreign competition can now seek protection in international agreements. This opens up a possibility of securing the English market to the English producer, free trade notwithstanding, even where English goods do not surpass foreign goods in cheapness or quality.[2] But even in these cases it has so far been an essential preliminary that concentration in England should exclude competition among home producers, and that similarly close monopolist associations should have been formed

[1] 'Economist,' Feb. 13, 1926, p. 37.

[2] Macrosty, p. 63.

abroad with which international agreements could be made.[1]

This condition was fulfilled at an exceptionally early date in the case of steel rails, which were concentrated earlier than the rest of the heavy iron trade in the hands of a few immense undertakings. Everything consequently favoured combination among the chief producing countries. In the early eighties there were in England 18 to 20 firms which rolled heavy rails.[2] In 1906 there were only 9 left, though production was about the same.[3] A similar process of concentration has taken place in all other rail-producing countries, especially in the United States.

As early as 1883 the English manufacturers formed an international rail syndicate with Germany and Belgium.[4] The syndicate several times broke down, but latterly became more and more a permanent institution for the regulation of the international rail market. In 1905 the United States, England, Germany, Belgium, and France were all members. In May 1907 the syndicate was renewed for five years, and since then Russia also has joined.[5] Great Britain, in which all the works except one belong to the syndicate, enjoys under the agreement the fullest security from the competition of its most important foreign rivals. Each country retains its own home market, while

[1] The 'Report on Trusts,' 1918, says (page 26): "There is ample evidence that, in industries subject to foreign competition, that competition acts as a check upon any tendency on the part of combinations in the home trade to raise prices unduly. But its importance can easily be overestimated. Industrial combination has no frontiers. Before the war British and foreign manufacturers of many staple articles had their understandings, agreements and associations embodying arrangements for the regulation of prices and the delimitation of markets."

[2] Macrosty, p. 63.

[3] Ryland, pp. 791-3. The firms were: Ebbw Vale Co., Moss Bay Haematite Iron and Steel Co., Barrow Haematite Steel Co.; Walter Scott; Bolckow, Vaughan & Co.; North-Eastern Steel Co.; Steel, Peech & Tozer; Guest, Keen & Nettlefolds; and Cammell, Laird & Co.

[4] Macrosty, p. 64.

[5] 'Manchester Guardian,' March 6, 1909.

the export trade is so divided that each member of the syndicate receives a region in which he is free from competition. Naturally this agreement exercises a considerable influence on prices in England. When steel rails rose in 1907 from £6 15s. to £7, after costing £4 to £5 during the three preceding years, while at the same time American home prices were only £5 12s., a good many Englishmen began to realise [1] that, free trade notwithstanding, the English price was no longer fixed by rates quoted in other exporting countries. Prices were clearly favourable for the export of American rails to England, but though a considerable number of rails were in fact exported from America in 1907, none of them came to the United Kingdom. This was in sharp contrast to what occurred in 1900 and 1901. Then, too, English prices had far outstripped American, the average price in 1900 being \$36.01 in England against \$32.29 in America.[2] As a result American export statistics showed a growing and hitherto unknown export of rails to England.[3] In November 1900 a trade paper stated [4] that "for some time past the British Steel Rail Makers' Association have kept prices up at £7 to £7 5s. per ton, but the Americans have been recently underselling them, and now the home makers have relaxed their conditions, and given freedom to makers to lower their prices at once. This has been immediately done, and some makers are quoting as low as £6 net for heavy sections." In 1907 the difference in price between American and English rails was even greater, and, as in 1901, America exported about 300,000 tons; but the whole of Europe only received a beggarly 474 tons!—a clear testimony to the international syndicate, whose arrangements barred export to England.

[1] 'Economist,' 1907, p. 871.

[2] 'Report of American Iron and Steel Association' 1906, p. 87.

[3] 'Exports of Manufactures,' Washington 1903, p. 3615. It amounted to over 20,000 tons.

[4] 'Memoranda,' etc., p. 326.

The world war has naturally dissolved this international cartel, in which the German output had an important place. Early in 1926 an International Steel Rail Syndicate was set up afresh. The British quota is now fixed at 43 per cent., the Franco-German at 40 per cent., the rest going to Belgium and Luxemburg. The price situation in England will be now under the same controlling influences as those already alluded to as existing before the war.[1]

THE TOBACCO TRUST

The history of the international tobacco monopoly is very different from that of rails or soda. The struggle was much more intense, one might almost say more dramatic, and its result led to a far closer form of organisation, an international trust.

The rise of this Anglo-American Trust has been described from the English side by Mr. Macrosty, in its connection with the American Tobacco Trust by Mr. Jacobstein, and more recently, in even greater detail, in an official American Report.[2] It will be sufficient to quote their conclusions.

On the ground that the American trust, the American Tobacco Company, were endeavouring to capture the English market by price cutting, the thirteen chief English firms united in 1901 to form a defence organisation called the Imperial Tobacco Company. This company had a capital of £11,957,022, and bought up several more firms in 1902. After a sharp struggle with Ogdens Limited and the British Tobacco Company, which had been bought and reorganised by the Americans, the Imperial Tobacco Company came to an agreement with the Trust. From 1902 on the company, now amalgamated with Ogdens, was left in undisputed possession in England,[3] while the Trust was

[1] See 'Economist,' March 27, 1926, p. 616.

[2] Macrosty, 'Trust Movement,' p. 235 ff.; M. Jacobstein, 'The Tobacco Industry in the United States,' New York 1907, pp. 113-115; 'Report of the Commissioners of Corporations on the Tobacco Industry,' 1909 *passim*, and pp. 166-176.

[3] 'Commissioners of Corporations' Report,' pp. 303-4.

given a similar immunity in the United States. A new third company, the British American Tobacco Co., conducted the export trade, the Imperial Co. holding one-third of the shares and nominating six directors, and the American Trust two-thirds of the shares and twelve directors. So far the object of this common undertaking has been to form branch trusts in the great import countries, Australia, Canada, and South Africa, possibly following herein the example of the American Trust, which formed a branch trust in 1902 in Cuba—the Havanna Tobacco Co.[1]

The English tobacco monopoly is therefore organised as follows: The English combine has an unchallenged outlet for its goods in the United Kingdom, as the American Trust has in the States. In certain organised foreign markets mutual competition is further prevented by their common representation, the British American Tobacco Company. The possibility that this division of markets might be rendered nugatory by the intervention of a third party was foreseen in the agreement of September 27, 1902, and it was laid down in paragraph 18 that "None of the parties should sell any tobacco products to any person, firm or company, who they had reason to believe would export the same to the territory in which the sellers had agreed not to sell such goods, as herein provided."

By the formation of this combine the English tobacco manufacturers gained the exclusion of the greatest, and in many articles the only, foreign competitor. The peculiarities of the English consumption of tobacco and tobacco products had for years made America the chief source from which leaf tobacco was imported. While Germany drew the majority of its import from the East Indies, Brazil, and Cuba, England drew almost all its leaf tobacco from North America. As tobacco manufacturing extended and became cheaper in America, the export of certain manufactures to England naturally increased continually. In 1902 it represented a value of $1,403,482; in 1906, though the

[1] Jacobstein, 'Tobacco Industry in the United States,' p. 112.

total American export showed no decrease, it had fallen to $333,584.[1] Clearer testimony to the effect of the mutual understanding could not be required. Once more the decisive factor was that in both countries production was strongly concentrated. The Trust had been dominant in America since the nineties.

In England a similar concentration had taken place, as the fact that in 1904 the Imperial Tobacco Company (which then included eighteen undertakings) represented half the total production[2] shows. Of the purchase price of the thirteen firms amalgamated in 1902 in the company, £6,999,221, or more than half, was for the great firm of W. D. & H. O. Wills in Bristol. Some important firms remain outside the English tobacco trust—such as Gallaher, Cope Bros., Godfrey Phillips, the Ardath Co., R. & J. Hill, Albert Baker & Co., S. Norris & Sons, Benson and Hedges, Singleton and Cole, and J. Hunter, Morris & Elkan. These firms together represent a capital of some £3 million,[3] while the Imperial Tobacco Company in 1925 had a paid-up capital of no less than £42·8 million.[4] Smaller tobacco factories, of which there are a few hundreds in England, play no important part in competition.

One cause of concentration in tobacco manufacturing has been the increased use in recent times of machines. "Wherever possible," says the American report,[5] "machinery has been substituted for hand labour, and the greatest success of the combine has been in those lines of the industry where the greatest use of machinery is possible. In little cigar and cigarette production, where almost all the processes are performed by machinery, the monopoly of the company was more readily established than in any other branch except snuff." The monopoly was the least complete in cigar making, where hand labour is still extensive.

[1] 'Exports of Manufactures,' Washington 1907, pp. 41 and 29.

[2] Macrosty, 'Trust Movement,' p. 237. [3] 'Statist,' Sept. 25, 1923.

[4] 'Economist,' Feb. 13, 1926, p. 307.

[5] 'Report on Tobacco Industry,' 1909, p. 266.

The same thing undoubtedly influenced concentration in England, though the monopolist use of patents was not so prominent as in America.

A second reason lay in the fact that as the potential productivity of undertakings increased, the necessity of developing production on a large scale by every possible means also grew. Every big firm endeavoured by advertisement to obtain the wholesale consumption of its goods. The change has been described by Mr. Archer, a director of the large firm of Hill mentioned above, in the following words:[1] "When I was first in business some thirty-five years ago competition among tobacco manufacturers was almost entirely as to who could produce the best quality and the best value for money, and considerable experience and practical knowledge of the business were necessary for success. All this is completely changed, and now competition seems to have resolved itself into a question of who could afford to spend the most money on advertising."

A special advantage of the English trust is that to provide itself more cheaply with raw material it has for some time had its own purchase company, the Imperial Tobacco Company of Kentucky. By taking over the large firms of A. I. Jones & Son and Salmon & Gluckstein it has come into possession of a great number of retail shops. The last-named firm alone has 170. The trust has set up a bonus system under which a premium is allowed to the small dealers who are tied to the trust. In 1914, when the system started, £241,000 was paid out as bonus, in 1920 £915,000, now over a million.[2] The efficient technical organisation of the trust, its cheaper purchases of raw material, its practical association with the retail trade, enable it, in the opinion of the 'Statist,' to drive the outsiders easily to the wall. But probably the trust is restrained from the open adoption of such a procedure by ulterior considerations. While its profits are so brilliant as

[1] 'Financial News,' March 5, 1909.

[2] 'Statist,' Sept. 25, 1923; and 'Economist,' Feb. 13, 1926.

in these past years such a policy may appear unnecessary. The high dividend of 35 per cent. in 1913 has not been repeated, but in 1925 it was 24 per cent. on the common capital, a net profit of £8,884,990. This is one of the most successful of all British trusts. Its power to influence prices is undoubted. An official Report of 1919 on tobacco trusts says that "conditions in this industry are such that the Imperial Tobacco Company is in a position to dictate prices which the great mass of consumers, habituated to certain brands of tobacco or cigarettes, will continue to pay. A business of such magnitude and with such large reserves of capital has it in its power, by cutting its profits for a time, to force prices down to such a point as to drive all of its rivals out of the trade and to establish at once or very soon a monopoly in the tobacco business.... We are further informed that the comparative Customs duties upon manufactured and unmanufactured tobacco are so adjusted that importation of certain standard kinds of tobacco or cigarettes is not feasible. In order that new competition should be rendered possible we are told that a firm stand must be made against the establishment of a monopoly." There has been no change since the publication of this Report.[1]

VARIOUS INDUSTRIES

To what has been said about the most important monopolist organisations in the chief English industries, a few facts may be added relative to combines and amalgamations in some of the smaller or secondary industries.

In 1920 an official inquiry was ordered into the match trade, which was found to be controlled by three groups of manufacturers. The first group, at the head of which is

[1] Fitzgerald does not share this view. He says (*op. cit.* p. 151) that trusts cannot "dictate" prices. He does not give any particular proof of this opinion, but merely points to the relative prosperity of rivals of the trust. But here, too, a distinction must be drawn between the actual power of the trusts and the economic policy pursued by them, which need not be co-extensive.

the well-known firm of Bryant & May, embraces seven concerns, the second five, the third three. Two large employers stand outside. Soon after the publication of the Report Bryant & May absorbed the other two companies. The British Match Manufacturers' Association has existed since 1907, and has brought together most of the employers. The Report of 1920 states that this Association controls prices and fixes a partition quota of output. The Tobacco and Matches Control Board set up during the war, and the prohibition of imports of foreign matches from 1916 to 1919,[1] doubtless contributed to strengthen the building up of a combine in this industry. Recently importation has been active, and special reference is made to it in Bryant & May's report.[2] But the understanding arrived at with the Svenska Tändstiks Aktiebolaget, its most important foreign competitor, has favoured English competition in its best markets. The parties have bound themselves together into a Society of Match Manufacturers to which—and this was not the case with the Association above mentioned—foreign manufacturers may belong. It is well known that on the side of the Swedish trust there is no undercutting of the prices of the English cartel.[3]

Long before the war the locomotive trust was important. We may call this also a "sheltered industry," since the type of the British locomotive and the special requirements of the railway engineers as regards its construction are such that foreign makers working with standardised types cannot invade the English market. This has been experienced in the case of imported American engines.[4] Locomotive building itself belongs to that group of industries which from the beginning bear a strong concentrated impress founded on the unification of large modern businesses. In 1908 there were only eleven English firms in this branch of production. These undertakings were amalgamated in 1903 into the

[1] See 'Statist,' Sept. 22, 1923. [2] 'Economist,' May 2,1925, p. 857.

[3] 'Statist,' Sept. 22, 1923.

[4] Lawson, 'American Industrial Problems,' London 1903.

North British Locomotive Company. Before the war these employed about one-third of all the labour in the business.[1] We have here the beginnings of a trust.

The glass industry, especially the manufacture of glass bottles, is another example of monopolistic organisation, which must be classed with monopolies having an international element. In 1907 a union was founded under the name Association of Glass Bottle Makers of Great Britain and Ireland. Its aim from the beginning was to exercise an influence on prices. It soon knit up agreements with foreign manufacturers, and the English combine joined the European Union of Glass Bottle Makers, founded to acquire the European rights of the American Owens patents. A special English union, the British Association of Glass Bottle Manufacturers, was started, its membership practically identical with that of the Association above mentioned, and concluded both national and international agreements. In 1912 an amalgamation, the United Glass Bottles Manufacturers Ltd., was brought about, which represented sixty per cent. of the total business of the first-named cartel and half the share capital of the second Association.[2] The war brought forth a great number of new undertakings in the glass bottle industry, and these were incited to act together during the high range of prices.[3] In 1919 a somewhat tardy reorganisation of the above, apparently not of great expert capacity, took over this undertaking and included a number of glass-blowing works which had not joined the Glass Bottle Association. As they were excluded from the use of the Owens patents, they bought up the Trust—the United Glass Bottle Manufacturers—at the end of 1919. Soon after there set in a general depression in the industry, and these newcomers brought down with them the hopes of a maintenance of the good times. A sensational slump took place in the Stock Exchange valuation of the share capital of the British Glass Industries Ltd. from £3·6 millions

[1] 'Economist,' Feb. 20, 1909, p. 34. [2] 'Statist,' Sept. 29, 1923.
[3] Schuster und Wehberg, p. 161.

to £183,000! In 1921 the Company was compelled to reorganise itself.[1] The high cost of buying up the new patents weighed heavily upon the trusts and cartels in the English glass industry, but the buying up of many small undertakings and the formation of one union was based upon the hope of establishing a monopoly through the use of the patents and of obtaining a dominating position over all competitors. The European Union of Glass Bottle Manufacturers still belongs to the trusts of an international character. It includes German, English, Czecho-Slovakian, Austrian, Dutch, Hungarian, and Scandinavian producers, and aims above all at the systematic execution of technical novelties in production.[2]

The soap trust is important, though not of fundamental significance in the scheme of England's large industries. It was first known by the name of Lever, and has been fully described by Fitzgerald.[3] An official report of 1921 states that the control of 80 per cent. of English soap-making was in the hands of the United Kingdom Soap Makers' Association. Of these firms 39 belonged to Lever Brothers combine —the well-known Sunlight soap makers—which stood for about 90 per cent. of the Association's output, and from 70 to 75 per cent. of the whole English production. Fitzgerald corrects these figures for later dates, stating that the main output of Levers is household soap, and that since 1920 new purchases by the trust have brought its control up to nearly 90 per cent. of the whole output of household soap in England. The influence of this trust on prices has often been a matter of controversy. Fitzgerald examines its significance with much caution and impartiality. It cannot be denied that Levers have a powerful hold over market conditions. Fitzgerald writes: "Evidently the combine can extract with impunity very high prices, looking

[1] 'Statist,' Sept. 29, 1923.

[2] Cf. Deutschlands wirtschaftliche Entwicklung im ersten Halbjahr, 1926, published by the Reichskreditgesellschaft, p. 21.

[3] Fitzgerald, pp. 59-71.

to the necessity for their productions, but such an increase would be checked by foreign competition and by the relative ease with which new competitors could set up in the trade."

We have now arrived at a certain conclusion in our investigation. We have tried so far merely to set out clearly the conditions under which large industrial monopolies can nowadays arise in England, and for this purpose we have taken the history of the most important and most lasting syndicates, cartels and trusts as our guide. No attempt has been made to describe associations whose monopolist character is as yet but slightly developed or whose persistence may still be open to doubt; for we were not concerned to give a detailed and exhaustive picture of all combines past and present, but rather to extract from a consideration of the chief instances some conception of the circumstances which at the present day, after so many years of unadulterated competition, fix the limits within which monopolist organisations are possible in English industries.

Before the results of this examination can be summarised, one further question remains. The financial success of a monopolist organisation depends primarily, but not solely, on a more or less definite control over production. The fact that by co-ordination or amalgamation production can be monopolised does not in itself show how the new association will profit by the advantages of its situation. Its structure and detailed equipment—its form, its administration, the number, relations, and capacity of its directors, the division of output and sales between the various members, and the financial position—are here all important.

CHAPTER X

QUESTIONS OF ORGANISATION

All the types of monopolist organisation known to the experience of other countries are to be found among the chief English monopolies. We see every stage of monopolisation, from loose understandings terminable at any moment or the more definite agreement for a fixed period, to the yet closer unions of the syndicate with a common place of sale and common regulation of production and the amalgamation into one undertaking of all the firms in favour of monopoly; that undertaking in its turn perhaps forming new syndicates and cartels with important outsiders. Each variety is distinguished from its predecessor in order of completeness by the greater number of functions formerly exercised by separate firms which it usurps and subjects to a common monopolist control, until, finally, in the "horizontal" combination, every single function is transferred to the trust.[1]

The general experience in Germany has been that problems of organisation are more complicated in associations of independent makers than in amalgamations and trusts. Once private interests are sunk in a single undertaking, the difficulties of settling the form of administration seem to be nothing compared with those of the time in which the directors are continually faced with the thorny questions of division of production, consumption by a member of the association, common places of sale, and so on. In England,

[1] See 'Report on Trusts,' pp. 17 *et seq.*, 38 *et seq.*

too, in former times, the Newcastle Vend, which was an association pure and simple, was much more complicated in organisation than any of the monopolies of modern times.

But at the present it is not the cartels and syndicates which prove in England the most difficult to organise, but the trusts. In Germany combinations are usually composed of a large number of undertakings gradually amalgamating into a trust; in England they have, as a rule, only a few members. As many examples have shown us, the possibility of raising prices by monopoly is much smaller than in countries in which natural monopolies in raw material, protective duties or high freights on competing goods, make such a policy especially attractive. It is, therefore, relatively difficult in England to unite 30, 40, or 50 interested parties in a combine; much more difficult than in countries where the probable monopoly profits of each are so high as to overshadow completely any objections which might be raised to the surrender of all independence. Accordingly, it has been found imperative in England to form a trust where, as in textiles, salt, soda, and Portland cement, many undertakings were affected. On the other hand, where there was only a very small number of firms, and private interests opposed to association were slight, monopoly has been achieved by a mere association in spite of the fact that the prospective profits were small. In the steel trade, especially in ship plates, boiler plates, and rails, in industrial spirit, and in cables, monopolies have been firmly established by mere syndicates and cartels.

As these syndicates and cartels only include a small number of members, usually of about equal power, their organisation offers far fewer difficulties than on the continent, where cartels embrace works both "simple" and "mixed," and of unequal economic and financial stature. But the organisation of English trusts, which have in several cases involved the amalgamation of a great number of firms each working under different conditions, has often proved to be very much more complicated, for instance in the textile industry.

In this case every single firm had to be allowed a large measure of independence as a branch of the trust. The English Sewing Cotton Company left each member its own individuality. Every partner or director of a former firm remained responsible for his own branch in addition to becoming a director of the whole trust. The organisation was in every way the opposite to the highly centralised firm of Coats, and its initial failure to rival the success of the latter was not least of all due to this division of powers. It was not until the company was reorganised with the help of Mr. Philippi of Coats's, and provided with central management and a common place of sale for all works, that an end was put to the evil system by which each separate firm went its own way without a thought for the interests of the whole. It was the same with the Manchester Bleachers. According to the prospectus, each firm was to deal personally with its own customers, direct its own works, and even receive a percentage of the profits. But the most loosely knit of all textile trusts was the Calico Association. It had a directing body responsible to the shareholders of 70-80 persons, 128 "vendors" of the 46 firms forming the combine each retaining the right to run their works for five years independently of the managing directors, and, finally, a number of managing directors. Although the association represented a financial amalgamation, in its inner constitution it resembled a badly organised cartel far more than a uniformly constructed trust.

Defenders of the theory that English manufacturers are by nature individualists might perhaps claim this scrupulous retention of individual functions even after the formation of a trust as a further proof of their thesis. But this interpretation of the case is hardly justifiable. The peculiar organisation of the textile associations is explained by the simple fact that certain firms enjoyed a special repute which it was not desired to destroy ; and accordingly their outward form was preserved, certain persons cognisant of the special wishes of customers were secured for the trust, and, no doubt to encourage sales, manufacturers were often assured a special share in the profits of their former works in the form of percentages. The decentralisation merely meant that the amalgamating firms possessed advantages for the sale of their special products which they did not wish to surrender, and which the trust did not wish to lose.

Economic advantages, therefore, sufficiently explain the form of organisation which the textile associations first adopted. Experience was necessary to prove that the immediate attractions of decentralised management were overshadowed by its drawbacks, and that important gains expected from the combination of undertakings could not be realised under this system. Economies in directors' fees, the allocation of production to the most efficient, and of orders to the most favourably situated as regards freights, the limitation of output in times of over-production, and the other advantages of combination, could only be effected if the trust was centrally managed. The first development of the new English monopoly combinations and amalgamations, especially in the textile industries, is everywhere faced by the problem of internal organisation. In the first decade of this century a reorganisation of trusts was in many cases effected on the lines of centralisation. This was the case with the Sewing Cotton Company in 1906-7.[1]

Its reports enumerate the following results of "concentration."

1. A linen thread mill was sold to round off the trust's sphere of business. 2. The production of the Egerton Mill was transferred, the report explaining that the trust "had sufficient reserve productive capacity at other mills to enable them to deal with the trade conducted at that branch." 3. The plant of the Belgrave Mill at Oldham was

[1] See its Reports for 1907 and 1908.

removed, and the site and buildings sold. 4. Finally, " a further concentration took place by the transfer of the business of R. F. & J. Alexander to one of the other branches of the company." A special account of such transactions was kept (Closed Works Account). Contemporaneously with this policy of concentration output was centralised by the connection of the Sewing Cotton Co. with Messrs. Coats, and the system of common sales established in 1906 through the Central Thread Agency.

The Calico Printers' Trust had also its teething troubles with organisation. In 1902 there was a consolidation of the boards of directors, but it was only in 1908 that a more centralised organisation was carried out. This was the work of Mr. O. E. Philippi, who had played an important part in the organisation of the Sewing Cotton Company and the firm of Coats. It was decided to give up the old division of separate administrative units and individual management of works and to set up a single central body.[1] That the whole stimulus to this reorganisation was due to the strong personality of a single member shows that in England, as in America, a type of " trust organiser " has arisen whose special organising capacity gives him a predominant influence over the structure of the new combination. It was astonishing to see how the problem of centralisation was solved in the new chemical trust composed of many strong individual manufacturers. When a combination of the leading men of the Imperial British Chemical Industries Ltd. took place the 'Manchester Guardian Commercial' came out with a somewhat ironical article, " The Who's Who of Directors." [2] The combinations of employers in the heavy chemical industries, the dye makers, the different branches of soda production, their arrangements with artificial silk and explosive manufacturers and with coal owners show again an undertaking of such ramifications that they include other trusts in order to attain their

[1] Cf. 'Manchester Guardian,' Feb. 25, 1909, p. 12.

[2] 'Manchester Guardian Commercial,' Nov. 4, 1926, p. 554.

objects. The problem of organisation was much more complicated than in the ordinary syndicate or cartel. Among the employers were well-known leaders like Sir Alfred Mond, Lord Ashfield, Sir John Brunner, Mr. H. J. Mitchell, Mr. Henry Mond and others. But to-day there is so much experience that the problem of centralisation is likely to be solved in favour of the enterprise as a whole, and the crises of decentralisation which occurred in the past will in the future probably be avoided.

Another important problem connected with the organisation of English monopolies has always been that of capitalisation.

We have already pointed out that the formation of a trust can come and has, in fact, come in England at several quite different stages of concentration. If the trust arises whilst the competition of numerous less efficient concerns still exists it to some extent anticipates natural development. Manufacturers hope to avoid the ultimate result of the movement towards concentration, and, without fighting the competitive struggle to the death, to enjoy the advantages of the surviving fittest. In other words to limit the total production of all existing firms to a few working at much lower cost owing to technical expansion, economies, and so on, and to fix prices on a monopolist basis by the suppression of many competitors. If competition is unrestricted, this consummation is achieved by the gradual extinction at a heavy capital loss of the less efficient firms; but if a trust is formed these firms are bought out at prices depending on the trust's expectations of profit from the new business. Supposing those expectations are not fulfilled, the combine has an ever-increasing dead weight of over-capitalisation round its neck and its entire financial success is endangered.

The development of trusts in the nineties and up to the beginning of this century was undoubtedly often characterised by heavy over-capitalisation.

The Calico Association appears to be an instance in point,

owing largely to the failure of its organisation to save as much by concentration as was expected when the shares were allotted. Another instance is the Portland Cement Association, owing apparently to the importation of cheap natural cement of which its founders had not dreamt.[1] In a third instance, that of the Salt Trust, both these two factors combined to produce over-capitalisation. For the ten years up to 1907 it paid no dividend. The average dividend between 1898 and 1914 was no more than 1¼ per cent. on the original share capital, though this had been written down. The United Alkali Company paid only 1 per cent. on the average between 1896 and 1913, the newly-founded Dyestuffs Corporation, in spite of state help, paid no dividend from 1920 to 1924; and similar examples abound, especially in the development of smaller trusts and combines like those in the steel industry.[2] A particularly gross case of ruinous over-capitalisation is that of the new Glass Bottle Trust in 1919.

The causes of over-capitalisation are numerous. Anticipated increase in price proves impossible. New competitors arise, foreign or domestic. New processes of manufacture are discovered—a potent factor in the poor financial success of the Alkali Company. Organisation is bad. But all of them come to this; that whether because it is harder to monopolise output and sales than was expected, or because the monopoly is not so energetically used as it should be, the rosy views taken of the prospects when a combine is started are not in practice realised. It is the story of the older monopolies once more. They too suffered from over-capitalisation and their founders also, the "projectors" as they were then called, to gain the grant of a monopoly and its protection by duties and by prohibition of import took upon themselves financial responsibilities which they could not discharge, and which finally destroyed them and their

[1] 'Statist,' Feb. 23, 1907, p. 381; 'The Baillie,' Feb. 6, 1907; 'Economist,' Sept. 12, 1908, p. 478.

[2] Cf. 'Statist,' "The Position of Combines," Sept. 30, 1924.

projects. As Mr. Price says of Mansell's glass monopoly,[1] " a large proportion of this [capital] was water, for at least three patents were bought up which would have possessed no value if markets had been open to all. And Mansell had bought out his own partners upon the basis of the speculative value of monopoly." Monopoly making is always a speculation ; but the more irredeemable capital liabilities have been piled up, the greater will be the discrepancy between the original capital basis of an industrial monopoly and its actual results in the gloomy days of continued ill-success.

Very many English combines have not, of course, met with these financial difficulties. In textiles, for instance, Coats & Co., the Fine Cotton Spinners' and Doublers' Association, and the Bradford Dyers' Association prove what financial successes monopolist associations can be. The Dyers' prospectus in 1908 stated that in every year from 1900 to 1907 " the net amount available after payment of the debenture stock interest has been more than twice the amount required to meet the dividend on the preference shares, and the profit-earning capacity of the Association has steadily increased." The profits ever since have been extremely good. The Calico Trust, after achieving its long-needed organisation, has now an assured profitable position. Courtaulds has enjoyed extraordinary prosperity. The same is the case with the Whisky Company, the Distillers' Company, the oil companies and the tobacco trust. The author of the 'Statist' articles, to which we have frequently alluded, says that the monopolist organisations formed before the war were most profitable where the danger of over-capitalisation was the smallest. This is, with some exceptions, still the case. He points out that the chief fault of the old amalgamations was that their working methods did not produce the estimated results, but that too often the efforts to co-ordinate different concerns resulted in waste and confusion. He

[1] Price, ' English Patents of Monopoly,' p. 81.

adds, nevertheless, that "the pre-war amalgamations worked very well, and though they have not yet made the most of their advantages deserve more praise than blame."[1] On the other hand, the close of a successful war has given an opening to company promoting, which has brought into existence some singular and sometimes quite unjustifiable undertakings. "It is certain," says the 'Statist,' "that if depression had set in directly after the war, or even had been anticipated in industry, there would not have been founded many of the 'house' concerns which have not fulfilled their original intentions, or must soon find themselves at a disadvantage with foreign competition owing to their unfavourable financial conditions." In general it may be laid down that the formation of a trust runs the greatest financial dangers when it buys up at high prices businesses which would undoubtedly collapse within a visible time under the stress of competition. Under such conditions the attempt to precipitate by a trust the monopoly which must in the natural course result from the slow but steady concentration of plant and business frequently leads to a financial fiasco. The position is different if the monopoly is organised at a stage in the movement towards concentration at which only a few very efficient undertakings survive.

It appears, therefore, that the monopolies resulting from the combination of a few very powerful firms are also the most successful financially. One of the most flourishing monopolist associations, for instance, in English industries is the Whisky Trust, in which a single firm engineered concentration for several decades, not by buying up inefficient competitors, but by entering into partnership with the strong survivors of a very bitter competitive struggle. The history of Coats & Co. is similar. If they had from the beginning bought up weak outsiders, they might well have suffered the disadvantages of over-capitalisation, which, in fact, appeared in the amalgamation of those same outsiders

[1] 'Statist,' Sept. 30, 1924.

into the English Sewing Cotton Co. Where it is a question of quite modern industries, as in the case of the artificial silk industry—in so far as they do not, like the English dye industry, rest on insecure assumptions and in themselves hold out little promise of profit—the presence from the outset of a great industrial organisation, which admits only a small number of competing concerns, means an extraordinary simplification of the process of trust-formation; and this explains the special financial success of the great English artificial silk industry.

It would also seem that large separate firms associated only in a cartel are more likely to pay their way in such cases and increase their profits than a trust including under the same financial control a greater number of firms of an inferior though productive type. No doubt an over-capitalised trust may be able gradually to close inferior works bought up at a heavy cost in favour of the better works, but this retards that increase of productive power by the reduction of working expenses, which is the more desirable for a trust, because the cheapening of production is one of its main defences against the rise of smaller undertakings, and goes to secure its monopoly.

The 'Report on Trusts,' 1919, pays special attention to the reduction of working costs as the legitimate function of monopolies, but the connection between the purely organising and financial questions of monopolies and their activities and their capacity to bring about in practice these greater economies in output is still too little realised. Yet it is evident from the difference between the old pre-war concerns and those of the short-lived company-promoting period that the organic and financial bases of concentrated undertakings may determine whether the will, which as a rule is present, to put the industry on a sounder footing by purely technical improvements, has any prospect of success.

CHAPTER XI

THEORETICAL CONCLUSIONS AND CRITICISMS

The basis of English cartels and trusts is in every case concentration, the restriction of *increasing* production to an ever *decreasing* number of factories and undertakings. Add to concentration immunity from foreign competition, and all that is essential for the creation of monopolist associations is given. To explain the real importance of concentration in connection with English monopolies, it is only necessary to contrast the conditions which characteristically precede monopoly in Germany, America, and other countries with those in England. Concentration has been at work abroad too; but while in England the movement towards monopoly only begins when the number of producers has shrunk to 40, 30, 20, or even less, foreign monopolies have often been formed at a much more elementary stage of concentration, and in some cases even when both production *and* the number of producers were increasing. What is the explanation?

We have considered two lines of enquiry bearing on the possibility of industrial monopoly. We asked under what circumstances could English manufacturers maintain a monopoly in their home market against foreigners, and we asked under what circumstances could they suppress domestic competition. We must now examine the results of these enquiries.

1. As to immunity from foreign competition.

England is much more exposed to foreign competition

existing so long as it shares the monopoly profits, but also while in competition with the monopolists of keeping its profits low, it may be lower even than those of the separate firms before combination. It was on the existence of such conditions that the classical economists based their doctrine of tendency to the equalisation of profits. If this, in fact, always governed industrial monopolies, monopoly could not at the present time exist in England, for as we have seen, monopolised raw materials are practically non-existent. They are at any rate unknown in almost all the monopolist organisations which we have considered. The textile trusts, the coal associations, the artificial silk and chemical trusts, the whisky and industrial spirit makers, the cable cartel, the wall paper trust, and the other monopolies may all have to face outsiders who—with certain exceptions and apart from the natural fluctuations of the market—can obtain raw materials and other necessities for production at the same prices as the combines, and can work them up in their factories at approximately the same cost. Even in the case of minerals like salt and cement, the natural supplies are so great that neither the Salt Union nor the Cement Association ever attempted to monopolise them. Yet all these cartels and trusts, and others not here discussed, started with the well-founded expectation of permanently suppressing competition or at least maintaining their existing " incomplete " monopolies.

An authority on American economic conditions, Dr. Vogelstein, has expressed the view [1] that " inelastic capital resources are the point at which monopoly, pure and simple, and a preponderatingly monopolist economic system with legal freedom of trade meet. . . . The possible monopoly of cartels and trusts rests almost entirely on the natural scarcity and inelasticity of an element of production." Whether this generalisation can be legitimately drawn from the position of American trusts is doubtful,[2] though most

[1] 'Archiv für Sozialwissenschaft,' 1905, pp. 346 and 348.

[2] Cf. Levy, 'Amerika als Wirtschaftsmacht,' Leipzig 1923, p. 75 *et seq.*

of them certainly fulfil the condition laid down. For England, the theory is certainly incorrect. The question of a natural or artificial inelasticity of supply is here quite unimportant, special cases excepted.[1] In England it is the size and productive power of an undertaking which produces a tendency to monopoly. The large capital investments which concentration encourages make the foundation of competing firms increasingly costly and difficult. Further, and this is perhaps the more important fact, every new competitor fit to keep pace with the gigantic creations of concentration means such a very large increase in production that to find a market there must either be an enormous increase in demand or an immediate drop in prices to a level unprofitable to both the new firm and the monopolists.

The moment the increase in the productive power of a business technically and economically profitable outstrips the growth of the demand, the tendency among existing undertakings to form a monopoly is checked. This has very often occurred in England where concentration of industrial units, horizontal and even vertical combination have of recent years immensely increased the capital resources and productive power of individual undertakings. To compete with firms representing 10, 20, or more per cent. of the entire output under conditions of production and distribution as favourable as those which their enormous organisation gives them, requires a certainty of finding a profitable market for a correspondingly large output. Assuming that the necessary materials can be acquired at the same cost, any one who can raise sufficient capital can set up an opposition firm producing at approximately the same cost. But if demand rises slowly he is digging his own grave. If a combination of these enormous concerns has further resulted in a trust or cartel, the demands on the fresh competitor become even more excessive. Even with a monopoly, attempts at greater efficiency persist, and

[1] Cf. *infra*, pp. 303-4.

sometimes the very size of the combination, witness the case of the Calico Printers or of Lord Furness's project, helps to decrease working expenses by better organisation of production and distribution. Naturally a new competitor need not by any means be prepared to equal the combine in productive power, for very possibly some of the combined firms are not of an economically profitable size. But it must at least be of the same productive power as the firm working most cheaply, and that alone implies a very great size where an industry is highly concentrated.[1] A recent example is the British Enka Co., which has set up a large scale competition in artificial silk. And if the advantages of combination have reduced the average cost of production to the combine to a level below that at which the cheapest producing firm can work in isolation, the new competitor must produce on a large enough scale to try conclusions on this basis. He must make his undertaking larger than the biggest of these combined in the monopoly, and thereby add to the risk of not being able to find a market for the increased output.

Let us take a hypothetical case.

Case I.—Assume an output of x goods per firm, the actual cost of making being £7. Assume further a selling price, if there is only one producing firm, of £31, and that every additional x reduces it by £2. With twelve firms, therefore, the price is £9, and the addition of a thirteenth firm will drive the price down to the unprofitable level of £7. Accordingly, twelve firms, producing $(12 \times x)$ goods, and selling at £9 would be the largest number that could exist, assuming that no further competition could arise unless it were possible to sell at a profit. But now let us assume these

[1] It is not in itself inconceivable that high prices might call forth undertakings inferior in organisation and technical appliances to the most profitable undertakings. But this does not in practice often happen where materials can be obtained at similar prices. Where the supply of materials is inelastic, and the high working expenses of a new undertaking are due to the fact that it can only exist at all by exploiting less favourable sources, matters are different.

twelve firms organise a monopoly, and, by reducing output, force up the price to £11. At once a new firm can spring up, and without hurting itself reduce the price to £9 again by its additional output. The attempted monopoly has failed; in fact, if the original twelve firms again put their full output on the market, there will be over-production and a general fall of prices to below the cost of manufacture. The attempt to form a monopoly would therefore be ill advised.

Case II.—Let us now, however, assume that concentration produces an amalgamation of each group of four firms, each unit, owing to increased efficiency, producing $(4 \times x)$ goods at £24 instead of £28 $(4 \times £7)$. On this basis a new-comer will have to produce $(4 \times x)$ goods and will in consequence depress prices even more than before. If, instead of reducing the price by competition to £9 for x goods, the three new groups formed out of the former twelve firms now combine, a new firm will not pay till prices reach £15 for x goods. At any lower rate the additional output would drive prices down too low for there to be any profit. At £15 the new supply would produce a reduction to £7 for x goods, and make a profit of £4, the cost of manufacturing $(4 \times x)$ goods being £24. The unit of manufacture being increased, the monopolist combination could merrily drive up prices to £13, provided it kept in mind the danger of fresh competition, and that competition was governed solely by abstract reasoning.

The actual degree to which the monopoly would be worked depends, of course, on the amount of output which produces the largest total profit. In Case II. the combine producing at £72 (£24 × 3) would rather sell $(10 \times x)$ goods at £13 per x goods, than $(12 \times x)$ at £9, or $(11 \times x)$ at £11, and would regulate its output and price policy accordingly. Suppose now demand increased. In principle the position is unchanged. In Case I., with twelve separate firms, if, instead of $(12 \times x)$ goods $(13 \times x)$ goods could be sold at £9, a new firm would spring up. In Case II. the monopolists would primarily profit by the increase in demand to sell their otherwise unproduced (or possibly dumped) 11th or 12th x goods at £13, and no fresh competition would arise. But if demand continued to increase till a 13th x also could be sold at £13, a new firm would pay, as its additional output of $(4 \times x)$ goods would only reduce the price to £7. So strong a demand would therefore reduce the limit up to which monopoly, with due regard for security from competition, could raise prices. An understanding with the outsider would, of course, again enlarge the monopolist's range.[1]

[1] The argument may be put in tabular form thus; the brackets representing the result of combination on the number of firms and the cost of manufacture.

Number of firms each with a productive power of x.	(combined)	Selling price. £	Cost of manufacture per x. £	(combined)
1	1	31	7	24
2		29	7	
3		27	7	
4		25	7	
5	2	23	7	24
6		21	7	
7		19	7	
8		17	7	
9	3	15	7	24
10		13	7	
11		11	7	
12		9	7	
13	4	7	7	24
14		5	7	
15		3	7	
16		1	7	

For clearness, various facts which might alter the situation in given cases, though not the principle, are here omitted. Under given circumstances, for instance, a trust might be able to meet an increased demand beyond its existing productive power by the addition of smaller concerns, not in themselves profitable industrial units. A wouldbe rival of the American Beef Trust would have to establish, in addition to enormous slaughter houses, secondary branches to dispose of bye-products, trains fitted with cooling apparatus, staff, and so on, equal to those of Messrs. Armour and Swift. But the latter could certainly themselves build new slaughter houses if the demand rose without requiring to increase their output at once to the extent that a new-

It must be remembered that we are only dealing with a tendency, and a tendency not often realised, if only because the founder of a new undertaking does not always know in advance what its influence on prices will be, or will not recognise it until mutual competition degenerates into economic suicide. At the same time not only the theorist but the student of actual industrial history will find the recognition of this tendency instructive. We have seen that the formation of monopoly depends largely on the number of existing manufacturers, and now we see why it did not result earlier, even where that was small. It is not the absolute number of competing firms which is decisive, but rather how far they could maintain a monopoly if they combined. If a relatively small concern is economically profitable, so that a slight increase in demand or price gives a new competitor a fair chance of existence, existing makers cannot maintain a monopoly even if they can obtain it. A monopoly is only conceivable when concentration has steadily increased each single concern's share in the total output. Whether the innate tendency of every such concentration to lead to monopoly actually develops to the extent that the permanent existence of a cartel or trust is possible, depends on the degree of concentration and the nature of the demand. Organisation to exploit its advantages is only attractive if existing undertakings are so large that for many years it will be unprofitable to set up a fresh undertaking in spite of an anticipated increase in demand.

In the desire to emphasise the protective effect of concentration, other factors which have in England worked in the same direction have for the minute been neglected. It is necessary, therefore, to recall the fact that the trust and

comer starting from the beginning would have to do. The fact that large firms have opened new slaughter-houses, therefore, in no way contradicts, as Vogelstein thinks it does ('Archiv für Sozialwissenschaft,' 1906, p. 555), my view, based on this very instance, that trading on a large scale can in itself have an element of monopoly.

cartel movement has often arisen in industries in which concentration was by no means the only security for a permanent monopoly. In the salt industry, though monopoly, it is true, first appears with the expansion of private undertakings resulting from the acquisition of transport and the consequential concentration, yet there was still a relatively large number of rival works in existence and the increased monopoly price at once stimulated further competition. In this rather exceptional case the possible profits of monopoly were great, and the question of their permanence was therefore of only secondary importance. Nor must it be forgotten that in a few cases, even in England, inelastic supplies of the requisites for production—for instance water-power in that of the Bleachers' Association—can check competition. The Bleachers' Association included more firms (53 in all) than any other of the textile monopolies, and showed therefore a much smaller degree of concentration than was necessary for most English trusts and cartels. Finally, the reputation of an established firm, with its own special brands and regular clientele, or the inherited skill of a special class of operatives, or its recently developed bonus system, tying the retail business, form in certain circumstances an element in a monopoly which must not be undervalued. Firms enjoying such advantages can sometimes, even if the protection of concentration is still insignificant, form a combine without fear of immediate competition. But the protection of a tradition is immeasurably smaller than that of inelastic material resources, which makes it hopeless *ab initio* for a new competitor to obtain what he requires for the purposes of manufacture at the same price as his antagonist. When the supply of such things, which exercises so much influence on the erection of monopolies in Germany and America, is so little limited as in England, the essential protection from fresh competition must lie in concentration, though naturally even in England subsidiary inducements can accelerate the day on which a concentration will actually result in the formation of a monopoly.[1]

It remains to draw a few conclusions. The development of cartels and trusts in English industries is restricted within narrow limits by three facts, the absence of a protective tariff, the comparative insignificance of freights, and the rarity of slowly reproduced mineral products likely to form national or international monopolies. Manufacturers can only set about the monopolist organisation of an industry when it is free from foreign competition, owing to the lowness of the cost of production, to the manufacture of special qualities, to traditional dexterity, or to international agreement. Even in such cases monopoly is subject to certain conditions. On the one hand the profit

[1] The latest and very capable chronicler of the English trust and cartel movement, Mr. P. Fitzgerald, admits the theoretical importance of my argument, but doubts its practical significance. He contends that the possibility of starting new businesses is much easier than it was thirty years ago. It seems to me that the development of great concerns in every branch of English industry in which the tendency to concentrate is established, shows the opposite. There are, broadly speaking, as is shown in Fitzgerald's work, no " near trusts " existing in rivalry with the great trusts and combines. I have never denied that many very small competitors may profit by and flourish under the price policy of the great trusts. But the question is how long such a development—which I traced long ago in the case of the American Steel Trust—can continue. My object was not to confront the trusts with the small ring of relatively backward outsiders, but to suggest the possibility of really effective competition, able to rival the competitive capacity of the great concerns. Fitzgerald has unfortunately neither made this distinction nor taken it into account. It is strange that Fitzgerald, after his own exposition, should say in this connection that " nothing shows that the trusts are the most economic industrial units." Here, too, there is a confusion. There may, of course, be badly managed, premature, over-capitalised trusts and amalgamations, which spell a failure, and over which even smaller competitors have an advantage. But to generalise from such possibilities means turning topsy-turvy the whole modern movement towards concentration. Exceptions, unfortunate incidents, and exaggerations are no proper criteria. We must look to the essentials of the new forms of organisation. See Fitzgerald, pp. 199-202.

is relatively small, compared with what it is in countries which are not without the three features mentioned above; and on the other hand the industries affected are such that their materials can be acquired at equal or even less cost by others, whereas many of the most important monopolies abroad are in industries whose materials cannot be multiplied at will, and can be monopolised. Therefore, even where prices could be raised so far as foreign competition is concerned, a successful monopoly can only be established when, in the first place, the number of competing firms is relatively very small; and in the second place, when the rise of fresh competition, even if prices are good, is either out of the question or only to be expected after a considerable period. Both conditions can only arise under the existing industrial organisation after concentration—in other words, when the number of undertakings decreases while production increases, and the most satisfactory economic unit can satisfy to an increasing degree the total demand for a given class of commodities. Concentration of works and undertakings is the foundation stone of English cartels and trusts. The conditions which made monopoly possible in other countries, even where concentration was but slightly, if at all, developed, being wanting in England, until the recent growth of concentration it was inconceivable. England presents the curious contradiction that, in the days when cartels were unknown in Germany or America, she had quite a modern cartel in her coal trade, based on freight advantages. When the rest of the world was being satiated with cartels and trusts, free trade, the improvement of transit—a very important factor in so small a country—the transition to the preponderating production of manufactured goods from imported raw materials and similar causes kept her from monopoly. The change came gradually after about 1870, in many trades even later, with the growing tendency of industrial capitalists to concentrate production in a few undertakings. For those who wish to study the effect on monopoly of that concentration by itself, all other influences being excluded, England now offers the ideal field of inquiry. There alone it is seen over a whole economic area, with nothing to obscure its working.

The war and its consequences have only strengthened the conditions conducive to concentration. The same tendency must doubtless be counted among the chief factors of monopolisation in other countries also. But numerous examples show that in those countries monopolies were conceivable owing to other conditions, even without concentration, or arose at a comparatively early stage in its development. And further, given strong concentrating tendencies, their influence is hidden by the existence of other conditions of monopoly. For instance, the fact that a Bessemer Steel Rail Works in America requires an annual output of 400,000 to 600,000 tons to pay, and that existing concerns had as early as 1903 a theoretical productive power of over 3,000,000 tons, must certainly dissuade people from starting new works. They would need to be confident of finding a market for the additional output of the new works not only during a boom but in average years, while in fact in years of depression the consumption of iron rails often fell far below 3,000,000 tons (1903, 2,100,000 tons; 1908, 1,350,000 only!). This state of affairs must, of course, have aided existing concerns to maintain a monopoly, but its effect in actual fact was almost entirely overshadowed by another factor, the monopolist control of the iron ore deposits, which gives existing undertakings a power that practically precludes the rise of new Bessemer Steel Works, even if such a thing were in itself profitable.

In other countries commercial policy, transport facilities, the chance existence of slowly reproducible minerals forming national or even world-wide monopolies, and other similar factors not essentially connected with the natural development of modern industrial capitalism can cause monopoly. Its rise under such conditions is not peculiar to a certain advanced stage of capitalism. Like the early cartels in English coal and copper mining, and so many

German cartels and American trusts, such monopolies may be shortlived phenomena vanishing with the disappearance of some accidental or temporary condition. In England, on the contrary, the creation of monopoly is directly connected with the most modern development of industrial capitalism, and is its logical consequence. The recent rise of cartels and trusts must therefore be regarded as essentially the pure result of that economic law which we have called the movement towards concentration.

And so it is that a few modern industries, like the young dyeing trade in England, assuming at the outset dimensions of business and financial importance, have succeeded straightway in establishing concentration.

There is no reason why the recently invented international cartels should not produce the necessary conditions for monopoly in England just as well as in other countries, inasmuch as international agreements have the same practical effect as a protective tariff. But up till the present time, as we have found, they have only appeared where concentration was already in a highly advanced stage.

In dealing with the sphere of free competition we traced the possibilities of concentration in England, its rapid progress in some industries, its complete non-existence in many, and the probable continuance of that state of affairs in the near future. We have seen, too, that owing to the absence of those artificial aids which stimulated it in other countries, concentration developed comparatively late in England, and that English industry as a whole by no means represents the most advanced type of combination now in existence.

Very different would the picture be if England broke with the free trade system. Protection would increase the number of trades in which the creation of monopoly would depend solely and singly on the amount of home competition. A great many industries in which at present concentration has very largely reduced the number of firms, but in which foreign competition has so far prevented a monopolist combination, would, under a tariff, straightway be in a position to found cartels or trusts. As it is, many industries threatened by foreign competition now find it easier than it used to be to suppress home competition; and in proportion as this is so, the probability that protection would be the last thing requisite for a monopoly increases.

Sir W. P. Rylands stated in a noteworthy article on the English steel industry, in the middle of 1926, that many presidents of the Iron and Steel Institute share this opinion. But the view that " in default of a certain restriction of imports it is extraordinarily difficult to induce individual manufacturers to give up their complete personal independence " cannot be accepted as of general application. We have seen cases enough in which amalgamations can and do take place without protection and in spite of individualism. On the other hand there are industries in which, notwithstanding protection, there is no monopoly. The motor car industry, now protected in England, is one in which the great number of manufacturers of about equal magnitude has made a combine impossible. It is true enough that from the point of view of the iron and steel trade protective duties would give an impulse to a rise of prices and check the formation of larger combines. But it is going too far to attribute, as Sir W. P. Rylands does, the strong iron and steel trusts in Germany before the war entirely to the effect of protective duties and dumping in foreign markets. The preoccupation of the trust to improve the technique of German wholesale business and its early installation of mixed works is at least of equal importance. The question remains whether, even if England set up protective tariffs for her iron and steel industries, the technical business structure of these industries would be strong enough under this impulse to establish a unified national monopoly.[1]

[1] See hereon Sir W. Peter Rylands on "Orderly Marketing in the Iron and Steel Trade," 'Manchester Guardian Commercial,' July 8, 1926, and my reply in the same journal of July 22, 1926. Also my article on "Concentration in German Industry" in the issue of September 2, 1926.

In any case, the prospects of monopoly building in such industries would be much brighter than in the days when the main problem was to suppress domestic rivals. For this reason, free trade is much more important as a defence against monopoly than it used to be. Moreover, duties on half-manufactured goods and raw materials stimulate vertical combination, and so artificially hasten the tendency to concentration. Finally, a tariff would, as in other countries, encourage the monopolistic combination of far more firms than is now possible, because the attraction of monopoly would grow with the possibility of profiting by the protective duty, and therefore monopolies would be conceivable in England even where little or no concentration had taken place. British tariff reformers are so well aware of this connection that they often desire a protective tariff simply as a means to creating trusts which they consider to be the most advantageous form of industrial organisation—a view strongly criticised on economic grounds by Prof. von Schulze Gävernitz.[1] Whether sound or not this project has no great influence on the practical development of English economic policy. It is true that some struggling English industries look upon a trust protected by a tariff as the remedy for dumping by foreign cartels and trusts, but the great bulk of the people, warned of the effect of trusts on prices by the experience of other countries, display no sympathy with such schemes. But a change of view has come about since the war. It can be shown that economists of different schools, and above all English official economic policy, have for some years past ceased to regard combines and monopolies as the bogey of altogether pernicious things, but have recommended them as methods of organisation. The 'Report on Commercial Organisation after the War,' 1918, emphasises repeatedly the advantage of cartels. It mentions them as one of the instruments of German success, and says that it is a method entirely adaptable to British industry. It draws particular

[1] 'Englischer Freihandel und Britischer Imperialismus,' pp. 270-77.

attention to the fact that a sub-committee for the machinery industry had suggested that manufacturers ought to be content to work together in the form of amalgamation or common agreement or an equalisation of their resources.[1] The Report by John Hilton, appended to the 'Report on Trusts,' takes a broad and long view of English monopolistic combines, and by no means adopts the attitude that they are merely dangerous.[2]

This is not contradicted by the fact that in another part of the Committee's Report there is a demand for strict supervision and control over combines in order to guard against possible abuses.

The Stevenson rubber scheme, under which the growers of rubber combined to effect a limitation of output, was prepared and supported officially by Government, and shows that if monopolistic measures seem to have a business-like object they are not regarded with hostility,[3] though the object here was to raise the price of raw rubber. It is worth noticing that the 'Report on Trusts' contains a special memorandum by Sir John Macdonell explaining the legal position as regards trusts and cartels in England. As is well known the common law opposes all monopoly as being "in restraint of trade." Sir John Macdonell investigates the old interpretations of this doctrine, shows how it has had already to be modified, and proposes far-reaching legal reforms in view of modern economic conditions. He adds that these reforms should "follow the teaching of the economists."[4]

Free traders no less than tariff reformers value the advantages of combination as a matter of organisation; but they maintain that under free trade alone can monopolist organisations produce desirable economic results. This opinion finds support among English, German, and

[1] 'Final Report,' pp. 12, 13, etc. [2] p. 16 ff.

[3] 'Statist,' Sept. 6, 1924.

[4] 'Report,' pp. 31 *et seq.*

American economists alike.[1] It rests on the argument that under free trade a monopolist combination cannot aim at raising prices, which must sooner or later provoke foreign competition, but only at reducing expenses, and thereby increasing profits. The facts which we have considered, however, show that foreign competition may be neglected in considering English industrial monopolies entirely in some cases, and in the rest up to a certain degree. The aim of such combinations is, at least in part, nothing more nor less than to profit more by freedom from foreign competition than would be possible if home competition continued unchecked. Just because they result from concentration it is an undoubted characteristic of English cartels and trusts that by economies and better organisation they produce especially large reductions in the working expenses of an undertaking. In many cases this may have been the chief object of the founders of great combines. But that does not alter the fact that even such combines, if free from foreign competition and strongly entrenched at home, occupy a monopolist position, which no one prevents them

[1] Hirst, 'Monopolies, Cartels, and Trusts,' p. 169. He holds that English combinations cannot raise prices above the "natural" level, *i.e.* the level of import prices, and therefore are harmless. But in the case of goods which were cheaper in England than abroad, foreign import prices might seem to the consumers "unnaturally" high. It is rather utopian for the 'Economist' to say (July 4, 1908, p. 16): "It is next to impossible for combinations to maintain prices in a free trade country above the legitimate (*sic*) level determined by the conditions of demand and supply." Mr. Pierce, in his very remarkable book, 'The Tariff and the Trusts' (New York 1907), p. 57, says: "That trusts exist in free trade countries as well as in protectionist countries is undeniable, but while in the former the economy in production which results from their promotion goes to the benefit of the consumer in the shape of reduced prices, in the latter they are identified with high prices to the consumer and large profits to the producers." Prof. Brentano ('Die beabsichtigte Neuorganisation der deutschen Volkswirthschaft,' p. 278) also thinks that under free trade "cartels are limited in their beneficial effects." Compare also Dietzel, 'Sozial Politik und Handelspolitik,' 1902, p. 23. On the other hand, the 'Statist' (July 26, 1924), at the end of its oft-quoted series of articles, finds in the experience of to-day a far-sighted and assured adherence to free trade as one of the only assured bases of security.

from using. As we have seen, this commanding position is not so strong, especially in the matter of prices, and its profits are not so great as in countries with high tariffs or heavy freights or natural monopolies in minerals. But we have also seen from examples that it may have effects not in principle different from those of trusts and cartels in other countries.[1]

It is admittedly a matter of very great difficulty to estimate the effects of English cartels and trusts on prices. In protected countries import price *plus* freight and duty are the measure of monopoly price, and it has been proved that in certain circumstances a trust or cartel has succeeded in raising the former competitive price by the whole amount of the duty. But in England prices often stand below the import price in spite of a monopoly rise, or, again, they develop quite independently of foreign prices and themselves fix the price in foreign markets, in which case no measure of the prices of English monopolists can be gathered from a comparison with foreign prices ; while the absence of accounts of expenses makes it impossible to compare prices and costs before and after the rise of monopoly. The history of various cartels and trusts points, however, to the following tendencies.

In the first place, the fixing of prices exclusively by competition is in general superseded by a more or less entire autonomy of the monopolist combinations, even where there is no complete monopoly. The decisive factor in prices in the particular industry affected is the price of the cartel or trust, whose power is no doubt definitely limited, but whose influence on prices is large and systematic. We find it almost universally stated in the reports of trade papers and similar documents that monopolist combinations have tried to " raise," or " reduce," or " maintain " prices. In other words, prices no longer depend merely on the results of unrestricted competition.

[1] For a special example of dumping by English associations see 'Report on Trusts,' p. 7.

In the second place, monopolist combinations usually achieve their avowed aim of raising prices above competitive prices. For this purpose cartels generally adopt the well-known device of assigning to each member a given quota of the authorised output; looser combinations rely on agreements to limit production, more particularly when demand falls. The object is often greater *steadiness* of prices, but the result is also a *higher level* of prices than competition would have allowed.

Finally, monopolist combinations show their influence in the division of markets so characteristic of trusts and cartels in other countries. Through a bonus system they seek to monopolise retail trade and to influence prices in such a way as to make combined dumping possible.

Such a policy in prices, which is very different from what prevails under competition, can only be undertaken by monopolist combinations. Nearly all of them have announced in their prospectuses that "price cutting" would be abolished. Very often they guaranteed not to use their monopolist position in developing prices, or, as the Dyers' Trust expressed it, not to "assume the rôle of monopolists." The industrial spirit cartel was represented to be "a quite innocent combination of manufacturers to prevent the depression of prices." Similar assurances accompanied the foundation of every trust that announced its appearance openly. Even Lord Furness thought it necessary to explain in connection with his projected trust in 1908 that they were not aiming at an "artificial level of prices"; and Messrs. Coats once declared that "they did not intend to get higher prices than those of the separate undertakings (of which they were an amalgamation), but that marked improvement in prices must naturally result where they had been unduly (*sic*) depressed by unfair and immoderate (*sic*) competition." Explanations of this kind make it obvious that it depends solely on the will of the monopolist combinations to put in practice a monopolist regulation of prices; and who is to guarantee the consumers that when a large monopoly is founded, and perhaps over-capitalised, the possibilities of monopoly will be neglected, and that the interested parties will take advantage only of the cheapening of production resulting from the amalgamation? It is sufficient to read the following passage in the report of the Calico Printers' Trust advocating a reorganisation after three years' existence:

"The disadvantages referred to . . . make themselves felt in most cases where a business is converted into a public company, and to a greater degree when a large number of businesses are combined and sold to the public. The necessity of meeting outside competition is no longer felt to the same extent, and the incentive to work the business economically in order to obtain an adequate return on the capital employed is seriously lessened. Too much reliance is placed on the possibility of obtaining higher prices, whereas it is in the case of a public company of the greatest importance to supervise every item of expenditure." Unfortunately it is not often that a trust is driven to such admissions about itself. It can only happen when, owing to even monopolist prices not giving the desired return, efforts must be made to increase profits by reducing working expenses.

Mr. Macrosty's contention that the higher prices obtained by English trusts and cartels can only be attacked if it can be proved that competition prices are healthy prices seems to me open to criticism. It depends entirely on what "healthy prices" as an economic term is to mean. Apart from practical impossibilities there is little to be gained theoretically by the calculation of the excess of prices over cost of manufacture to which he pins his faith. Very often we have to deal with a monopoly which has intervened in a slow process of concentration which would ultimately end in the survival of the fittest, for the very purpose of saving from sudden extinction firms which can no longer face the prices produced by competition. In such a case higher prices would be justified on the basis of normal profits by the higher cost of production compared with more favoured works. But whether the continued existence of such firms is economically desirable is no more settled than whether a nation should or should not preserve its decaying industries by protective duties.

There is, then, no reason to manifest a special economic optimism with regard to English cartels and trusts. It must be again emphasised—as was done in the 'Report on Trusts'[1]—that people may be conscious of the dangers of trusts, without assuming a purely negative attitude towards them. There are in England some radical opponents of concentration. Professor Gregory, Dean of the Economic Faculty in the University of London, says in a recent speech:[2] "All industrial combinations begin with a heavy financial charge which they get back from the community in the form of higher prices or from the shareholders in the form of watered capital. The trust movement hinders the development of industry." Such an opinion must be considered erroneous. How can we regard opposition to amalgamation as always advantageous to English industry when we look back upon the catastrophe of the coal dispute of 1926, its effect upon English trade, industry, and finance, its loss of business and waste of labour, its menace to the international position of the English coal trade, etc., and remember that the 'Report on the Coal Industry (1925)' throws much of the blame upon the splitting up of the industry, and concludes with proposals for amalgamation of the pits?[3] We must recognise that in the long run free competition tends, and is bound to tend, to concentration. And yet this process in view of foreign competition and of the complicated social problems of an industry, often continues too long, to the economic prejudice of the country. The alternatives of "higher prices or watered capital" are equally irrelevant. The idea of "high" prices is not solely

[1] p. 11. See also Fitzgerald *passim*.

[2] Quoted in the 'Free Trader,' Dec. 1926, p. 304.

[3] 'Report,' p. 233.

mathematical. The stability of prices is often of more importance. Such concentrations as we are dealing with can and do bring about lower costs of production which must in the long run result in lower prices, and in any case mark advance and not stagnation or retrogression. Without doubt the movement towards concentration renewed since 1925, and in German industry more strongly than ever, envisages this possibility. The methods it adopts are the rationalising and commercial simplification of business with the view of increasing or accelerating production, and it remains only for the State to intervene in case of any inconvenience which may result to the public if a monopolist price policy does not pass on to society some of the benefits of these technical improvements. The hitherto successful British monopolies which have not been over-capitalised have paid very high dividends without raising any clamour about exorbitant prices. In these days of great capitalised concerns there is the double object, lower costs and higher prices. But this double purpose may become single. In studying the price policy of trusts we must take the long view, and distinguish between times of a slump in demand and commercial crisis and times of increasing demand. Cartels and trusts are more dangerous in the second case than in the first, for in times of crisis their chief interest lies in a revival of demand which can only be aided when reduction of costs can bring about moderation of prices. In times of prosperity a monopoly makes hay while the sun shines. It is precisely because the post-war period has become one of depression, and one in which every intelligent industrialist must do his best to increase demand, that we must assume that monopolists in their own interests will not take advantage of their position to aim at small turnover with high prices. In this province of economic policy, too, the principle applies that stereotyped conclusions are to be avoided. Rather must the possibilities and estimate of development be considered with reference to an economic and industrial situation which is not constant, but is continually changing. At the very least what is here needed is a comprehensive foresight, as opposed to comprehensive judgments, especially when these judgments are based on somewhat antiquated theories.

On this ground alone—and others might be added—it seems to me that a general verdict on the economic effect of the actual prices obtained by English monopolist organisations is impossible, though there is no doubt of their monopolist trend. And to my mind its main importance lies rather in the methods adopted than in the actual level of prices reached.

For the first time since the earliest days of capitalism a large section of English trade has become overrun with monopolist organisations. What in those days rested on legal privilege, is now, though trade is free, the natural result of economic and more particularly capitalistic development. The analogy is not complete, for the monopoly of the present day is not full fledged, but rather competition reduced to semi-monopoly. Yet it is true to say that at a higher stage of development capitalism has returned to the form of organisation peculiar to its infancy, with closely similar results. In the seventeenth century the privileged entrepreneur, the "monopolist," regulated prices "at his pleasure." Now it is the cartel or trust which so far as it can "fixes" prices in large areas on monopolist lines. Separate rates rule in separate markets according to the degree of monopoly obtained, just as in the seventeenth century the monopolists fixed district prices for salt. As in the sixteenth and seventeenth centuries the grant of monopolies artificially increased the power of certain capitalists and forced capital to concentrate by uniting in the hands of a single person or company the few existing capitalist concerns, so now cartels and trusts outstrip concentration, and attempt to obtain at once the monopolist advantages to which concentration would ultimately in the natural course lead. Undertakings spring up financially dependent on the speculative value of anticipated monopoly profit, and as hazardous as the old monopolies for whose patents courtiers had paid too heavily. Again we are faced with the question, Does the consumer or finishing manufacturer actually benefit by the reduction of cost promised when the monopoly is started, or is it true, as Davies said in 1641, that "the interests of the subject and the settled price decreed by the Patentee cannot consist"? The revival of these long-forgotten problems marks the ebbing of the age of competition whose everlasting continuation no man doubted for a whole century, and the beginning for a second time of an age of industrial monopoly.

The world-war, its aftermath, and the world-wide economic crisis, lasting now for more than six years, have strengthened these tendencies. It is precisely now that we find ourselves at a time which seems to demand more urgently than ever before that international industry should of its own initiative do something to cure the ills from which it is suffering, because those ills—according to the 'Survey of Overseas Markets'—are undoubtedly due to the excessive producing capacities of the world's industries. War industries, States (newly founded since 1918) which all do their utmost to be self-sufficing, the strong protectionist spirit overseas, as well in the United States as in Japan, South America, and the British Dominions, all these have worked together to the excessive enlargement of industrial power, while the world demand and purchasing power have remained in a relatively backward state. The movement towards concentration may be regarded as the means, or one of the means, of bringing about a new organisation of industry, keeping only the works best equipped for production and so lowering costs and prices. It would be a hazardous matter for England were she to overlook this aspect of amalgamations and to see in the movements towards concentration in other countries an almost "un-English" proceeding, possibly intended only to do harm to English industries. Instead of such a revival of competitive jealousy it might well be more to the advantage of

English industry to attach itself to so powerful a movement, and by this means to assist in a course which may in the end succeed in curing the economic ills from which the whole world is suffering. Fear of monopoly ought not to cloud these associations or to act as a deterrent. England also will undoubtedly come to recognise, on the ground of the development which we have described, that a revolution has broken out in the most important areas of industrial organisation, and that this revolution calls for new departures in economic and political thought and policy.

APPENDIX I

A CARTEL AGREEMENT OF 1835

(' Report of the Select Committee on the State of the Coal Trade.' House of Commons, 2nd August, 1836, pp. 7-9.)

It was handed in, and was as follows: Articles of agreement made this day of 1835, between the several persons whose names are subscribed, being owners or lessees of certain collieries within the counties of Northumberland and Durham.

1st. The owners or lessees of each of the undermentioned collieries, will by a written document appoint a representative, with full powers to act for such colliery, and to bind the owner or owners during the continuance of this agreement.

2d. That the representative shall have such an acquaintance with the general management of the concerns, and the money transactions of the colliery he represents, as to be able at all times to state correctly the quantity of coals sold, and the price actually received for the chaldron or ton, of both round coals and small, and shall be responsible for any irregular allowance or other deduction from the price at which his coals ought to be sold, or for any other violation of either the letter or spirit of this agreement.

3d. That the owners or lessees shall have the power of changing their representative, upon giving notice in writing to the chairman,

4th. That a committee for the Tyne, consisting of nine members (selected from the representatives), shall be appointed by lists to be sent from each colliery, to act for one year, subject to re-election at the expiration of every 12 months; but though it is desirable that the committee should consist of the number above stated, for the purpose of settling the basis for the respective ports and collieries, the committee shall nevertheless be competent to form among themselves a sub or execute one for the purpose of carrying the provisions of this agreement into effect, so that such committee shall not consist of less than three for the Tyne.

5th. That five constitute a quorum, that the votes be taken by ballot, and that the decision of the majority shall bind the parties to this agreement in all cases, except where an appeal is allowed.

6th. That the parties to this agreement will adopt the existing basis for the collieries, whose quantities are now fixed, till such quantity shall have been objected to by the committee or the representatives, and finally settled by the referees, and in settling the quantity to be allowed to any colliery, the committee or referees to be guided by the powers of working and leading proportion of the different sorts of coal, their respective selling prices and facilities of shipment. But that in estimating the powers of the respective collieries for the purpose of fixing the basis, such portions of their respective powers as are applied to the producing of coals sold, foreign or land-sale, shall not be taken into the account.

7th. That impartial reference shall continue to be the great leading principle on which the arrangements of the trade must be governed, and that it must be applied to settle the quantities between the different ports or rivers, forming parties to this agreement, as well as between individual collieries.

8th. That before an appeal be entertained from a river or district, a majority of the representatives of the collieries of such rivers or district must have declared their conviction of the propriety of it, and have made such request in writing to the united committee.

9th. That the dissatisfied river or district shall name their referee, and that the united committee shall do the same, and that those two gentlemen shall name a third as umpire, previous to their entering upon the inquiry.

10th. That the whole expense shall be equally divided between the appealing part and the trade at large.

11th. That the referees shall have power to reduce or to augment the quantity of such appealing river or district, and such decision shall be final.

12th. That the above principles which are to guide the reference in the case of rivers or districts, shall be applied to individual collieries appealing from the decision of the respective committees in the district to which they belong, except that it shall not be necessary for any individual colliery to obtain leave of the committee of the river to which it belongs, to make an appeal from their decision.

13th. That as soon as this agreement shall be signed, the rivers and districts shall be at liberty to appeal to the present united committee, but in case no appeal is made previous to the commencement of 1836, that then no change of basis as between the rivers or districts shall take place, except at the commencement of each year, and then only in case the river or district shall have given four months' notice to the then existing united committee of their intention to make such appeal.

14th. That in the case of individual collieries, they shall be at liberty to appeal also as soon as the agreement shall have been signed; but in case no appeal is made previous to the commencement of 1836, then no change of basis shall be made except at the termination of any six months, and then only on the representative of such colliery giving three months' notice previous to the 1st day of January and the 1st day of July in any year to the respective committees of his intention to make such appeal.

15th. That the decision of the referees shall take effect in the case of rivers or districts from the commencement of the year, in the case of individual collieries from the commencement of the six months succeeding the period when he shall have given such notice.

16th. That the committee or referees shall have power to summon the parties to this agreement, or their agents, to answer any interrogatories, and to produce any documents necessary to enable them to give full effect to this agreement, but such power not to justify calling for the private accounts of the colliery.

17th. That the parties so summoned shall, for non-attendance or refusal to answer or produce such documents, forfeit £20, to be returned only in cases where an appeal to a general meeting of representatives the majority shall decide in favour of the party appealing, the committee at such meeting not to vote upon the appeal against their decision; the votes at such meeting to be taken by ballot.

18th. That the relative prices of every description of coal be fixed by the committee and the representatives of each colliery, subject to an appeal to referees.

19th. That no colliery, without leave of the committee, shall vary the fixed price agreed on between such colliery and the committee, as the selling price of that colliery, under a penalty of 5s. for every chaldron so sold, subject to an appeal to referees in case of dispute.

20th. The committee in concert with the committee of the Wear and Tees, and the other parties to this agreement, shall make such issues of round coal from time to time, as may be necessary to meet the demand.

21st. Any colliery where particular difficulties of shipment may be reasonably apprehended at particular seasons of the year, or other causes, may be allowed such quantity, from time to time, in anticipation thereof, as the committee shall deem proper; any colliery thinking itself aggrieved by the refusal of such leave, the claim to be decided by reference.

22d. All coal to be sold by weight, either by the ton of 20 cwt. or the chaldron of 53 cwt.; any colliery found by the inspector giving over-weight to be fined 2s. 6d. for each and every cwt. of excess on an average of 10 waggons; every colliery to have a weighing machine, in proper order, in a convenient situation, under a penalty of £20.

23d. Any colliery exceeding the issue beyond 100 chaldrons, or 2 per cent. upon the basis, to finish a ship, shall forfeit for every chaldron so exceeding 5s., and such excess shall also be deducted from the issue to the colliery for the next month.

24th. That each party shall deposit, in the hands of trustees, a promissory note, payable on demand, to the amount of £20 per 1000 on its respective basis, as a security for the payment of fines and the general performance of this agreement, the committee to fix the amount of fines in every case not specially provided for; the trustees to consist of the chairman and the committee.

25th. That the inspectors of the Tyne, Wear and Tees, shall, as often as the committee of either river may deem it expedient, examine together the measure of all the collieries of the different ports comprehended under this agreement, that the weight per chaldron may be kept moderate and uniform, as provided in rule 22d.

26th. No freighting or upholding freights or prices to be permitted without permission from the committee of the river or district in which the respective collieries are situated under a penalty of 5s. per chaldron on the quantity of coals so vended, subject to reference.

27th. That all the parties to this agreement shall strictly adhere to such regulations as to the sale of coals in London by the coal-factors as the united committee shall, from time to time, agree upon.

28th. That if, at any time during the continuance of this agreement, the united committees shall deem it expedient, for any temporary purpose, to grant an additional issue of coals to the markets upon the coast, they shall have power to do so under such modifications and upon such terms as they may consider expedient.

29th. That it be imperative on the committee to enforce the penalties incurred under this agreement, and collect the same once a month, and pay the same to the Newcastle secretary for the general purposes of the trade.

30th. This agreement to commence on the 30th day of January 1836, and to continue from year to year, during the pleasure of the parties hereto, any of whom may withdraw, on giving six months' notice, in writing, to the united committee previous to the end of any year after the first year, and thus terminate this agreement.

31st. If circumstances should arise to render it expedient that this agreement should terminate otherwise than before provided for, and that, at a meeting of the representatives of the three rivers, and the other parties to this agreement, called for that purpose, four-fifths of the parties hereto shall so think it expedient, then this agreement shall terminate.

32d. No party to be bound by signing these rules until they shall have been agreed to and signed by the proprietors of every colliery upon the Tyne, and until the coal-owners of the Wear, Seaham, Tees, Hartley, Cowpen and Netherton, shall have signified their willingness to act in concert with the Tyne committee upon the general principles of this agreement.

33rd. That in case any difference of opinion should arise between the respective committees, or any individual coalowner and the committee of the district to which he belongs, upon the construction of any of the above articles, or upon any other point not herein provided for, that the same shall be submitted to reference.

APPENDIX II

COMBINATION OF WORKS. LORD FURNESS'S SPEECH

(Report of the Eighth Annual Ordinary General Meeting of the Shareholders of Richardsons, Westgarth & Co., Ld. Held on Tuesday, Dec. 29, 1908).

THE usual routine with regard to our annual meeting has this year been interfered with on account of a proposal which has been made to your Directors for the amalgamation of our business with those of several other engine building firms on this coast. I may at once say that I was in no way responsible for the proposal, and am neither directly nor indirectly interested in the scheme except as your chairman and as a shareholder in your Company, but the commercial possibilities of such an amalgamation are in the opinion of your Directors so important, that we feel it our duty, even at the sacrifice of very considerable time, to investigate the position thoroughly and to take part in what are proving to be very prolonged negotiations.

You will, I know, agree with me that the past year has been one of the most disastrous in the annals of the North-East Coast, involving as it did the practical stoppage of the engineering industry for no less than seven months by the engineers' strike, this in our own case being preceded by partial stoppage and complete disorganisation owing to sectional strikes in the shipyards. We have lost, in fact, an entire year, and the immense efforts we have made in laboriously building up additional branches to our business by the creation of new departments for the manufacture of steam turbines, pumping machinery, steel works' equipment and electric installations, have been ruthlessly upset by one of the most ill-advised and calamitous strikes on record. The general public have grown so accustomed to the continuous succession of strikes that nothing short of the stoppage of the nation's railway system or coal supply creates more than ordinary interest, but the alarming fact remains that British industries are being jeopardised and British capital destroyed to an extent unparalleled in British industrial history. Take our own case as an example. We have three works, in Hartlepool, Middlesbrough, and Sunderland, with staffs of highly trained technical experts for the conduct and development of our various manufactures, each department having an organisation of designers and draughtsmen complete in itself. To supervise the actual manufacture there is a further organisation of works managers, departmental foremen and assistants, and in addition the usual commercial and clerical staffs, numbering in all some 250 men, whose services cannot, of course, be dispensed with the moment the general body of employés decide to go out on strike. At the commencement of the strike it also happened that we had an unusual number of important contracts in process of erection in various parts of the kingdom, and at a stroke everything was brought to a complete stoppage, this being followed by the virtual paralysis of our entire business for seven weary months, each successive month bringing possibilities of settlement by various proposals, including the intervention of the Board of Trade, whose good offices were so flouted by the men as to result in the resignation of Mr. Barnes, the General Secretary of the Amalgamated Engineers' Society. For ourselves, we were compelled to see our profits turned into losses, grass actually growing in our yards, our customers disappointed and disgusted, and our prospective business brought to a dead standstill by reason of our inability to accept orders. In the town, as you know, men were brought to beggary, women and children to the verge of starvation, and tradesmen's savings reduced almost to vanishing point. This, then, is the sorry picture of a strike for which there was no justification whatever and which was blindly persisted in notwithstanding many friendly efforts, including those of a Cabinet Minister and the men's leaders.

We are still among the wreckage, but let us hope that this epidemic of strikes is over, for otherwise it will be quite impossible to maintain the prosperity which has hitherto been associated with the engineering industry on this coast. Indeed, even with a mutual desire to recover lost ground, it is problematical whether we can do so unless we adopt methods by which the cost of production can be reduced by the elimination of wastage. The position we have to face is one of intense competition, and what that competition means is well illustrated by the fact that our once highly-remunerative forge department, together with many others in the district, is now practically closed, as we can obtain forgings at considerably lower prices than we can either produce them ourselves or buy them in this country. This competition will surely spread to other departments unless we adopt wise measures, and the points we must always keep prominently in view are—that there must be no strikes, that greater individual interest must be taken in the day's work, that contract dates must be kept and the confidence of buyers restored, and that the cost of production must be reduced.

If commercial success is to be achieved by any scheme of amalgamation, however, it is obvious that it can only result from increasing the excellence of our manufactures and decreasing the cost of their production. Any attempt at artificially creating a range of selling prices higher than the market standard prevailing at any given time is foredoomed to failure, as we should deservedly lose our trade by sacrificing the goodwill of our friends and customers. The one objective must, therefore, be to beneficially influence the shipbuilding industry by supplying machinery at prices which will compare favourably with those of other competing centres, and at the same time secure, if possible, a fair manufacturing profit. It is unquestionable that marine engine building presents an ideal proposition for the application of such a scheme, and if it becomes an accomplished fact and is carried out with an enthusiastic determination to make it a great success, then, in my opinion, it cannot fail to have a favourable and permanent influence on the shipbuilding industry on this coast.

Experience has shown that the highest success in any manufacture can only be obtained by specialised production in large quantities under expert management. The production of marine machinery, and the mass of detail in particular connection therewith, involves so many trades, each requiring a separate department, that specialised production in bulk under highly concentrated management becomes practically impossible for the average engine builder ; but under an adequate scheme of amalgation the entire proposition is simplified and is feasibly desirable. For example, the firms considering this scheme have, during the past seven years, supplied complete engine equipment to 1206 steam-ships, having an aggregate horse-power of 2,150,000. The detail alone in connection with the yearly output of 172 sets of machinery is enormous, and were it standardised and manufactured under modern conditions, profits would be obtained which, under the present conditions, are quite impossible.

In view of the highly progressive nature, not only of the manufacture of marine and other machinery but also of its design, every single builder is now constantly face to face with heavy expenditures for plant in order to keep pace with the times. Take another example : since this Company was formed, seven years ago, we have spent £133,000 in new machinery and buildings, besides another £140,000 or thereabouts in maintaining our three works in a high state of efficiency, this expenditure being entirely apart from the cost of our turbine works, which are practically independent and constitute what is to us an entirely new business, and which have involved an outlay of fully £50,000. We are, of course, not alone in this expenditure, as all firms recognise that it is necessary for their very existence, and, heavy as it is now, it will undoubtedly become more so in the future by reason of the ever-increasing severity of competition throughout the industrial world. By amalgamating several of these big businesses, however, and localising, as far as practically possible, the manufacture of standard details, this enormous aggregate expenditure could either be very greatly reduced or, if spent as freely as at present, would inevitably result in far greater profit-earning capacity. This is to my mind the most important requirement of the present-day engineering manufacture. Experience has proved beyond question that in order to exist at all every engine manufacturer must, no matter how well his works may be equipped at present, continue to spend money very freely, and the essence of the contemplated scheme of amalgamation is to spend that money in such a manner as will enable a united body of manufacturers to meet competition with far greater success than is possible as independent units, each repeating the other's work in a fashion which, in years to come, will be regarded as tantamount to commercial suicide. The suggested amalgamation is therefore a commercial proposition of the first order, its anticipated effect being to conserve and ultimately to considerably enhance the value of the capital embarked in the industry, an effect which will apply equally to all the capital invested in engineering works on this coast. This is possible because an amalgamation offers facilities for the high development of an organisation on commercial, technical, and practical lines quite beyond those afforded by independent competitive units. Of course, any scheme of amalgamation decreases internal competition and automatic benefit would accrue under that head, but it would be a mere bye-product in comparison with the central aim and object, viz.: decreased cost of production. It would, of course, require time and immense energy on the part of everyone concerned to organise a new departure, but there would be compensation in the fact that the energy would be centred in the useful channel of progressive construction rather than in competitive destruction, and, therefore, it would beget that enthusiasm which is invariably associated with success.

It is a pertinent fact that all the firms on the coast buy many details in this country cheaper than they themselves can produce them, and yet the manufacturers of these details make very substantial profits. They do so, of course, by specialised production and concentrated management. Again, we all make details which cost us just as much as we could buy them for, and we content ourselves with the thought that they contribute their quota to our working expenses. To obtain the profits we now lose, however, is only possible if the scheme of amalgamation is sufficiently large, so that unless all the firms at present interested in the matter are in agreement it cannot be carried through.

Under the present system engines and boilers are built by each of the firms to the requirements of the several classifications, and whilst the average result of each firm's productions closely approximates that obtained by the others, yet each builder has some points of excellence, either in design, method of manufacture, arrangement of parts, quality of material or of workmanship, which in combination would yield greater excellence, and being reflected in the higher general efficiency of the entire machinery, would tend to place British construction on a higher plane in the markets of the world. Again, each firm has an expensive staff, producing designs practically identical with those of its competitors, as well as pattern-shops producing equally identical patterns. The useless expenditure under these two heads alone may be estimated from the fact that the designs and patterns for a cargo boat's engines cost about £500 to produce, and for passenger steamers a correspondingly higher figure.

It is impossible for me to enumerate within the limits of a speech all the sources of economy that are open to such an amalgamation, but its possibilities are sufficiently indicated if you consider the matter on its broad lines. The adoption of a single scheme of buying under the control of the commercial directors would alone tend to a considerable diminution in first cost.

With regard to the works, one system of organisation would be established, all antiquated tools would be replaced, and the latest methods of manufacture adopted. Overtime, which is at all times highly expensive, would be abolished as far as manufacturing conditions permitted, and night-shift at high rates of pay only resorted to when it was warranted by the conditions of trade and obtainable prices—the productive capacity of the whole of the works acting in union would in all ordinary circumstances dispel the conditions which lead the individual to resort to overtime. Broadly, the leading principle would be to limit the working hours to the standard length of the working week and to divide the work amongst the various shops to that end—an arrangement, one would suppose, that would be as satisfactory to the workmen as it would undoubtedly be to the employers.

An important advantage to the shipbuilders would result from contract deliveries being strictly maintained, as in the event of local pressure relief could always be given by one or other of the amalgamated works. There would also be no reason why ships should not always be engined in the port in which they are built, as the same standard of workmanship would prevail in each of the amalgamated works. Last year the expenses incurred in this connection alone amounted approximately to £18,000 for insurance, towage, etc., all of which represents unnecessary cost, apart altogether from the loss involved by the delay in completion consequent on the ship's absence in a distant port for approximately a fortnight.

It is intended to retain the identity of the several firms as at present, and each firm would therefore trade under the name upon which its business has been built up, and by which its productions are known and celebrated the world over. Moreover, the local boards of management would continue and the executive staffs would be retained, as only by their united efforts could the new scheme of organisation be developed with despatch and success.

I would again emphasise the fact that I am simply putting before you the proposition which has been put before your Directors, and before all the firms interested in this matter, and it is only by force of circumstances and not by intention that it falls to my lot to give public expression to the views which prompted any of us to give the scheme our consideration. I am convinced, however, that if we are to advance our industries and protect the capital invested in them we must recognise facts and modernise our methods, and in dealing with this scheme we must also endeavour to sink personal considerations of every kind. We cannot but realise that the industrial world is advancing at a pace unparalleled in its history. To have been told ten years ago, or even five years ago, that Japan would be building, and building with the greatest success, her " Dreadnoughts," her fast torpedo boat destroyers, and her 23-knot passenger liners, would have been regarded as a dream, yet they are accomplished facts. Continental competition is also, as you know, increasing by leaps and bounds, but in spite of all I am convinced that we can hold our own, nay, more than hold our own, if we will but shake off the incubus of our stereotyped industrial methods. In Germany, which is in the forefront of industrial progress, there are some hundreds of amalgamations of one kind and another, so there it has been amply demonstrated that the secret of commercial success lies in a policy of combined effort. At this stage I cannot say whether the scheme will mature or not ; if it does it will involve an adjustment of our capital to a basis which, it has been decided, shall be the standard basis for every firm, although on that point I am unable, and it is altogether unnecessary that I should say more on the present occasion. Your Board propose to you that this meeting shall stand adjourned until a convenient date, and that in the meantime you will patiently await the maturing of the negotiations that are now afoot, relying upon the ability and zeal of your Directors to safeguard and protect your interests in every possible way, and as soon as the negotiations are sufficiently advanced we will lose no time in putting the matter fully before you for your final decision.

APPENDIX III

ORGANISATION OF MONOPOLY. THE INDUSTRIAL SPIRIT CARTEL

(Ridley's 'Wine and Spirit Trade Circular,' Nov. 8, 1907, pp. 828-9.)

THE INDUSTRIAL SPIRIT SUPPLY COMPANY, LIMITED

UNDER the above title a "Trust"—as some people may be inclined to dub such an association nowadays—has been formed, through the hands of which will pass all the spirits sold for methylation or for use for industrial purposes, by the following firms :

ENGLAND.

London : J. & W. Nicholson & Co., Ltd ; Hammersmith Distillery Co., Limited (Haig & Co.).

Liverpool : Preston's Liverpool Distillery Co., Limited ; A. Walker & Co., Vauxhall (now merged in the Distillers' Company, Limited).

Bristol : Bristol Distilling Co., Limited.

SCOTLAND.

Bo'ness : Jas. Calder & Co., Limited.

Edinburgh : The Distillers' Company, Limited.

IRELAND.

Belfast : United Distilleries, Limited.

The only firm manufacturing spirits for industrial purposes which is absent from the above combine as shareholders is that of Messrs. King, Howman & Co., Limited, Derby ; but an arrangement has been made under which all their output, which is not very considerable, will pass through the hands of the new distributing centre. The secretary is Mr. C. Honeywill, and his firm, Messrs. Honeywill Brothers, of Mark Lane, London, E.C., will act as agents for the Company.

This Combine is perhaps in some ways the most important movement which has ever taken place in the spirit trade, and viewed in conjunction with the drift in Scotland and Ireland towards a " Trust " of all the manufacture for beverage purposes of spirits by the patent still process, must be accepted, for good or evil, as another step towards a gigantic spirit trust, embracing the manufacture of patent still spirits in the three kingdoms.

The Combine may partly have originated in the competition, which from time to time has existed, of the methylators among themselves, which competition was accentuated and aggravated by the fact that every now and then, when a surplus of grain spirit had to be got rid of in Belfast and in Scotland, not to speak of Liverpool and Bristol, the surplus was generally placed by a cut under the figure at which the regular makers could quote. The whole difficulty, competition, or whatever it may be called, has now been accommodated by those who caused the trouble having been admitted into the Combine, and receiving shares in it, their fraction having, of course, to come out of the share of the regular makers of the old informal association. In its immediate effects upon trade profits in the methylated business the new move is to be commended in the interest of all concerned. The methylator will have to compete as usual, but he will not have to compete with a rival who has bought his spirit at less money.

The Company is not a Company for profit; profit must be made or not made at the distillery. It is purely a distributing concern at a price to be fixed, from which there is to be no departure to any individual buyer, no matter how large the purchases of that individual methylator or manufacturer may be.

The advantages of such a combination are obvious. In the first place, as just mentioned, a uniform price is ensured; secondly, a great saving of carriage is made. It will be at once seen, that to have the nearest outlet for the spirit appropriated to the particular distillery which can with least carriage serve the customer must mean a great saving on the whole to the Combine. It will be none of the members' interest to increase, at the expense of another member of the Company, their output; that is defined by the proportion of orders to which the member is entitled to by his share in the Company.

It will at once be asked by those who know anything of the methylating trade, what provision has been made for dealing with those distillers who themselves methylate the spirits they make? Such distillers would obviously have a small pull over those who had to pay a commission to the agents on sales to the methylators or manufacturers. This has been met by providing in the Articles of Association for the payment into the Company's funds, by the distillers who methylate, of a sum per gallon equal to the selling commission payable by the Combine to the agents.

The point just mentioned is the only resemblance to the well-known " pooling " process, by which those who sold more, paid into, and those who sold less than their proportion received, out of the " pool," so much per gallon.

That the Industrial Spirit Supply Company is in itself apparently not a formidable engine of capitalism would seem to be shown by its registered capital being £1000 in twenty shares of £50 each. In fact, as at present constituted, it is merely an invoicing office, through which all the output of spirits sold by the above-named distillers for methylating or manufacturing purposes must pass. We share then the declared opinion of the promoters that it is at present a most innocent association of manufacturers formed to prevent undercutting of prices, and to afford buyers of spirits for industrial purposes a guarantee that there is no lower price than the one at which they are buying.

It will be able to regulate the inflow and outflow of spirits, with Messrs. Honeywill's hands, as it were, on the tap, so that the possible inroad of the German Centrale may be controlled, by a fall in the price on the one hand, if that Spirit Ring wants to send in spirits here, or be provided with spirits from this side, if the surplus here, and the price over there, warrant the shipment to the Continent of British spirits.

While we indicate above that apparently the general effect, at present, of the new Supply Combine will be of benefit to the traders concerned, we cannot conceal the view which must present itself to the mind of those who have studied the question of monopolies, that they always begin by disclaiming any intention of, at any time, bearing hardly on those whom they supply, and thereby bearing hardly on the dependent industries, and finally on the public. We know of a certain place the way to which is paved with good intentions, and we cannot but foresee that this monopoly within another nearly organised monopoly, may turn out ultimately of anything but advantage to the industries which may be concerned in the production and distribution of industrial and methylated spirits.

Fortunately, perhaps, for those branches of our national commerce which have to look to supplies of cheap alcohol in competition with Germany in particular, where the alcohol used for purposes other than drinking is subsidised and thus rendered artificially cheap for the industries using it, and for consumption for motive power, lighting and heating purposes, we, in order to enable our manufacturers to compete, have lately granted the same drawback to spirits industrially used as to those exported.

As the new Combine heralds an approaching rise in the price of industrial spirits, we see foreshadowed in this a movement which might become dangerous, if the distillers should become too desirous of profit. Happily, however, there is a constant check at present existing in the German article, which will be always on the watch to come in if the price here of the British article is unduly pushed upwards. At present, the Combine would be quite safe at some pence higher, but it is quite likely that in another six months to a year the volume of German production may again bring down the figure over there to a dangerously low point. However, a move up or down becomes now a matter of twenty-four hours with the central bureau of the new Supply Company.

APPENDIX IV

ADDENDUM TO THE REPORT OF THE COMMITTEE ON TRUSTS

(Cd. 9236 of 1919, reprinted 1924; by Mr. Ernest Bevin, Mr. J. A. Hobson, Mr. W. H. Watkins, and Mr. Sidney Webb.)

We have signed the above Report because we find nothing to disagree with in its recommendations; but we feel that it does not adequately express the gravity of the situation, and that the proposals fall far short of what—in the terms of reference to the Committee—will be necessary to safeguard the public interest.

The fact is that Free Competition no longer governs the business world. The common assumption that the rivalry of traders affords a guarantee that the price of commodities will oscillate closely about the necessary cost of production—whatever may have been its degree of truth in the past—is now, in this country, nowhere to be implicitly relied on. It is nowadays open to doubt whether we ever buy anything at the cost of production. We find that capitalist combination, in one or other form, and at one or other stage of production, transportation and distribution, now loads in varying degrees the price of practically everything that we purchase.

Such a conclusion has momentous implications. The consumer cannot be sure that he is charged no more than is required to defray the necessary costs of production and distribution. The wage earner cannot be convinced that any reduction in the expenses which may be effected by labour-saving machinery or other improvements will be reflected in a fall in price to the consumers. The Government has no assurance that any new tax will not be made a pretext for the levy on the public in enhanced prices of much more than the return to the Exchequer. The primary object of combination or association between businesses in a trade is to raise the level of profits by eliminating competition among the various firms. The larger gains which are admittedly thus obtained are attributable mainly to three sources :—(1) The saving of wasteful costs of competition ; (2) the reduced expenses of production by better technical and business organisation ; (3) the monopolistic fixing of prices at " what the trade will bear." We may observe that this last source of gain, involving usually an actual rise in prices, almost always and of necessity involves a lower aggregate production than would have emerged had the arrangement not been made. It amounts, in fact, to restriction of output.

The importance of the first and second gains suffices to explain why combination is not always followed by an actual increase of selling prices, but sometimes even by a reduction. An effective monopoly may sometimes find it more profitable to abstain from a reduction of prices that it could well afford to make than to raise prices, which would cut down its sales and lessen the economy of large scale production. In general, however, it is found that the formation of a combination or agreement is attended by a " regulation " of output and an actual rise of prices, due to the fact that most of the organisations control articles or services so essential to the community that the elasticity of demand is slight.

These surplus gains, whether due to an actual rise of price or to a failure to reduce price in correspondence with reduced costs, are got at the expense of the whole public of consumers, whose interests the Committee is enjoined to safeguard. We believe that they amount, in the aggregate, to a very large sum annually.

We do not suggest that any action should be taken to prevent or obstruct combination or association in capitalist enterprise. Apart from the experience that no such interference can be made effective, we have to recognise that association and combination in production and distribution are steps in the greater efficiency, the increased economy, and the better organisation of industry. We regard this evolution as both inevitable and desirable. It is, however, plain that the change from competitive rivalry to combination calls for corresponding developments to secure for the community, both safeguards against the evils of monopoly, and at least a large share of the economic benefits of the better organisation of industry which it promotes.

It has not been possible for the Committee, in the time and with the means at its disposal, to work out a programme of what will in the near future be required for these purposes. We think that this task should be the first duty of the suggested Trusts and Combinations Department of the Board of Trade. We may, however, indicate the following directions in which, as it seems to us, remedy might be sought.

I.

Profiteering may in some cases be kept in check, without preventing the better organisation to be obtained by combination, by the existence of a rival who cannot be persuaded to enter the combination, and who can be relied upon to serve only the public interest. The Co-operative Movement, which returns to its customers in proportion to their purchases all the surplus that it makes over cost, serves incidentally as a check on profit-making combinations, into none of which will it ever consent to enter. The national factories have been found by the Government extremely valuable in this respect during the war. If they could be continued in peace for the production of certain essential commodities, for the protection of the public of consumers, their value in serving as a check upon capitalist combinations might be considerable.

II.

In considering the prevalence of capitalistic combinations in British industry, it is impossible to leave out of account the check upon profiteering which may be afforded by foreign imports. This operates, however, only so long as the foreign producers are not also brought within the combination. Whilst the imposition of import duties would increase the power of combinations to raise prices, " Free Trade " is not, in itself, a complete safeguard against it.

Nor is the objection to the profiteering of capitalist combinations removed by the imposition of a tax which diverts to the Exchequer some or all of what is unnecessarily extracted from the consumer. Such a tax, whilst levied apparantly upon profits, may be held to make the Government *particeps criminis* in these overcharges. Such a tax has the further evil that the Government has even an interest in the increase of his gains. It may be better to have an Excess Profits Duty than not to have it, when there are Excess Profits about ; but it would be far more profitable to the community (and, therefore, also to the Exchequer) if there were no excess profits to tax.

III.

The only effective safeguard against the absorption by a capitalist combination of more than the necessary return appears to be the control of prices. We regard the experience, during the war, of the full and precise " costing " of every part of a commodity as affording valuable suggestions for the future fixing by

Government Departments of a Maximum Price for particular articles which can be standardised. Where, as in the case of gas and electricity, such a prescribed price can be made to vary with the amount of profit taken by the capitalist producers, such a " sliding scale " of prices and dividends appears a useful expedient. It involves, it will be noted, the full application of two principles which may be destined to ever-wider application in business, but to which the business world is at present hostile, namely, Publicity and Measurement.

IV.

Where, as is evidently the case in various highly organised capitalist enterprises, competition is being rapidly displaced by combination, largely monopolistic in its structure and powers, and tending to restrict output with a view to raising prices or preventing their fall, we hold that it is contrary to the public interest to allow such enterprises to remain in private hands. In some cases their functions may more advantageously be assumed by the Co-operative Movement. In others their place may be taken by Municipal Enterprise. Where the enterprise is national in scope, and especially where its product enters into practically universal consumption, we see no alternative to State Ownership. But State Ownership does not necessarily imply State Management. In some cases it may be preferable to lease the enterprise, with prescribed schedules of price and wages, and other necessary conditions, for management either by a Local Authority, a Co-operative Society, or a joint stock company. The subject, in our view, urgently needs further study.

(Signed) E. BEVAN.
J. A. HOBSON.
W. H. WATKINS.
SIDNEY WEBB.

24th April, 1919.

LIST OF AUTHORS REFERRED TO

ABBOTT, G. *Essay on the Mines of England.* London. 1833.

ANDERSON, A. *Geschichte des Handels.* Riga. 1778. (Translation from English edition of 1764.)

ASHLEY, SIR W. J. *History of English Industry.* Leipzig. 1896.

—— *The Adjustment of Wages.* London. 1903.

BABBAGE, C. *Economy of Manufactures.* London. 1833.

BAINES, E. *History of the Cotton Manufacture.* London. 1835.

BANFIELD, T. C. *Industry of the Rhine.* London. 1848.

BEACH, C. F. *Monopolies and Industrial Trusts.* St. Louis. 1898.

BERNOULLI. *Reisebeschreibungen.* 1784.

BOSENICK. *Der Steinkohlenbergban in Preussen.* Tübingen. 1909.

BOWLEY, A. L. *National Progress in Wealth and Trade.* London. 1904.

BRAND. *History of Newcastle.* London. 1789.

BRASSEY, LORD. *Papers and Addresses.* London. 1894.

BRENT, N. *A Discourse of Free Trade.* London. 1645.

BRENTANO, L. *Arbeitsverhältnis gemäss dem heutigen Recht.* Leipzig. 1877.

—— *Die beabsichtige Neuorganisation der deutschen Volkswirtschaft.* 1904.

BRODNITZ, G. *Betriebskonzentration und Kleinbetrieb in der Englischen Industrie.* 1908.

BROWN, F. C. *Shipbuilding Depression.* 1926.

BROWNE, S. *The Laws against Engrossing.* London. 1767.

BUCHANAN, D. (ed.). *Wealth of Nations,* by A. Smith. 1814.

BUNNING, T W. *The Duties on Coal.* Newcastle. 1883.

BUTLER, D. B. *Portland Cement.* London. 1905.

CAHILL, J. R. *Report on Economic and Industrial Conditions in France* London. 1925.

CHAPMAN, S. J. *Work and Wages.* London. 1904.

—— *The Cotton Industry.* London. 1905.

CHAPTAL. *De l'industrie française.* Paris. 1819.

CLAPHAM, J. H. *Woollen and Worsted Industries.* London. 1907.
COX. *Staatseinrichtungen Englands.* Berlin. 1867.
CUNNINGHAM, W. *Growth of English Industry and Commerce.* Cambridge. 1907.

DAVIES, J. *An Answer to those Printed Papers published in March last by the late Patentees of Salt.* London. 1641.
DIETZEL, H. *Das Produzenteninteresse der Arbeiter und die Handelsfreiheit.* Berlin. 1903.
—— *Sozial Politik und Handels Politik.* 1902.
DODERIDGE. *The Tinners' Grievances.* London. 1697.
DUNN, M. *View of the Coal Trade.* Newcastle. 1843.
—— *The Coal Trade of the North of England.* Newcastle. 1844.

EDINGTON, R. *A Treatise of the Coal Trade.* London. 1823.

FECHNER. *Direktionsprinzip im Silesien.* 1900 and 1902.
FITZGERALD, P. *Industrial Combination in England.* London. 1927.
FLOWER, P. W. *A History of the Trade in Tin.* London. 1889.

GALLOWAY, R. L. *History of Coal Mining.* London. 1882.
GARDINER, R. *England's Grievance Discovered.* Newcastle. 1655.
GERBER, C. F. *System des deutschen Privatrechts.* Jena. 1852.
GOLDSTEIN, G. *Die Entwicklung der deutschen Roheisenindustrie seit* 1879. 1909.
GOTHEIN, E. *Konzentration in Kohlenbergbau.* 1904.
GRAY, W. *Chorographia or a Survey of Newcastle-upon-Tyne.* 1649
GROSSMANN. *Glasindustrie.* Leipzig. 1908.
—— *Bedeutung der chemischen Technick.* Halle. 1907.

HASBACH, W. *Zur Characteristik der englischen Industrie.*
HELM, L. *British Industries.*
HEUSER, E. *Pfälzisches Porzellan.* Speyer. 1907.
HEYMANN. *Die gemischten Werke im deutschen Grosseisengewerbe.* Stuttgart. 1904.
HIRST, F. W. *Monopolies, Trusts, and Cartels.* London. 1903.
—— *Safeguarding and Protection.* London. 1926.
HODGSON, W. B. *Competition.* London. 1870.
HOOPER. *British Industries.*
HORSTER. *Die Entwicklung der sächsischen Gewerbefassung.* Krefeld. 1908.

INAMA-STERNEGG. *Deutsche Wirtschaftsgeschichte.* Leipzig. 1901.

JACOBSTEIN, M. *The Tobacco Industry in the United States.* New York. 1907.

JEANS, J. S. *Trusts, Pools and Corners.* London. 1894.

—— *The Iron Trade of Great Britain.* London. 1906.

—— *British Industries.*

JUSTI, J. H. G. VON. *Polizeiwissenschaft.* 1760.

—— *Abhandlung von den Manufakturen.* Copenhagen. 1767.

KLOSTERMANN. *Das allgemeine Berggesetz.* Berlin. 1884.

KNAPMANN, K. *Das Eisen- und Stahldrahtgewerbe in Altena.* Leipzig. 1907.

KOCH, W. *Die Konzentrationsbewegung in der deutschen Electro-industrie.* Munich. 1907.

LAWSON, W. J. *American Industrial Problems.* London. 1903.

LEVY, H. *English Cartels of the Past.* 1907.

—— *Large and Small Holdings.* Cambridge. 1911.

—— *England und die Konzentrationsbewegung in der deutschen Industrie.* 1926.

—— *Einfluss der Zollpolitik auf die wirtschaftliche Entwicklung der Vereinigten Staaten von America.* 1906.

—— *Entwicklungsgeschichte einer amerikanischen Industrie.* 1905.

—— *Die Stahlindustrie der Vereinigten Staaten von Amerika.* Berlin. 1905.

—— *Der Weltmarkt* 1913 *und heute.* Leipzig. 1926.

—— *Amerika als Wirtschaftsmacht.* Leipzig. 1923.

—— *Concentration in German Industry.* 1926.

LEWIS, F. H. *The Cement Industry.* New York. 1900.

LEWIS, G. R. *The Stannaries.* London. 1908.

LIEFMANN, R. *Schutzzoll und Kartelle.* Jena. 1903.

—— *Kartelle und Trusts.* Stuttgart. 1920.

LIST, F. *Der internationale Handel.* Stuttgart. 1841.

MACAULAY'S *History of England.*

M'CULLOCH, J. R. *Dictionary of Commerce.* London. 1882.

—— *Treatises and Essays.* Edinburgh. 1859.

—— *Principles of Political Economy.* Edinburgh. 1825.

—— *Essay on the Rate of Wages.* Edinburgh. 1826.

MACROSTY, H. W. *The Trust Movement in British Industry.* London. 1907.

MALTHUS, T. R. *Essay on the Principle of Population.* London. 1817. (5th edit.)

MALYNES, G. *Lex Mercatoria.* London. 1622.

MARTIN, G. *La grande industrie en France.* Paris. 1900.

MEADE, A. *Coal and Iron Industries of the United Kingdom.* London. 1882.
MILL, J. S. *Political Economy.* 1848.
MISSELDEN, E. *Free Trade.* London. 1622.
MONTAGUE, F. C. *History of England.* London. 1907.
MORGENROTH. *Exportpolitik der Kartelle.* Leipzig. 1907.

NICHOLLS, H. G. *The Forest of Dean.* London. 1858.

PALGRAVE'S *Dictionary of Political Economy.*
PARKER, HENRY. *Of a Free Trade.* London. 1648.
PAXMANN. *Wirtschaftliche Verhältnisse der Kaliindustrie.* Berlin. 1907.
PIERCE. *The Tariff and the Trusts.* New York. 1907.
PORTER, G. R. *The Progress of the Nation.* London. 1851.
PRICE, H. HYDE. *The English Patents of Monopoly.* Boston. 1906.

RAFFEL. *Englische Freihändler vor A. Smith.* Tübingen. 1905.
ROBERTS, L. *The Treasure of Traffike.* London. 1641.
ROGERS, J. E. THOROLD. *History of Agriculture and Prices.* 1866, 1882.
—— *Industrial and Commercial History of England.* London. 1892.

SCHLÖZER. *Staatsanzeigen.* Göttingen. 1783.
SCHMOLLER, G. *Grundriss der allgemeinen Volkswirtschaftslehre.* 1908.
SCHULZE. *Chemische Industrie.*
SCHULZE-GÄVERNITZ. *Englischer Freihandel und Britischer Imperialismus.* Leipzig. 1906.
SCHUSTER UND WEHBERG. *Der Wirtschaftskrieg. England.* Jena. 1917.
SCHÜTZ. *Die alt-württembergische Gewerbefassung.* 1850.
SCOTT, W. R. *Records of a Scottish Cloth Manufactory.* Edinburgh. 1905.
SCRIVENER, H. *History of the Iron Trade.* 1841.
SMITH, ADAM. *Wealth of Nations.* 1776.
SOLGER, H. *Der Kreis Beuthen.* Breslau. 1860.
SOMBART. *Der moderne Capitalismus.* Leipzig. 1902.
—— *Die Deutsche Volkswirtschaft.* Berlin. 1903.
SOPWITH, T. *The Award of the Dean Forest Commissioners.* London. 1841.
SPICER, A. D. *The Paper Trade.* London. 1907.
STEIDA, W. *Die keramische Industrie in Bayern.* Leipzig. 1906.

STEUART, SIR JAMES. *Principles of Political Economy.* London. 1767.

STILLICH, O. *Steinkohlindustrie.* Leipzig. 1906.

TAYLOR, J. *Statements respecting the Profits of Mining in England.* London. 1825.

THOMAS, D. A. (Lord Rhondda). *Growth and Direction of the Foreign Trade in Coal.* 1903.

THOMAS, F. MOY. *J. and R. Morley.* London. 1900.

THUN. *Die Industrie am Niederrhein.* Leipzig. 1879.

TOOKE AND NEWMARCH'S *History of Prices.* 1838-1857.

TOYNBEE, A. *The Industrial Revolution.* London. 1884.

TROELTSCH, W. *Die Calwer Zeughandelscompagnie.* Jena. 1897.

TUCKER, J. *Cui Bono?* London. 1782. (3rd edit.)

UHDE. *Produktionsbedingungen des deutschen und englischen Steinkohlenbergbaues.* Jena. 1907.

UNWIN, G. *Industrial Organisation.* Oxford. 1904.

—— *Gilds of London.* London. 1908.

WARDLE, T. *Report on the English Silk Industry.* 1884.

WEHBERG, 261, 275, 292 ; *see* Schuster.

WHITE, A. G. *The Electrical Industry.* London. 1904.

WIESE, VON. *Entwicklung der Rohzinkfabrikation.* Jena. 1903.

WILKINS, R. *The Sope Patentees of London's Petition opened and explained.* London. 1694.

INDEX

PRINTED IN GREAT BRITAIN BY ROBERT MACLEHOSE AND CO. LTD.
THE UNIVERSITY PRESS, GLASGOW.

For Product Safety Concerns and Information please contact our EU representative GPSR@taylorandfrancis.com Taylor & Francis Verlag GmbH, Kaufingerstraße 24, 80331 München, Germany

Batch number: 10725973

Printed by Printforce, the Netherlands